HOW TO LIVE A MEMOIR-IN-ESSAYS

HOW TO LIVE

A MEMOIR-IN-ESSAYS

*

KELLE GROOM

*

TUPELO PRESS

North Adams, Massachusetts

How to Live: A memoir-in-essays
Copyright © 2023 Kelle Groom. All rights reserved.

Library of Congress Cataloging-in-Publication data available upon request.
ISBN-13: 978-1-946482-83-9

Cover and text design by Ann Aspell.
Cover art: Michi Meko, *Alone in the Vast,* 2021. Private collection. Used by permission of the artist.

First paperback edition October 2023

All rights reserved. Other than brief excerpts for reviews and commentaries, no part of this book may be reproduced by any means without permission of the publisher. Please address requests for reprint permission or for course-adoption discounts to:

Tupelo Press
P.O. Box 1767
North Adams, Massachusetts 01247
(413) 664-9611 / Fax: (413) 664-9711
editor@tupelopress.org / www.tupelopress.org

Tupelo Press is an award-winning independent literary press that publishes fine fiction, non-fiction, and poetry in books that are a joy to hold as well as read. Tupelo Press is a registered 501(c)(3) nonprofit organization, and we rely on public support to carry out our mission of publishing extraordinary work that may be outside the realm of the large commercial publishers. Financial donations are welcome and are tax deductible.

for Larry Collins

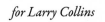

CONTENTS

HOW TO LIVE   A MEMOIR-IN-ESSAYS

Nothing will tell you
where you are.
Each moment is a place
you've never been.

—Mark Strand, "Black Maps"

On the door it says what to do to survive
But we were not born to survive
Only to live

—W.S. Merwin, "The River of Bees"

EMERALD CITY

I owned a house once, for twenty-four hours. In Syracuse, New York. Snowiest city in America. Vapor from Lake Ontario rises into sky, freezes, snow fall continuous, a wall. Emerald City, Salt City an older name—Jesuits tasting the salty springs. Home of the Onondaga Nation, firekeepers of the Haudenosaunee.

I never lived in the house I owned for a day. Never saw it. *I bought you a house,* X said on the phone. *Yesterday.* House not right for some reason. Frantic calling of the realtor. Sale cancelled. The day I owned a house, I didn't know it. I lived in a pink apartment in Florida, having left X, the man I loved. Just for a time I thought. Until we have our own house, until he's divorced, until his moods don't swing. Until the right medication is found.

The first time I saw him, it was a picture in a book. Yellow light of a now-dead bookstore, his poems in my hands. Familiar—I felt related. Photograph black and white. Dark hair. Gaze clear, as if he could see me from inside the book. Every time I went to the store, I'd look for it. Under a spell. I'd forget the title. Run my hands over the skinny spines, recall a letter. Forget his name, but not the poems, his face. Until one day, I bought the book, took it home.

5

July, we meet in a writing workshop in Provincetown, Massachusetts. He is like his photograph. Every day, when I arrive late—rushing from the east side of town—there's only one seat left. Always closer to him. As if the circle draws us near. Until by the last day, we're side by side. On the Fourth of July, I walk down to the harbor to watch fireworks. Anniversary of the day I died, came back to life. Before I stopped drinking, got sober. Ash falls on the water. Invisible until I hear, *Kelle. Kelle.* He comes toward me on the crowded street. His seeing brings my atoms together, makes me human again.

Back in Florida, I work at the opera. Little lights come on in the orchestra pit like underwater torches. Some nights, I wear a watery green ball gown with small roses in a line across my breast. In my seat, the fabric puffs around me like a sparkly blanket. Hundreds of paper flowers are flung in the air for Cio-Cio-San. The same bad deal being made over and over. Baby of straw rocked and sung to by a grief-crazed woman. People come from heaven in the upper balcony. Voices rise after everything is lost.

Before I'd come to marry him, I'd often fly to visit. Once we watched *Groundhog Day,* and it became our constant wish at the airport. For my flight to Florida to be cancelled, and we could have another day together. And because it was winter in Syracuse, and because we were lucky, my flight was often cancelled. The gift of another day together always made us joyful, giddy. On one flight, I boarded, but there was some delay. In the terminal, he waited for me to take off, staring at a photo of me in his hands, crying. A woman watched. When, after an hour, we deplaned, the woman said, *Oh, you can see her again!*

His words are unlike any I'd ever heard, sometimes all we do is talk for hours in restaurants. He tells the hostess that we have business to discuss and asks for a quiet table. We laugh to ourselves. I think he even has a briefcase.

I propose to him on small piece of paper. He proposes in a note that I read on a plane.

He calls me *the sweetest of all sweethearts.* He says, *You are 44 Anna Kareninas.* He says, *I am still falling in love with you eight minutes after telling you that on the phone.* Snow coming.

My engagement ring yellow plastic with a large watermelon gem circled with aluminum turrets from a gumball machine. Or it is one from the set of juice-colored rings with long-lashed eyes that open and shut.

*

The Gachalá Emerald has a turquoise sea inside and its own sun. Unseen until 1967.

*

Wake up, wake up, is that what my grandmother means when I sleep in his house? I haven't seen Nana since she died. But one morning, she comes back. Her death a mistake after all. Her face right above mine. All I have to do is open my eyes to see her, but I'm sleepy—eyes heavy, sun from some summer with her on my face. No rush, she's back. Then I wake in the narrow bed surrounded by photographs of the dead, a staring gallery of people I've never known, having waited too long. She's gone.

He says that he wants to live with me anywhere USA. He says *it is very flooring.* Says, *I still feel a glow from it.* The city in celebration has printed posters with bright bulbs and words like stars that spell *42 Nights of Joy*. He hangs one in our borrowed house. The downtown has a few new shops open between all the shuttered ones. But so many lights are strung among the streets—as if the town is one big tree—it is hard to see the darkness.

Lake water freezes in the sky. November, the light still silver. Air so cold, I feel unconcealed, and someone in a hall hands me a paper cup of tea. Buildings medieval as if we've gone back in time. He wants to hide me even as he introduces me. Not divorced yet. Hide a kind of hall. A hull where I grow older and think of the calendar in his kitchen with the periods marked of his last wife when they'd still been together. Days magic markered as she'd planned for a baby that never appeared. He'd found that after several years one could reuse a calendar from long before, and somehow the numbers, days and weeks all lined up exactly again.

He had so little vanity, the light blue raincoat—sky colored—that he wore to a reading was unlike any article of clothing I'd ever seen. Like a sky tent with a belt. As if he'd come from the future or the past.

It's the closest I've ever been to marriage. Red wool scarf, Kentucky coat. Night sky snowing heavy on my hair, letting it fall like quiet hellos. Inside would be sadness again, his green sweater torn at the sleeves, collar, worn day after day, comfort of the familiar. Though when he touches a fall sweater in the mall store, delighting in something new, I secretly buy it. And he wears it all the time. As if he'd just been waiting for something beautiful to arrive.

When my father phones, asks, *How are the lovebirds,* my father is so happy. I have forgotten what that is like. *The love nest,* my father calls this place. I am in the love nest while the man I am in love with says, *Sometimes, I'm so depressed it's like I'm alone in the house.* He says this when I am so close, I could blow on his eyelashes and watch them flutter. Watch him blink. And he means right then, he feels alone.

He says, *You are still my sweet girl.* Moon out the window. We spin our bodies on the bed as it moves across the night sky. So that the moon is always in our sight through the dark square while he sings to me. He says, *My heart to you.*

At Christmas, he holds the tiny tree in his hand. Gifts on the coffee table. Miniature statues of men and animals at play. I give him an instant camera because he'd wanted to stand outside a house, see something in the window. A pair of jeans I'd measured with my own body, trying them on in the Army/Navy store, forgetting to adjust for height. The hem hits his shins, never worn. Years later, he tells me that that day—when he was a man in his late fifties who had had three wives—he says that our coffee table celebration in the dilapidated city with the beautiful old houses during the 42 Nights of Joy was the best Christmas he'd ever had.

Emerald is my birthstone—stones in a watch, a necklace from my grandmother. He types our names together because he wants our names closer. He finds us a house in Geneva, a house west of Syracuse, a house one hour east door-to-door in Rome. The snow is coming down. He says, *I love you.*

Before we arrive at the gas station in Verona, our gray car parked by the pumps, a thought had come to leave the earth for the lake. To drown in it. Step into the water at Green Lakes in my running shoes, let it cover me. But I remembered I'd been a person before all of this happened, before X—I had to save that person. I'd run back to the car. At the station in Verona, I want to hurt him, the one I love. Want him to see what it would look like without me. So while he is inside the faraway yellow light to pay, I walk quickly to the restroom, outside door. Without telling him. Knowing he'll look for me, see the absence. Have a little panic. It may not seem like much. But that intent to hurt the one I loved so sickened me, the turn.

The Onondaga have a casino in the dark ahead, but from there, it was lights to us, or snow—a whole nation inside this one. Before Verona, all I'd felt for him came out of tenderness. As I open the restroom door I see him bent over the car door—maybe he was going to use that sharp voice that isn't his, the one he used at the lake. But the car is empty.

There was no one else I wanted. Even when he is afraid I'll leave him, mad at the deep cleavage of a black sweater I wear on a plane to meet him. I only wanted him. When he walks into a room, his light lights others up—people are so glad to see him in meetings, the grocery store, anywhere. He is beloved. When I tell him, he shakes his head.

Maybe we could have let it slide off, maybe we could have just breathed quietly in the gray car. It felt familiar, that meanness that rose up when I felt backed into a corner, the equivalent of a punch, some old thing I thought I'd given up. He says, *I'm forgetting to tell you something.*

I never tell the man I loved my thought to be a lake. Instead, he drives us home, and I pack my suitcase. I unpack it. Pack it again. In the airport, he is like a desolate child. We sit on a little couch curved like a comma in the center of a hall, and he cries uncontrollably. Wailing, bent over at the waist. Inconsolable. People stare, concerned. As if I am going away to war, never to return. I hand him tissues. I fly away for good. When I'd packed my suitcase, we spoke of my return. But he was always smarter than me, knew the truth especially if unspoken. That's why he could cry like that.

He says, *Come home!* He says, *Could you bring yourself—and a few thousand kisses—your laugh / your brightness / your light / your smile.*

I know you will bring all of you which is one reason I love you among many many.

He says, *A kiss is floating near your refrigerator.*

I never go back to live in Syracuse. For a couple of years afterwards, when I still visited, laying eyes on him in the airport tunnel, he'd look slightly electrocuted. At first. Hair on end, eyes sparking. Then he'd calm, reveal himself. Or, it took a while for me to be able to see him.

*

Ten feet of snow expected when I lived there. Darkness at four o'clock. Some light always arrives, gray lifting before it falls again. *I can't draw,* I say. *Why don't you draw a flower for your Nana?* So I do. Sit with him at the long dining room table for hours, night after night, drawing flowers. White light overhead. We cover all the cabinets and tables with our flowers, a garden surrounding us.

He says, *hmmm, hmmm, hmmm—trying to hear your breath like that.*

I haven't made a snow angel since I was a child. He opens the back door on the black night, and I lie down in the snow. Wave my arms until I have wings.

THE CITY BEAUTIFUL

1.

The motel over the bridge could be demolished as early as spring, and a dollar store there overlooking the river and what I saw—a woman propped between two men. Her body looked stiffly drunk or drugged the way she was hustled upright with the posture of a fence. Held up by the men on either side like posts. Heavy, older. She walked as if there was something unmended inside her. A bar across the highway, but I didn't see them there—it was just after they'd crossed the white line, as they entered the motel parking lot, headed toward a door. Her blond hair like a wig from the back, frozen with hairspray. The way a pregnant spider can be frozen with a spritz of hairspray, then killed, so that even her babies will freeze too, not stream about from her dead body. There wasn't anybody else around at dusk the time falling. I didn't drive my truck into the opposite end of the curved lot to face the men through glass at their end of the arc, didn't meet her eye. Afraid I could wind up in that room. Be skin over a boat, then just skin. But before they reached a door, why didn't I call an emergency number and say I saw suspicious activity? Why drive on, as if she wasn't real? Something in me frozen too. I let the woman go. Maybe they're just helping her back to her room, I thought, though they'd gripped her like something caught.

2.

In 1998, after my grandmother died, and I stood in her bedroom, my uncle Dean said, *Come out of there.* He said, *You're like me.* I saw it in how open his eyes were, sleepless. But I turned away to take everything of hers that I could carry— her clothes meant for the Cancer Society Thrift Shop, her quilt, a painting of Gloucester harbor on the wall. I still have it all—her slippers, sweaters, flight bag, diary. I carry them everywhere. When I stood in the Yarmouth post office surrounded by her things, weeping, no box for her painting, the postman said, *I like art.* He took the painting from me, wrapping it like a body in rolls of brown paper, talking in a constant low tone. The spooling out something I could listen to. I don't know how to let her clothing go—I have no idea. Nothing can be worn. I tried, and it made the veins in my wrists hurt.

3.

I saw her before she died, Mary of the violet eyes. Her mother hadn't wanted to go the hospital either, their deaths preventable. But they sat in the house, endured. My father says I should be careful when I write about other people. I don't think he knows how careful I am. Mary with her open eyes too. Her parents from Finland. I remember her brother, my grandfather, and his silence. The strongest man I've ever seen. And my mother, his child. Her rules—the winters I watched from inside, the house I can't enter, her hundred years and more of worrying. And then the relative in Finland who went into the bedroom and stayed for seven years. Unable to come out. The months I didn't want to move. Blood slowing down. I'd thought, *I wonder how bad this can get?* As if my body were a dress I'd been fond of, taken off.

4.

Someone I loved was moving across the sea, to another country. Leaving Orlando. The City Beautiful. And as I drove to his house, on the road where the disappeared groves still stood, I looked into the green, the bright oranges I'd known since I was a child, and talked to God. I was afraid for my friend's safety—but he wasn't the only one—and I'd been trying to address/correct the fear with prayer. If I didn't, anything could happen. I asked God if I could stop this, I needed to stop. I could get down on my knees in the orange groves and beg for it to stop. I said, *I'll just trust you to keep everyone safe.* And when the fear came, instead of words, I'd remember the moment of trust beside the oranges. The whole grove already damaged, doomed by freeze upon freeze. Growers spraying the trees with water in winter, so ice could keep them warm. It worked for ten years. When the fear came back, the grip was worse than childhood. The death of my grandmother undid me. The house full of white flowers drawn on white paper. When the bank froze my money, I hung my clothes from trees. I sat in the Quaker meeting house one night a week, and it calmed me some. The wood gleamed, and I looked into where it shone.

5.

The New England Algonquins were buried with things. Ninety-four round glass beads make a necklace for the baby. A spoon and bowl, two bells, small square bottle, three glass rosette buttons, and a body but no mention of age or gender. Just a baby and a body to the right, about 18 inches apart. Why would the baby be apart? Why isn't the baby in the body's arms? Closer? If the baby will need a necklace in the next life, surely he/she will need to be held. Another body in another grave had hair eight to twelve inches long that fell away when the blanket was removed. A small kettle. Head facing southeast. Another grave, 120 shark teeth. Nails. Graves lined with matting or blanket. At home in Florida, I felt surrounded by things, as if I were in a museum of my life. The photographs were the worst—I couldn't recognize myself anymore.

6.

Under his bed in a box, a soon-to-be-ex-boyfriend had photographs of his previous girlfriend. When I'd arrived, he emptied the box on his bedspread, photos scattered. In some, she was nude. He didn't like them—seemed to think she'd been showing off. There was a strange prudishness to his voice, as if he'd become a Calvinist, clothed in invisible severity. He had a pair of scissors and was cutting the photos up, angles all over, so that you couldn't see what was what. His skin had been my only way in, but when I touched his arm, his chest, I didn't feel anything. As if he was trying to cut me up too. Like I wasn't there. Then, I wasn't.

7.

After 9/11, I flew to New York a lot, the risk always orange. That winter I tried to cut up photos of the man I loved and me—we looked so unhappy. But I'd only cut a corner when he stopped me, as if it were bad luck.

8.

When a woman is arrested in Miami, held against the police car, I heard her say someone has stolen her eyes, and she must get back to ancient Rome. The cop says, *Re-lax*. But CNN does erase her eyes, her face fuzzed out for anonymity, nowhere to look.

9.

I thought about going to a grief group to see if it would help. If they had any tips. My widowed neighbor belonged to one, all widows. I'd thought there would be different kinds of grief. The widows dance with the Elks on Friday nights. My neighbor said in their grief group all they talk about is sex. *It's disgusting* she says. *Not the sex, but that they want it too soon.* The widows say they want to be taken care of, but my neighbor thinks they should spend some time alone and learn to take care of themselves. Maybe she wants the widows to take care of their own loneliness the way a baby left alone learns to comfort itself, waving his hands, learning to sing. She said, *You remember my daughter died,* but I'd forgotten. *You remind me of her.* When I told my neighbor about my sadness, about my son's death, I was sitting at her kitchen table, tea drunk, ready to go. She had no words at all. Her mouth opening and closing. Maybe she said sorry. And she kept knocking on my door. Even after I moved, she'd come by and knock on my door.

10.

I was late for work when men were making their way toward my house in their white shirts. When I drove past them clustered at the neck of a driveway like a brooch, one man lifted his hand in forgiveness. But just before, another man beat me to my car, pamphlets in hand, and said he saw my rush, *But here, this one is about Mary.* She's younger than me, wise, too modern for the ancient world. On page eleven is the answer to "Can the dead harm the living?" But it's not very helpful. A man believed in spirits, but now he doesn't. And bad angels who came to earth without permission and married, so the Flood came to wash them away, forced them to live in Tartarus which the article says is not a physical prison but a state of suffering and complete darkness. The Flood washed away their children too—hybrids, the article says—called Nephilim, and the women who seemed guilty of nothing more than marrying bad angels. All destroyed. The point of the article seems to be "don't dabble in spiritism."

There's a drawing of Cain walking away from Abel whom he has just killed. Abel looks like he is sleeping on the ground, head resting on his forearm, while Cain turns sideways to glare maniacally, in a thick grass skirt, his ribs visible in his turning. I wonder who else was around then, who Cain could talk to after this. The pamphlet says Abel was the first man to ever die.

11.

When someone dies, I think what is the good of learning from that now that they're gone? I stopped seeing a friend because he wanted to marry me, and then he died, and now I can't see him. He sat with me for many nights in a diner. One of those nights, I had a terrible fever and couldn't find my way out of the ladies' room, and my friend came to the door looking for me, but I was winding all the towels out of the machine, I was all in white.

12.

Somewhere in Turkey, my friend worked for years near a river, and I can see his city that I don't know, the name like a bridge, in charcoal and some tough filigree in a past that looks engraved. Everything happens in twenty-four hours, or under forty-eight, and the bus left at 8:45 this morning. But in another years ago, he and Irina from Bucharest and a filmmaker from Florida, Olga from New York, and a painter born in the Middle East, who went to the Tropical Sensations porn store in the aqua cement block on A1A to buy a magazine to paint a woman's body from—and flipping through kept saying, *No, no, more graphic, more graphic* because she needed to see inside, and wound up painting in tans and mud and a kind of rose, a woman holding her feet, displayed in a way like Tranströmer's vaults within vaults, though his were first in a cathedral and then the spirit in each person, the body a beginning (though even that preceded by a field of energy) opening exponentially—this painter, and the three other women, and my friend would come over nights to sit on my porch beside the ocean or walk on the beach. They repeated a question I had for my soul, and someone made it into a song.

13.

When I had to leave someone in trouble, when the decision to abandon him demented me, my friend said, *You've given yourself too big a part to play.* Cradling a delicate neck, as if I could be a sea, a house, bed. Mattress and umbrella. The cars rushing by in the night, the night. Shoes, letters to be named, nursery, and coastal town. It's a familiar feeling—this awful adrenaline upset. But when there was difficulty, he'd told me the moon knew about it long ago.

14.

Once before dinner, in the living room of a friend, the sun was going down. A stranger was going to walk on my back, but he said, *You're too weak.* He held my face in his hands, told me I had three guardians. He said I could see them if I wanted to. There were freckles somewhere on his face, striped cotton shirt. He didn't look like someone who would die, but he died. He said, *You never have to be afraid. Ever.* Bodies hovering over you. Stroking your hair, murmuring your name. How do I see them? I forgot to ask him that. I thought all I had to do was be willing to see them, and the guardians would appear.

15.

I was fever-sick, in the basement of a strange house in a new city. I knew my son would be here soon. He was running toward the room I was in. He wouldn't know I was his mother. It was as if he'd lived, been raised by others, and I'd just come to visit. I worried I wouldn't know what to do or say. He came from the right, around the corner, still running. Two years old, or three—a little older than when he'd died. I reached out my arms, and he was in them. I lifted him up. And he let me, the way a small child does. The center of my body opening/deepening to a place beyond my body. Making room for him. He'd been eating crackers in another room. I found an oval cracker in my hand, and held it to his mouth the way I'd held a bottle the day he was born. He hadn't been hungry then. This time it took a moment, but he ate. He was so light to carry, but real, a real boy. He had that same lightness when he was born—weight part of it—though really something else. It was around us too, and us. My left arm still holds the warmth of him where his back rested against my skin. Thirty years since I last held him. But just today, he was in my arms. Never sick. He'd never been sick.

16.

Exposure is part of the cure. If you have a fear of your house burning down, you watch it go down. If you have a fear of stabbing yourself to death, you open yourself to the knife. I have a fear of numbers, of money, the account empty. The way it disappeared once and now that bell keeps ringing. Low-balling when I could have my hands deep in the abacus, that clarity. It's the disappearance of you that most concerns me, that I think may break me in two. How do I expose myself to this? My own disappearance, brain a slew, some distance behind. I've tried looking at an empty yellow field. When the thought comes that I can save you with a prayer, I think it's then that I have to let go. Not to imagine the world without you—I'm not capable of that. I have to let go of the fear of your leaving, the possibility, and my complicated net to save you. Once, in a recovery meeting, I sat in a chair in the crowded room, wondering why I was there. Antsy. Not like the early days—I could stay—it was more that I was still more in the outside world. The group of chairs on my side of the room faced the main hall, people in the chairs before me facing front, profiled. A girl sitting in the back of the room leaned her chair against the wall. Tipped it back. I'd never seen her before. She said that we're loved more than we can know. I think of that almost every day. When I'm terrified that someone might come to harm, I think of her leaning back, her ease. I think that no matter how much I love someone, how tight my fear to keep them safe, everyone is loved more than I can know. Each person a flame I stare into.

MIRROR CITY

WASHINGTON, DC
NOVEMBER 2011

Sascha, the tall German Fellow, and I go on a tour of the Library of Congress. Both of us in residence here for the fall semester. We ride the elevator with the other Fellows, to the special top room—empty, as if waiting for a dance. Carolyn, the director, says, *Come stand in this spot and say something.* But people are shy. It's hard to know what to say.

Then the Russian girl with brilliant red hair stands in the spot and says, *Hello.* Which seems manageable. But Sascha can tell I still feel shy to walk out in front of the others. Speak in this spot, a kind of performance. He asks, *Do you want to go together?* So we do. And our voices carry out and back to us. Sascha says there's a place in a church where people pass out from this—it's called the parabolic effect—all the music in the whole church lands in that one spot, and it overwhelms the people who sit there. A vortex. You become the place where all the music resides, reverb knocking you senseless.

*

Bright blue sky again. Wet red brick sidewalk heaped with leaves—cherry and blood, yellow and black-purple of liver, organs deep inside. Some fall face first, curl like stars with tan backs. Color disappearing. We don't have this in Florida. All this leaf-death feels like a celebration, petals strewn before me on my walk on Capitol Hill. This is the place Sascha found for me to live. I have a white bedroom in a brick townhouse painted the cream of a cake. A tower room with three windows on the street. Dark mahogany front door. Black iron handrail attached to the white doorframe. Fire-red stoop. Aqua of the house door next door washes up against ours.

I share the townhouse with my landlady. She's small, compact, a retired teacher who watches murder shows at night with her cat. Sometimes her face tightens with what I think is disapproval. When I moved in, she offered to pick me up. Pouring rain. Double-parked. Under the eave, I stop to greet her. *Hurry!* she said. When we entered her foyer, she said, *I don't want you damaging my wall with your suitcase. You'll have to take your clothes out down here, carry them up.* Her staircase narrow, my suitcase large. A lot of bossiness right off the bat.

My landlady shakes her head as if in a hair commercial. I don't know what she wants. Brochures on my dresser for drives in neighboring states to watch the leaves change. I don't have a car here. I walk. To the museums. The Capitol. Union Station. Round trip to the Lincoln Memorial is five miles. Among the crowds, I feel we all have the same destination, like birds in flight. I walk up the higher streets, with restaurants, a bakery, theater, old firehouse. Spend weekdays in a cubicle at the Library, reading. Still, on weekends, I love going to bookstores. Breathe easier around books. Voices I can hear. Walk to a used bookstore near my landlady's house. In a back room, books piled low on a table. Open a sky blue one with Indians on horses.

The next summer in Wyoming I'll see the plains, but I don't know this yet. I'll remember the cover of this book, *In a Barren Land.* Inside are the words of Kicking Bird of the Kiowa who, in the mid-nineteenth century, said the earth would be destroyed without Indians: "It is our mother and cannot live when the Indians are all dead." The mother cannot live without her children. Black ink inscription:

> *to terry:*
> *In these days*
> *you were like a mother*
> *to me*
> *thanks for all*
> *DIEGO REMUSSI*
> *8/26/2000*

It makes me want to mother Diego myself, or at least see how he's doing. Unlike my distant relatives, he's relatively easy to find (or like my relatives, the Diego I find may be one of many Diegos) on Facebook. He's from Buenos Aires, and in his profile pic is holding a small child. His interests include the University of Maryland which is in the neighborhood of here, so I think I've found him. So fast. He is *a papa*, one caption says. They all show this, a handsome man with thinning hair. A baby in his arms, who grows in the photos—a royal baby in one. Velvet red dress with her pacifier hanging from a white loosely braided chain of yarn like a Tudor emblem, a crest. Papa's eyes a little red here, but more handsome with his sweater ajar. This was so easy, I know so much in seconds that it's time to stop.

*

Crossing Fourth Street, nervous of the big vehicle slowing down because I'm not walking fast enough. But it's L who says she's going to get pizza. Do I want to go with her to get pizza? I do. In the shop near my house where I usually eat alone at the counter, self-conscious, deferential to the pie-maker, L tosses her hair with even more force than my landlady. Leans against the brick wall, brusque with the man who takes her order. She keeps her eyes on me. For the first time in this place, I don't feel freakish in my solitude. Grateful for her company.

And her family is going to watch a movie, so I go over, and we watch *The Last Station*. Tolstoy. Helen Mirren as his wife. Sit on a red couch with the big screen in front of us. *We usually all just sit on the couch,* her husband said. *No room for shy people in this house.* At which point I am terribly shy.

But I sit, and there is enough room. A super soft rug on the floor of the bathroom, and when I flip three switches (one the light), a heater warms my feet in my flip-flops. Toasty. Fall now, I should be wearing shoes. L is long blond beautiful, wide laugh, but she makes me nervous. I don't know what she wants either. She's from this city, married, two kids, a comfortable wealth. I can't find my footing here, still quiet, lost.

As I leave near midnight, L tells me to buy pepper spray at a hardware store on 11th Street. Said her son's friends got mugged on Georgetown Metrobus in daytime. She walks me outside. Streetlamps turn the air gold. Bright yellow leaves still on the trees. The sidewalk glimmers. I live on 6th, but from L's house, nothing looks familiar. A big Baptist church appears, which I'm sure I would have seen on these weeks of walking home, the sign at least.

L asks, *Are you Southeast?* When I said yes, she explains that E. Capitol separates 6th from 6th. The streets are mirror images of each other on either side. I had no idea. I walk past E. Capitol, and it's the 6th I know. I live in a Mirror City. As in a fairy tale.

*

Amos Oz in the DC bookstore tells us his mother died, when he was twelve, and no word to anyone before her suicide, even though whenever anyone left the house even for half an hour they had to leave a note telling where they'd gone. Afterwards, I walk back to the car with L. She's parked down a residential side street, almost dark, but we can see. Trees around, and then the house to my left with a stag in the yard, nose to the grass. Like a deer statue except moving.

Even when L and I talk, the stag doesn't startle, just keeps going through the yard. I don't want her to know how alone I am. The deer walks. She presses me when I don't answer her. *I'd rather not talk about it,* I say. Loneliness one thing if secret. One moment it's unbearable, and then it's borne. Over and over. *How long?* she asks. Since I've been with someone. To say it in the open air unreels every untouched moment. Brings it into my conscious mind, instead of pushed down in the darkness. The clearer my loneliness, the more it is like L has a sharp little knife, and she is taking swipes at my hair, the skin on my arms, shredding my clothes.

L had told me a secret earlier, unasked, is desperate to balance her vulnerability with mine. She pulls it from me. Once she understands that I'm not seeing anyone, haven't in recent memory, once she sees how deeply it pains me, she relaxes.

I hated her in that moment. Hated her blond hair strong enough to make rope, her kind voice, little gifts. I stand there naked. Then the stag crosses the street, and comes back to the middle white line. Heads right toward us. He veers back into the yard—maybe trying to find his way home. I say, *It's going to be dark soon and then he'll be gone.* And then he is.

*

From the townhouse on Capitol Hill, I walk to the Holocaust Museum. Elevator walls like steel. I'm alone in there, going up. When the doors open, it's long bones scattered like sticks, people burned into one high pyre. I can look into it and see one person, another person. One of the train cars is cut in two, so I walk inside, walk through. Smell of must in the wooden train, though nothing else has any smell. I have to walk back through because I don't know where I've been. There's a boat, orange wood, small portholes, a hull the color of the black and white sky behind it. But a real boat that a family might take out on a bay, a fisherman to fish. In October 1943, *Danes rescued more than seven thousand Jews by transporting them to neutral Sweden.* But the Jews in a boat off Miami weren't allowed to land.

People sailed little boats out to be beside them, to see and speak to them. But the president said no, didn't answer a direct last appeal, and the people were brought back to Europe, left in different countries, where many of them were killed. The forests in Poland, the people taken in there, the walking in, the shooting. Near the end I'm late, closing time, and I'm still heading toward the exit, when I see the shoes. The must again. They cover the floor on both sides.

I walk between their shoes, all some shade of brown or

yellow now. It's only a small portion, like the wall of hair that is only a small portion of what was found tied up in packages for sale, for stuffing bedding, things like that. There are beds in this world filled with the hair of the dead. Someone sleeps on this bed. Earlier I saw the gate to a Jewish cemetery. White with gold rust in places, an ornamental gate, partially open, through which Jews were taken and killed and left there. It helps that there are many visitors, accents from different countries, people reading big white boards, black type, it helps keep me from breaking down. Trying to make sense of the words. It's a forty-one-minute walk from my landlady's house.

LAKE

2011

The Wounded Angel is carried, is blindfolded. But what is the wound? I stood on the median to cross Pennsylvania Avenue, Capitol shining like a spaceship to my right. Obama still running this country like a hero, like we'd have heroes for good. I'd left home for what I thought was nine months. But it would wind up being four years of traveling. I'd thought it was everything I'd ever wanted. To be free to write and read, to see places I'd never seen. Free of the daily workplace, endless paperwork. I'd minimized my need to be known. Seen. I didn't know I needed that. I'd always been around people who knew me. Twenty-two years living in Central Florida, another five in a small surfing town beside a National Seashore. Now I was in a city where I knew no one. I thought it would be exciting. Thought my life would start again. Something new.

That fall in DC, before I crossed Pennsylvania Avenue at the walk sign, I thought of brakes. Cars coming fast. In Orlando, when my own car had been without them, and I had no money, the car repair guy said, *I could turn you in to the police.* In traffic, I'd downshift, then pull the emergency brake. Knew it was very dangerous. Finally took $200 from rent money to a brake store chain, and they gave me used bad brakes that lasted a few months. My bills and coins all poured out on a newspaper in the store, counting out the two hundred.

I used to dream of not being able to stop the car on a circular highway winding like a Disney ride or Miami or the George Jetson future which should be here by now.

That day in DC, or one nearby, a man selling Christmas trees on the side street near Eastern Market had said, *You look exhausted.* I saw how lovely his face was even with my migraine. *It's just heavy,* I said, walking between the aisles of trees, like the green was leading me somewhere.

Across the street from the Library of Congress, my bag felt lighter, and my scalp tingled as if something were about to happen. Just half my scalp, but it was the feeling that seemed to accompany the very good, the unbelievably good happening, the tingle my awareness of it being real.

When I looked inside a doorway, I saw an angel filling it with his white wings. But then, it was a man between a staircase and a wall, porchlight on.

*

That thought I'd had on the Pennsylvania Avenue median, before I'd crossed, thinking of brakes. The dome of the Capitol to my right. The Starbucks man singing in baritone. Standing on the median, shivering in my yellow coat, the thought: *Walk into traffic. Your life is over.*

In Eowyn Ivey's *The Snow Child,* someone walks across the black glass frozen lake to the cliff. But she walks back. She comes back. The voice I heard said, *Die.* It said. *You don't deserve to live anymore.* I'd heard those same words when I secretly visited my son's adoptive parents in Falmouth to ask about his life. Why now? Why stronger? As if I'm breaking another silence and must be shamed, stopped. Or is this self-hatred? I don't know yet that this is my addiction again, alcoholism, trying to find a way to kill me. Slashes on the body. Sew around it, staying close to the edges to prevent raveling. Sew up the heel and the body. Sew the foot of the body to the sole.

*

After DC, I'll go to Vegas for a semester fellowship at the university, then teach in Lake Tahoe for nine months. Still in Nevada, but so high up a mountain, I can't get down. The mountain lake began with melting snow, then rain. A yellow inflorescence branches on this shoreline trampled by a glacier two million years ago. I'm nearly 7,000 feet up a mountain. To reach the village of Incline in Tahoe, you have to drive 10,000 feet, to the top, then come back down. *Bonanza*'s Ponderosa Ranch nearby, shuttered now.

When the show was filmed here, they had to haul all their equipment up Mt. Rose. It was such a hassle, they filmed most episodes in Virginia City instead, on the other side of Reno. But that opening scene, with Pa and Little Joe, all the brothers arriving on horses in a field—that was down the road from my rented condo. On TV, this place had looked like another country. Sometimes I shop beside the very rich because there's just one grocery store. In the cheese aisle, a woman's face looks caulked, masked with lead white Elizabethan paint. She stared at me with an unchanging horrified expression. As if unused to humankind. *It's money,* another teacher said. *There's a lot of money here.*

*

From space Las Vegas is the brightest city in the world. From space that place is burning bright, as if the center of life. Mountains all around a circle of fire. The second most popular tourist destination in the country. Suicide Capital of the U.S. Researchers found that just taking a trip out of town decreased the likelihood of dying by suicide by 13 to 40 percent. The Vegas Valley 2,030 feet above the sea, in the Mojave. A rainshadow desert. All of it covered with a chain of lakes eleven thousand years ago.

*

A thirty-thousand-year-old male skeleton, Mungo III, was found in an Australian lake. Knees bent, hands clasped, as if he is about to dive. One arm detached at the elbow, a knee in fragments. Red ochre in his empty chest. Skull now part and parcel of a square block of beachy sand.

*

In the Sierra Nevada Mountains, I'm exactly 6,225 feet up. Lake Tahoe at the end of my road, highest lake of its size in the U.S. Second deepest lake in the country, tenth in the world—1,645 feet down. Tahoe a mispronunciation of the Washoe tribe's word for lake, Da ow. Lake Lake.

I can see snow on the mountains around me. Roller coaster road. Gym on my left. When I park my jeep, it often feels nearly sideways. As if it might tip over. Ground tilted. Inside, the dance studio is ringed in glass, my first yoga class. I don't like group exercise, or groups, or my idea of yoga— some sedentary thing. The idea of calm exercise seems scrambled, useless. But last summer, another teacher had shown me the muscle in his calf, said it was due to yoga. I open the door, and a woman, Naomi, gives me a rubber mat with a swirly design. There's a man from school here, but he doesn't recognize me. *I'm Kelle,* I say.

He says, *I know, I've seen you at the dog park. No,* I say. *You have a big, black dog,* he says. I don't have a dog, have never seen the dog park. When I was a student, working in a health food store, I'd sometimes see a customer elsewhere—a library, the lake I ran around. The customer always surprised, unable to place me. As if I only existed in the store. Or changed when in another place. But no one really knows me here. The altitude and decreased oxygen makes me feel pixilated, not yet materialized.

I try to copy the way Naomi moves. When I can't follow and panic, she comes to sit beside me. I don't know the name of the difficult pose—all I can think is penguin. Try to fold myself into myself. Another time she touches my hip to lengthen it. Something like when a little girl touched my hand thirty years ago when I'd felt that I could float away.

Naomi reads a poem at the end that said we are like water. That night, some dark worry comes, but doesn't escalate. I feel steadier, belonging in my body. The thought there. And it goes away.

The next day, I want to try another class. On my drive, I pass a green field with people, dogs. I see a blond woman with a big, black dog walking toward the road. Maybe that's me, I think. The me that the guy from school recognized. Ten minutes late, I peek in the window of the dance studio door. See a guy with a canvas belt in his hand. Embarrassed to go in, interrupt. Open the door. There are only two students.

The guy with the belt and an older woman. The teacher, Rebecca, smiles kindly, nods as I roll out the yoga mat I grab from the box. Kick off my shoes, copy her—raise my arms, reach down, up, breathe. Afraid to look in the mirror. But lying on the mat, flat on my back, glance to the left into the glass. Surprised to see someone else. She reminds me of the beautiful familiar I saw years ago when she said she was my soul.

*

In the Great Lakes, the Red Ocher people lived, spoke a form of my 5th great-grandfather's language. Thomas Greenough.

*

In DC, I'd watched a film in a museum, the filmmaker there. She said a nine-year-old girl was reading a hard text, hard vocab, and the girl was unable to pronounce many words. The filmmaker said, *Oh, keep going.* Instead of another word describing women, the girl said, *artists,* and I opened up then to hear an auditorium of goodwill. A shifting camera helped convey the shakiness of the visitor in new land. Outside, flowers were bowing down including the yellow circle ones, the summer ones.

*

Vermeer used red ocher in "The Little Street," "The Milkmaid," and "A Maid Asleep." It can be a substitute for blood.

*

I didn't go directly from Vegas to Tahoe—a summer in between. Flew to Wyoming for that month, then a month in the Santa Cruz mountains. While there, Margot gives me a ride down the one-lane cliffside mountain to San Francisco. I walk to the museum.

Past the angels and fence, people gather around a woman in front of six black-and-white photographs. *What is happening here?* she asks. *What do you see?* I don't like her elementary school teacher tone, but I look. In the first photo, a man is balanced on two steel bars that make an X beneath his feet. His pants are almost the dark of the bars; his T-shirt almost the white of the sky. His head down. The man is at the top of a stadium. The second photo shows two others appearing on girders to the right. The man lifts his left leg casually, like a dancer at rest, too casually for this height.

He turns toward the others in the third photo, holds his arm out to stop them. Here you can see his hair combed with care. He's still young. It's 1971. One of the rescuers has his right knee bent, one arm resting on a beam. The other is above, both hands gripping a girder, his body parallel to the earth, crawling in the air toward the man. His legs appear to straddle a beam.

In the next row of photos, another rescuer appears from the left. He and the standing man from the right walk toward the suicidal man who now has both arms outstretched as if preparing to fly. As if he thinks he is a bird. His head has disappeared. In the fifth photo, he has bent so far over into space that he's almost only visible from the waist down, except for the white of his shirt as he looks down. As if he has dropped something and will go get it.

On either side of him, a man approaches. The rescuer on the left supports himself with one hand on a beam and the other stretched out to the man, to halt. The rescuer on the right has both hands on the beams, his left leg reaching toward the man. In the final photo, the rescuers have reached the man and hold him with their hands. Each has one hand on a beam, one hand holding the man. The suicidal man now holds onto the arm of one man, the leg of the other. *Couldn't he pull them all over?* asks one of the group surrounding the woman.

Yes, she says. *That's part of it, isn't it?* It looks a very long way back to the earth from the X's of girders, a lot of unsupported air around them. Their three bodies all bent over at the waist. The arcs of their reaching for each other make a kind of spider shape in the steel, one organism. The woman says that the photographer, Enrique Metinides, was a crime photographer, and this is how he came to be at the scene. The museum's keywords for *Secuencia rescate de un suicide en la cúpula del Toreo* (Suicide rescue from the top of Toreo Stadium) are "suicides," "crimes," "redemption," "saved," "saving."

*

I can keep a book of skulls in the house, but not a book of ghosts.

*

One of the oldest pieces of art is the hand of artist. Painted in a cave in France twenty-seven thousand years ago, fingers splayed, it looks as though the artist spray-painted red ochre around his palm pressed to stone. My own palm hovering over almost fits inside.

*

Twice I'd thought I could become a lake.

Long after I'd given up on dying. After the years of drinking, the dark years after sparked with light. Until I was in the light, grateful to be alive in a continual way—moments that were days, months, years. I had time.

But then, I had the thought to be a lake. The first time, I'd rocked without a rocking chair. I'd phoned John, my ex-boyfriend in South Carolina, but a woman answered. Refused to let me speak to him. Her laugh like a banjo. I could see him hazy in a doorway, afraid to hear my voice. *I was afraid I'd come back to you,* he said later. As if I were a drug, a bad habit. I hadn't counted on losing his friendship too, his love. Thought he could be counted on always. Forever mesmerized by those diamonds on my silver tights. Eyes locked on my legs as I took my seat, late. The shut door of him shook me. A strange woman's voice mocking me. Later, I'd say, *Mail me all the photos I gave you.* The naked, the in-love. He'd been shocked, expected to keep these images.

But when the lake thought came, when I rocked without a rocking chair, I drove to a room where I could hear one person talk at a time. Stared at the list of steps for staying alive, like a scroll unrolled on the wall by my chair. Surrounded by people in folding chairs, silent army of protection. Afterwards, I drove to a friend's house, said, *I can't be alone.* Sat beside her while she watched TV. I sat with her son, her dog. Sat while she cooked dinner.

The next day, I came back. Sat there all that day too, until I no longer thought about becoming a lake. I don't remember anything on TV, just my friend beside me, the solidity of her body. Someone who could be counted on. Who would stay.

The second time I thought to be a lake, to drown, it was green. Like Ophelia's river. Surrounded by a forest of trees that seemed enchanted. Instead, I went to the house where I was living and packed my suitcase. I flew away. X, the man

I loved, crying like a child in the airport, but I flew away for good. When Nana died I thought I could count on John. Then thought I could count on X. Transferred what couldn't be transferred to either of them—neither strong enough to love me like that. Love I could always feel in my body.

*

A bombarded cranium found in Lake Turkana is 3.5 million years old. It's the size of my outstretched palm. The chin has the uneven roots of a tree. One eye is a kaleidoscope, the other cascades into the middle of the skull. It's hard to know this is a face—the dome, deep cheekbones, no mouth that I can find. Bone itself flaking, crisscrossed like a city map seen from far above.

*

The Black Skull from Lake Turkana, blue-black manganese bone looks made of feathers or wolf, or the ash of burned trees, 2.5 million years old. Not human yet. Sagittal crest a helmet, a kind of crown. A tiny penguin stands on the right cheekbone.

*

In DC, I'd walked to another museum. The tapestries from the fifteenth century are sewn behind, over tears. The walls red and peopled. A story retold in thread differently than what was lived, so large like the planet of this battle day five centuries ago. Then someone sewing for a very long time. Eyes smarting, how many were smarting?

Lost, I talked to the guards with my straightened hair. The restaurant man said, *We're closed baby.* The kind eyes of F.

Scott Fitzgerald followed me. Twice the security guard told me to carry my backpack like a baby. *Baby,* he kept saying, *like a baby.* He held his hands in front as if he was a waiter with a tray held very low, at his knees, as if serving a baby.

I was pretty sure I couldn't hold any item in that position and walk, especially not a baby. And never mind being able to actually see anything in the museum since my view would only be two or three feet from the floor. Never mind that I would do almost anything to hold my baby. He said, *Someone's backpack knocked over a work of art worth two hundred and fifty thousand dollars.* When I didn't look impressed enough, he said, *It belongs to the government.* Later I see a man wearing his backpack on his chest as if it is his back and understand.

In Orlando, Mary used to tell me that gratitude is an action. Action—to do the things I'm afraid to do. In the atrium, I looked around for Whitman's office door, his view. But this room of glass was new, post his termination from the patent office. Voices at the table nearby: *Are you warm enough now? I'll never be warm enough. I'll be warm in the car.* A pamphlet said that the skylight above me is a block long, shining its shady light on us, me unseen. But as I left the museum, there's snow on the coats of a boy and girl entering the front door of the gallery. *It's snowing,* I said to them, and they turned, snowed on. They could see me.

Yes, they said. And then I stepped outside in the snow light, and it was snowing between the buildings. I walked out from under the awning, and it fell on my yellow coat; like the others, I was part of the snow world, snow globe.

THE SKY IS FULL OF HORSES

LAS VEGAS, NEVADA
JANUARY 2012

When I brought my bags to the skycap in Orlando, he said, *I'm afraid of you.* Joke-friendly, as if I'm a big gambler with my big hair, overpacked suitcases. Arrive in Las Vegas, Spanish for *The Meadows.* I have never seen a place less meadow-like, except El Paso. Another desert. *Miss America Pageant is tomorrow,* the cab driver says. Look out the window at tall hotels with the strange feeling I'm inside a TV, all the Miss Americas I saw as a child in pajamas. Women in satin gowns. Nervous as each one walks down those stairs in heels. Not looking down. Strange that it's real, that this is the place. I have a fellowship in Vegas for the spring semester.

In an Italian restaurant, I'm seated right beside the piano player and he's singing. The maitre d' had asked if I wanted to sit near the band. No art museum in Vegas. It closed, art dispersed among the buildings of UNLV. My fellowship at the university is January to May.

*

Am I on a mountain? The mountains are around me. I'm in a basin, but am I high up too? What is the altitude? So dizzy, I could lie down right now on the floor. A student at the soda machine in my dorm says, *I gave all my ones to that showgirl.*

The red mountains outside my window change color. Before they're shadow, they turn gold ocean sand, so maybe I'm not so far away.

Sea level: "The level of the ocean's surface, especially the level halfway between mean high and low tide, used as a standard in reckoning land elevation or sea depths." The elevation in New Smyrna Beach is seven feet. The elevation in Las Vegas is 2,030. I am 2,023 feet higher up in Vegas.

*

It turns out Nevada is one of three states where isotopes directly related to tsunami damaged reactors in Japan reached. They were measured on Flamingo Road, just off the Strip. Minute, they say—not harmful. It's where the Target is, and the Atomic Testing Museum: 1.4 miles from my dorm. Six minutes by cab. Just east of Paradise Road. The Museum has a store. One item is a yellow can labeled in thick red capital letters, "TOXIC WASTE" with green goo spilling out of the top, down the can edge. This is under the category of "Novelty Items" which includes "Candy, poker chips, dolls, and more fun stuff."

An image of a bomb cloud comes up out of desert: "November 1951 nuclear test at Nevada Test Site. Test is 'Dog' from Operation Buster. The first U.S. nuclear field exercise conducted on land; troops shown are 6 miles from blast." The way the men are crouched and darkened, thickens them, so that at first they seemed muddied or made of mud.

*

I'll go to Incline Village, Nevada, in July for ten days to teach. Returning in August as visiting faculty for nine months. Elevation there is 6,404 feet. Three times the elevation in Vegas.

DC's lowest elevation is sea level, on the banks of Poto-
mac; highest near the National Cathedral at 390 feet. Five
thousand two hundred eighty feet is a mile. Denver is a mile
high. Incline Village is over a thousand feet higher than Den-
ver. Dizzy the few days I once spent in Denver. The moun-
tains unreal and hyper-real like a movie come to life. Like me
in a movie, mountains appearing in between the buildings.
Bright bright bright. I could hardly look at the mountains
for long, their beauty and vivid presence exhausting. Craving
a dim room, a rest. You need twice as much water in Denver
for the altitude and because it's dry like the desert. I'm in
the desert.

There's 25 percent less protection from the sun, so you
need to wear sunscreen even in winter. "Because Denver is
closer to the sun, it can feel much warmer than the actual
temperature during the daytime, but then become very chilly
after sundown." What does that mean? Warmer than the ac-
tual temperature?

How close am I to the sun here in Vegas? In Incline Vil-
lage? Maile, who teaches at the university, mentioned the
radiation here. Thought she meant sun radiation, but also
desert radiation, the radiation of Las Vegas, the brightest
city in the country. Is that radiation too, lights? The nucle-
ar testing site sixty-five miles northwest in the desert. Maile
recommended sunscreen.

*

Joe, one of the graduate students, emailed me a Time-Lapse
Map of Every Nuclear Explosion Since 1945. Beneath the
video link, he wrote, *Hope this doesn't make you worried about
living in Nevada!* A Japanese artist, Isao Hashimoto, made

the map. It shows 2,053 nuclear tests and explosions. One is the bomb dropped on Hiroshima, one the bomb dropped on Nagasaki. The rest are practice. The U.S. is responsible for 1,032 nuclear explosions. They appear on the map over Nevada as a series of red blips, like a video game, or like someone is shooting at the map, and everything it hits blows up iridescent red. Hashimoto's aim in making the piece was *to show the fear and folly of nuclear weapons.*

*

So little water in the air, I find it hard to breathe. Opening a window helps. My fifth-floor dorm window only opens so far, so no one can jump or fall out. But the wind comes in, over the mountains, down in the valley. I was afraid to drive my old jeep from Florida to Vegas, across Death Valley. Name itself a pretty clear warning. Afraid I'd never make it. Even thinking about it made me thirsty. Steam geyser from the runnel around my green hood, cacti and snakes. The dying always on their bellies crawling. Instead of driving, I walk in Vegas.

*

One recovery meeting a week is in walking distance. Last night, I held hands with a woman who works in a morgue. Afraid she would still have the dead on her hands, but what could I do? She was freckled, sunburnt from her day off. When my hand was in hers I forgot about the bodies. I think she'd been telling me to live. Horatory is *advising*; hosanna *save*. She said things don't really matter that much. Debts, jewelry. Speaking as one who helps the dead.

In our circle, a three-week-old baby reclined under a

blanket making new talk while the woman from the morgue trailed off. In her ellipsis I saw quiet bodies around, stitched where they'd been cut, all their stuff at home: no more horse-radish, skim milk, headphone songs. Imagined us as a room of the dead, the woman on my other side without her hat. Not the baby—he kept living. Morgue woman took my hand, and it was like it always is—my hand in the room of possibility.

No kitchen in my $900-a-month dorm room, but there's a Chipotle across the street. I eat so many bowls of rice and beans in these five Vegas months, I can't stand the word "chipotle," nausea rising. Before I reach this saturation point, I run across the highway. Walk over handbills with photos of naked women, stars on their breasts. A boy winks at me, star-eyed.

Alone on the fifth floor, this old dorm recently renovated as conference housing. But almost everyone only rents the lower rooms. Once in a while, I'll hear voices for a few days. Door slams. One night, the insistent voices of several men wake me. There are men I don't forgive, I don't even try. It doesn't bother me to see their bodies in the cold room. I can think of it and breathe. In this valley, I wake up to the voices of strange men, and go to sleep to them. They are loud, angry even if they aren't mad. Close. One afternoon, on the sidewalk outside the door, these three men pass close by me, all smiling, though the sidewalk is wide.

Because there are no other voices here except my silent one, I have a biological reaction to a cough coming from their room across from mine, inquisition light under my door. It triggers something. I try to explain it to Josh, my friend from the English Department. Vague, I can't get at it.

His face wrinkles under his dark glasses. I'm afraid of their voices, how close they pass.

Alone at night, their voices, across the hall of red doors, are always argument. It pierces the center of my chest, hornet skewer. In my all-white bleachy bed, I am out of combat. Body on guard. Sometimes it acts hospitalized, waiting to be towed. Because we are meridians of light, what is happening here—to my light? Dizzy here, high up, held up. At the meeting, I thought I might say something to the morgue woman, but she ran from me to the baby. Stood beside her, and the baby was all we saw.

*

In a DC museum, I'd seen a woman made from marble in 1876. Veins in her neck where her blood flowed. The boy young on her lap, she holds his wrist, chest fallen back. Her hand supports his head, wet hair, her cloak fallen. Camisole strap thin and thinner, those holes in her eyes. Veins in her hand holding his just faint ribs, and he holds near the gem of her cloak, holds on so maybe he lives. There is a little swirl in her cap, a thread just one. I hope he lives.

All the loud excited little girls in the exhibit with me. A space like a white cave a white walkway and swirl in the foreground. The green of a river.

In another DC museum, a guy nearby says, *The sky is full of horses.* I hear him. Look up.

BLACK MOUNTAIN

LAS VEGAS, NEVADA
SPRING 2012

Maile taught me to gamble on the penny slots. She said, *All slot machines play in the key of C.* It's pleasing to us, the sound when you win. Various small parrots, electronic buttercups, gold coins. Smoke. A woman the color of driftwood. *Superstitions aren't mocked here,* Maile said. *It's a pagan town.* I have an office at the university's Black Mountain Institute and live on campus. From the windows of my fifth-floor residence rooms, I can see the green MGM and treeless mountains.

*

The Facial Action Coding System (FACS) is only useful sometimes—*only 43 percent recognized frightened faces.* How do I know how you feel? I guess you have to tell me. I have to ask. 43 percent. Not even half. In Joanna Bourke's history of fear there's a photograph of a naked woman dragged to her lobotomy in 1950. She's almost backed herself into a corner, but a smiling woman in a dark dress and no shoes blocks the corner with her bare feet in a kind of plié. The woman being dragged has her head thrown back against the wall, hair thick, curly. Her one visible arm across her breasts is lifted toward the wall; her fingers touch it in a dead way.

Because her head is thrown back, I can't see her face, just her mouth, open wide toward the ceiling. Appealing for help beyond the dark-dressed woman, the nurse reaches both arms toward her in an empty embracing gesture. The nurse's white tights sheen and glitter like a dancer's.

The nurse is the only one wearing shoes (white). She wears a dark leather watchband on one weakly reaching wrist. It matches the only item on the dragged woman—a leather belt cinched around her waist with a tiny light circle. Next to the circle embedded in the leather is an inch or so of leather facing downward toward her thigh, as a belted belt can have the extra unnotched piece folded over itself. Perhaps she is too thin for the belt—she's very thin. The belt has a strange holster that hangs from her waist halfway to her knee. It looks like it could hold half a rifle, a shotgun. But who would carry such a large gun on her body? Maybe there is more to this, more behind her. She has one foot (cut off in the photograph) on the wooden floor, one in the air, hidden from mid-thigh behind the nurse's wide white dress.

Though struggling, she has the appearance of a doll. At least three other people here—two women draggers, the photographer. *Where is her dress?* Why are the walls filthy, black mold climbing? The dark-dressed woman nearly has one foot in the black corner. Sixty-two years ago, the naked woman ended there. There is another wall behind the women attendants—it might be a door—gray/black with many scraped areas of white, as if knives have been taken to it, or nails. The caption: *Other patients have to be held.* The edge of the photo reads, *The Wellcome Trust.*

*

You may find that your thinking is characterized by more than one distortion. Intolerance of uncertainty is a common cognitive distortion. As is an inflated sense of responsibility. I want to find the author of my worry book, track him down at his anxiety institute. Ask if he saw that issue of *Time* that I found in a used bookstore about fifteen years ago (the issue much older). Yellow cover and either a winged image or hands in prayer (the steeple, inside all the people) or both. The cover article on the power of prayer, instances of prayer working, maybe even scientific proof (a study). The magazine disappeared when I went to look for it, replaced by a yellow cover of *Time* with the image of Jesus, his face all calm love.

Also, what about positive thinking and imagining what you want—visualization—to make things happen. What about that, Doctor? Are you familiar with the power thoughts are thought to have?

*

Chronophobia is the fear of time. People who suffer from this are often prisoners. They cannot speak, the world narrows. There are *overwhelmingly haunting thoughts.*

*

Another book tells me how to cure a fright: 1) Find the person who does the cure; 2) Get a red hot key. Be bled. Wear or drink hyacinth. You'll need a healer to feel the suffering in your pulse and temples. *Fear must be charmed out of the body.* It was thought fright could make a person so weak, a demon could enter, possess them. I remember a girl in a recovery meeting who had been in the Navy's detox program after me. Either she, or another girl who witnessed the event told me the story. While in treatment, the girl had been vulnerable, and a presence had possessed her. She said it spoke through her in their circle, in group. I remember thinking of darkness over their circle, swooping in on her, on a weakened space in her aura. I thought I have to be strong. Envisioned my aura like the weave in a coat. If torn, I'll have to mend it.

*

In Vegas, the place I rent on campus comes with a TV room and cable. The only shows I saw in DC were ones my landlady on Capitol Hill watched. Sometimes, when I came home from the Library, I'd sit with her and her cat in the living room. The couch very close to the TV. She sat in a puffy chair, a retired English professor. The shows almost always involved the abduction and torture of a young woman, and the efforts of detectives to find her.

It feels luxurious to watch whatever I like. *Mouth of Fire* begins with a scene of an old woman, Marte Herlof, tied to a ladder. She's pushed, falls face first into a fire. The real name is *Day of Wrath*. In the movie, old, black and white, another woman's eyes are wide with an inward slant. Something hidden. Shifting light on water. Hard to fix on. It's suggested she may have her mother's power of wishing, witchness. She's young, and her old husband, a pastor, who may have never loved her, asks if she has the power to wish things to happen. To curse.

She floats in a rowboat with her old husband's son whom she loves, but he abandons her. It's Denmark, 1623. She wears a white collar and cuffs, white brimmed cap, white apron even in the boat. She and the son hold hands. The movie is based on a play—*Anne Pedersdotter*—based on real life in sixteenth-century Norway; a real woman who fell in love with her old husband's son. The woman who plays Marte is eighty years old, sentenced to burn at the stake for witchcraft, for wishing harm to another. For harm happening.

The pastor in his dark robe keeps asking his wife if she has wished him dead. She looks cornered, eyes flickering with candlelight inside, and she says yes. She wished him dead. And then he immediately dies in front of her, a heart attack. She goes to court in what looks like a tomb. She appears to sit on the edge of a coffin to confess. We've already seen what happened to the old woman after being made to confess, the way they tied her to trees. Fire in front of her. Then her body raised on trees, the wooden frame. As if they were raising the wall of a house with a woman roped to the inner beams, tied down. And then, after it was perpendicular to the ground, the boy singers sang and watched her. The men below pushed the frame forward, and the old woman fell face first into the flames. She screamed going down, but once she hit the flames—silence—her mouth full of fire. Then no more mouth.

*

The next day, I meet Oksana, a writer from Russia, for coffee at the Coffee Bean & Tea Leaf across from school. On the news, I'd heard of many pedestrians struck down by cars. *It seems as if a week cannot pass without a motorist striking and killing somebody walking.* In the Las Vegas Valley, twenty-nine pedestrians have been killed this year. The highway across from my conference-housing dorm is the second busiest north-south street in town. My decision to live here for five months without a car was ill advised. I wait for a clear space, walk fast.

Oksana tells me about cursing. She says that even now in Russia, or in the very recent past, one could go to court and say they'd been cursed. The court would have to check it out. The curse investigated. Oksana says the pagan, the Christian, and the superstitious were hidden behind a wall of Communism. But not gone. Just behind it.

*

In Wyoming, Evan will tell me that if you are threatened by dogs in Bali, you should reach down as if to pick up a rock. You don't have to actually pick one up, it's just the reaching that's necessary, and the dogs will retreat. When Simen went to Bali, he could hear the dogs at night alone in his room. Began to think maybe he'd been poisoned.

*

Howard Hughes lived at the now demolished Desert Inn in Vegas. He stayed on the top two floors for four years straight. Bought the hotel. How easy it is to just stay inside. And then he disappeared in the night without being seen.

*

O my terrified my obdurate / my wanderer / keep the trail
—Adrienne Rich

*

In Vegas, I am drawn to a necklace, gold swirl interlocking with a brown leather cord—but it's Maile who says, *Is that a snake?* And it is, my fingers on the bumpy gold. I like touching what I am afraid of, wearing it around my neck. *Like a talisman,* Maile says. I'm not sure that's it. Maybe she meant amulet. Not to protect me against what I fear, but to wear what I fear. To move in the world with what I fear around my neck, unafraid.

*

Bring some luck to the table, the guy next to me says at my first roulette. Lit up, surprised that I might have some.

*

In "The Great Dog Massacre," Mark S.R. Jenner, said that one early attempt to combat plague was the large-scale slaughter of dogs and cats. People need something to do against the unknown, fear. They need an object. Then they need a task.

*

At the store near where Japanese radiation landed on Flamingo in Las Vegas, I buy a very soft dark blue blanket to cover my scratchy couch. But I put it on my bed at night, over the green blanket on which someone had inked a smiley face. I'd found it in a plywood closet, the face creepy. One wall is the color of grape soda. The sign outside my building says "Central Desert Complex." Instead of grass, there is a lawn of sharp rocks. Baseball sized, if baseballs were all edges, heavy. Outside are bushes that look like Cousin It made of grass instead of hair, rows of them all together: a family.

I have signs inside too. One in my bedroom; one in my TV room. Though the rooms are identical dorm rooms made into one unit—a small bathroom with toilet and shower in between. The bathroom doors both have signs that read: "OCCUPIED." The bedroom and the TV room each have a sink with a sign glued to the mirror that says, in thick red letters, "DO NOT PUT FOOD IN SINK." They're just regular bathroom sinks. I'm at the top of an old building. The long, glistening red hallway of doors, absent of other people, reminds me of *The Shining*. When I first arrived, I meet a man in the elevator, and he can't stop talking. Says, *You're the first person I've seen up here in months.* But he leaves the next day.

One night, I walk down the hallway to the elevators, trash bag to take out. A horrible smell in the hallway six or seven doors away, I'm already gagging. Reek of spoiled animal and what else? On a bike that summer, I'll pass a decomposing deer on a twice-daily basis. This is worse. A man is vacuuming the room. Door wide open. I hold my breath, rush past. Toss my trash in the ground floor dumpster, breathe fresh air. I have to get by the room again. There's only one way in. In the hallway, the man and I pass each other. He carries a big bundle of bedding, including a brown thing, maybe a mattress pad. All of it held slightly away from his body and putrid. Door shut, but the smell is still horrendous. I don't ask. I have no other place to go. Open my windows even though it's winter, cold. Even though one window has no screen, and Nevada has bats. The material of the green blanket I'd found is thick and weirdly stiff—extra flame retardant or flammable. Like felt with cardboard in it. I drape the ocean-dark blue over it. Let it touch my face, lean into it.

I leave Las Vegas in the middle of May 2012. My vastly too-heavy bags topple, jam the elevator door, then, the dorm's front door. Finally outside in the bare bulb desert air. The giant blue bag and medium black both tumble over like toddlers on the bright sidewalk. An hour's sleep. It's nearly a hundred degrees. Not the 100 degrees of Florida filled with water, skin a slide of humidity. In Vegas, the water is scorched out of you. An iron pressed down on the cloth of air. My blood vessels deflate. I want to lie down in a cool bathtub.

In the airport, I pass the slot machines, the circling attendant in black with keys jingling at her hip. Go in the restroom. Fingers achy from my clench/claw, dragging the bags. Shadows of small bruises blooming on my forearms from traveling with more than I can carry.

Exhausted, I hear the woman beside me at a sink mirror say, *I'm ready to leave Vegas.* I think she tells me how long she's been there. I tell her I've been here five months, and I'm going to Wyoming. She asks, *You just decided to go?*

Yes. Realize it sounds like I'm moving there. Carefree, almost romantic, with my bloodshot eyes and hair in every direction but down.

The woman at the mirror says, *Well, you only live once. Have fun.* It has not occurred to me for a long time to have fun. Even when I've said it, it's more a way of complimenting who I've been with, "that was fun" rather than actual fun. I remember Denise at Atlantic Center the summer before asking, *Can't you just wave your hands like this.* Her hands held high beside her temples. So we could both dance with Alan. Alan saying, *She won't come unless you do.* But I couldn't, that part of me was so far down I would need a shovel and a crane.

I miss the years when I wanted a bottom floor apartment, so I could dance at night without disturbing anyone. I danced on the second floor anyway, my feet pretty quiet. But now, it's more like I have to swim up from the bottom of where I've gone, swim up from below. I think of the woman in the Vegas bathroom. *Have fun.* She said it like gentle command. Something necessary. Or, like a wish.

THIS USED TO BE AN OCEAN

UCROSS/BUFFALO, WYOMING

JUNE 2012

> *Even this late the bones of the body shine*
> *and tomorrow's dust flares into breath.*
>
> —Mark Strand, "The Coming of Light"

In the summer of 2012, when I arrive in Wyoming, it's green. I've never even seen Wyoming on a map. Imagined one of the longer, rectangular states, dusty from the gallop of horses. Hills, a rocky summit knife flat, a dance floor. But wreathed like a crown. The Crow and the Sioux, these are their buffalo lands where I stand. High plains at the foot of the Bighorn Mountains.

For two years, I've been traveling to places I've never been before, where I know no one. Trying to understand what home is, where it is. For myself, who left Cape Cod as a child, traveling to a new state every few years, a new country in my teens. For my ancestors from Ireland and Finland, who left their countries and never returned. For my Native American ancestor, last of the South Yarmouth Wampanoags, who had his home taken from him. Is home the place you left, or the place you are now?

I've been invited to spend the month of June at an artists' residency on a peaceful twenty-thousand-acre cattle ranch in the majestic, wide-open setting of northeastern Wyoming.

I want to climb Medicine Bow northwest of Laramie. But the talk of bear and lightning strikes, rattlesnakes even in the field where I ride my bike, the cattle rustling to charge me on a minor hike, a little rise of land—it scares me off. Ruthie, the program director, drives me through roads of winding hills, hand out the window, blue tattoo at her wrist. She says, *All this used to be an ocean.* When I ask why she moved here, she says she'd wanted a new start.

The deer always run around me while I bike home from my writing studio at dusk, so I have to be careful to look for their bright eyes, bodies darker than air. All of us here together. On the butte above, Indians had stood on that flat, looked down. I wondered if the medicine men could see this far, this plain. Shoshone here at the foot of the Bighorns, then Crow, Arapaho, Sioux, Cheyenne. More cows than people in this state. When a boy is seen walking down the highway, neighbors phone house to house, call the police.

When I first arrived, I asked Ruthie if it was okay to drink the water. *We have Culligan,* she said. A bottled water dispenser in my studio. I'm surprised. We're on the prairie. The plains. The least populous state in the country. Over half of the ranch's lands are protected by a conservation easement held by The Nature Conservancy. We can't drink the water here?

It's on a drive to Sheridan, "King of the Cowboy Towns," that I begin to understand. Ruthie and I pass hulking machinery, an abandoned house, detritus left in the grass by the companies come to explore mineral rights beneath the land. Roads dug in. *What is this?*

Ruthie tells me you can own your land without owning the mineral rights. Someone could show up at your door.

Dig up your land. Frack it. This involves injecting pressurized chemicals mixed with water into the ground to extract oil or gas.

We stop at Ruthie's house on the way to town. She lives in a geodesic dome, an elfin, fairy tale house from the 1960s with unexpected little nooks. Ruthie never lets her two St. Bernards run free because they'd go after the cows, and cows come first in Wyoming. *They'd shoot the dogs,* she says as I pet them. The dogs press against the fence, watching us leave. *Most people only own surface rights,* Ruthie had said. And *mineral rights take precedence.* Like cows over dogs.

Until 2010, companies didn't have to reveal the names of chemicals used in fracking. Trade secrets. Wyoming was the first state to demand disclosure. According to Earthjustice, *78 percent of known fracking chemicals are associated with serious short-term effects: burning eyes, rashes, asthma-like effects, nausea, vomiting, headaches, dizziness, tremors, and convulsions. Between 22 and 47 percent are associated with longer-term health effects: cancer, organ damage, harm to the endocrine system.* All that quiet, and this underneath.

Recent reports prove fracking has polluted groundwater in Wyoming, and contaminated aquifers in Texas and Pennsylvania. A 2018 report on the harms of fracking includes increased risks of asthma, birth defects, and cancer for those near an active site. Hazards range from benzene in the air to "cleansed" fracking wastewater (which can be radioactive, flammable, and carcinogenic) released into local bodies of water.

The federal government owns nearly 50 percent of the land in Wyoming—that's a lot of leasable mineral rights. And the Stock Raising Homestead Act of 1916 means 11.6

million acres of private land in the state also has split rights. Surface rights are privately owned, but the federal government owns mineral rights. Energy companies can come on your land, tear it up, and there's nothing you can do. Plus, the water is sucked out of the coal seams to get the methane to come out. This drains aquifers, and it can take centuries to get them back. I see why I can't drink the water.

Earthjustice created a map of gas drilling incidents in Wyoming. They're called *fraccindents*. On the map, the fraccindents are marked by little white skulls with crossbones in black background circles. Wells tested near these areas contained petroleum hydrocarbons, as well as naphthalene, phenols, and benzene.

In July 2008, a well in Sublette County tested for benzene, a chemical believed to cause aplastic anemia and leukemia, in a concentration *one thousand five hundred times the level safe for people.* Tests showed contamination in eighty-eight county wells. Researchers sought additional samples, but couldn't open the wells, *so full of flammable gas, they were likely to explode.*

In the same year, benzene was discovered in an illegally operated pit in Rock Springs, WY. Three weeks later a rancher was hospitalized after he drank well water out of his own faucet. Tests showed benzene in his water.

In 2009, Pavilion, WY, residents were advised not to drink their water or use it for cooking. *To avoid explosions due to methane contamination,* precautions included *ventilation when taking showers.* In 2013, a man was severely burned in a flash fire explosion in Fremont County, WY. The next year, Opal, WY, an entire eighty-eight-acre town, had to evacuate after an explosion and fire at a natural gas processing unit.

Wells exploding. Water catching fire. These are a few of the skulls and crossbones on the fraccidents map.

On our visit to Sheridan, I tell a girl with a scar on her face that I am going to San Francisco when I leave Wyoming. Put my arms into a warm blue-gray coat, like a scissor-cut blanket with buttons. She calls to me from behind the dressing room door, *Hey, San Francisco, how're you doing?* As if my name is wherever I'm traveling to.

On one of our last nights, we drive twenty miles to Buffalo to hear live bluegrass at the Occidental. Antlers abound in this historic hotel, skins on the wall. Above my head the head of a deer is white and soft. I sit on a shellacked wooden stool made from a small tree for a tiny person. A framed note from a woman who stole two spoons from the hotel in 1919. The woman wishes to make amends, sending this letter of apology and two dollars in 1957. Also on display is a pack of Lucky Strikes, a tin of Prince Albert, a match dispenser with stars at the corners, the matches one cent. A lantern hangs over a photograph of Sherman and the Sioux signing a treaty, later broken when gold was discovered. Desire for money overriding.

Almost dark, I walk upstairs. Rooms unlit. But light comes from the windows and takes over. I feel like I will always see the white light in this room of the Occidental, walk on the squeaky floor, see these nineteenth-century dresses in the hallway. Handsewn baby clothes, white dresses with tiny embroidery. Smocked like gathering fog.

Some rooms are open with thick, fancy ropes across them, the kind you'd ring for a bellhop in a Cary Grant movie, but these horizontal ropes block entry. The famous stayed here: Buffalo Bill, Calamity Jane who made this her headquarters for a while. Headquarters for what? Maybe another word for home.

In 2017, President Trump will rescind the 2015 final rule on hydraulic fracturing. When he offers up for lease more than 12.8 million acres of drilling rights, in Wyoming alone, the number of rigs doubles. Methane release restrictions are relaxed. A fracking boom. Once the fossil fuel companies drill for oil and gas beneath the land, they can hold the leases indefinitely.

Downstairs, I ask another artist-in-residence, Moyra, if she wants to see the open roped rooms. She nods, but when we come back upstairs a quarter of an hour later, all the doors are shut.

I'm cautious of drinking the water at the Occidental. Order a Sprite. But what about the melting ice cubes? It's packed downstairs in the saloon as the bluegrass band sings "Amazing Grace." We stand as you would for the National Anthem. I saw the windows, all that last light in the minutes before those doors shut. Walked the stairs Calamity walked. In the back room of the saloon, I watched a woman whose husband died fifty-one years ago dance with boy after boy. Watched her serious dancing, unbroken eye contact. Closing time. My bed twenty flat, empty miles away. Even way out here where it seems no one could reach you, in the plains and prairies, and buttes and arroyos, a person isn't safe. Even water can catch fire.

OCCIDENTAL

UCROSS/BUFFALO, WYOMING

JUNE 2012

The white rose is for remembrance, the death of a child. Lilies, chrysanthemums for sorrow. It could be a bouquet, a basket, an altar covered in flowers. But I can't see it from here. The surprise of the lie blanketing.

I thought it was only live music in churches that I couldn't stand. Since that day in church with the flowers. The Sunday after my son died, and the flowers were for him. My surprise when the minister said my father's nephew had died. Instead of his grandson. As if I were not my son's mother. Reduced to a cousin. Invisible. My uncle's family had kept it a secret, where Tommy came from. Even now, after he'd died. Even three thousand miles away. The surprise, and then my disappearance. Empty dress in a pew. Everyone rose and sang.

In between there was a moment for the congregation to acknowledge my "cousin's" (son's) death. Even if it was just the moment/breath between the minister saying, "these flowers are for him" and "let us sing." Before we rise. I don't know if the hymn was for my son, in his memory, or in recognition of his loss.

I don't even know for sure if I cried as they sang, but

I remember having to push everything down. Later, in my gray Corolla, switching the stations on Orlando radio, the Christian music—church songs—would come on. I'd turn the dial, find a different song. But all those songs were for my son who we lied about in church. Even there, the disguise. In the car I was undisguised. The music all for him, and I am his mother.

At the Occidental Hotel there had been live bluegrass, folk. The last time I almost heard live music was with my son's adoptive parents, my aunt and uncle. November 2009, an Irish pub in Falmouth, and they were so happy. My aunt especially pleased there would be Irish songs and everyone would sing along. I was petrified—knew I couldn't sing anymore. That place of being able to sing was too far down, too buried. To sing aloud would leave me ridiculously vulnerable. When I'd think of those people rising beside me, singing in church, it was as if they'd all knifed themselves open, throat to belly. Chests open like cupboards, dark crested, each slick heart a little cake on a shelf. All believed they were loved. Even the memory almost unbearable. Their trust made them children. Innocent. Foolish. I would never be a child like that again.

For a while, I've been turning to stone. The woman in the Vegas airport bathroom telling me that life is short. *Have fun,* she said. And I'd been surprised at the idea, that it could still be allowed. That everyone isn't boarded up. In Falmouth, when I'd visited my son's parents, I'd been so relieved when the Irish band hadn't shown up. We left without singing, my aunt disappointed.

I don't know what would have happened if they started singing around me, my son's parents. Years of departing my body yet still hauling it around. My lips moved that Sunday in the Florida church after my son died. I did that sometimes, pretended to sing.

*

Calamity Jane drove freight wagons on the Bozeman Trail, stayed at the Occidental. It's near the Bozeman at the foot of the Bighorn Mountains. In 1887, she began writing letters to her four-year-old daughter Janey, who she'd given away to her friend Jim in New York. Calamity had paid him for all the expense of raising her daughter. In 1903, after years of alcoholism and depression, her beauty gone, she boarded a train for South Dakota. Calamity drinking a lot, going blind, dying. The same age as me. The train conductor "carried her off the train and to a cabin." After she died, they found a packet of letters, all the letters that she'd written to her daughter and never sent. *April 1902: All I have left are these little pictures of you...*

*

My housemate at this Wyoming ranch, Moyra Davey, a photographer and filmmaker who made *Les Goddesses,* said she likes live music. I once rode in a van from Orlando to Tampa to hear Neil Young live. We traveled in driving rain to get there. I ate bran muffins with too much honey, sat high up in the front seat of the van. Sugar made me dizzier and dizzier as we drove toward Tampa. Rain so hard, in sheets, my boyfriend had to just stop the van on a street in St. Petersburg. Out my streaming passenger window, a fancy hotel glistened. Gold glow, quiet. Like an underwater castle. The hotel off-season and affordable. Claw tub, nineteenth-century wallpaper—

tiny flowers, that old rose pink. My boyfriend like a servant who would do anything.

The next day in the sun, I saw a statue of Jesus with a missing arm and went in a quiet church with no people. Was it the first time that I'd been in a church since that Sunday in disguise against my will? If I had a will? So unvoiced, just the way I was. Still a surprise to be that invisible. In St. Petersburg, I didn't hold my breath. I was alone, I could breathe. Look around. Sat there and breathed a chant of plain music with the air. Dearly beloved, it was white, and no other person entered. All that quiet sewing stitched across the gap.

In *Les Goddesses,* Moyra Davey narrates a story about Mary Wollstonecraft: "Five months after her first suicide attempt, on confirmation that Imlay (Gilbert Imlay, her daughter's father) had a lover, Mary jumped from a bridge in rain-soaked clothing, to hasten her descent. She was saved by a boatman and briefly consoled by Imlay. But MW was lucky to find a friend in the person of William Godwin, a sage man who, according to MW biographer Lyndall Gordon, counseled: 'A disappointed woman should try to construct happiness out of a set of materials within her reach.'"

A disappointed woman should try to construct happiness out of a set of materials within her reach. I had been in Rome, NY, not Italy. A town where all the work had left. Darkness came early on all the big old houses, built when things were brighter. I wasn't betrayed by X with another woman. *I don't even know you're here. I can't even see you,* he said as I walked to his right in the dim house.

After I'd left him, I felt the desire for him lift, like the desire for a drink. *Can't you see he's like the bottle?* my friend, Terri asked. *The bottle*—a time pre-dating mine, 1950s. Like someone not an alcoholic describing addiction. But I could see him tall like a bottle, my extremes of happiness and despair.

Before the desire lifted, I kept wanting to walk to his house. Even though it was over a thousand miles, twenty-four hours door to door in a car. As if my soul kept making a break for him. Found itself caught inside my body. But then the desire was gone. All that was left was disappointment. During those long-distance, phone years, after I'd left him and come back to Orlando, I sat in one spot and didn't want to move. Freezing in place. Like those women who turn to stone or salt, I turned into a person who sat and read and didn't want to move. Once it got a little dark, I'd walk around the lake, but I didn't want anyone to see me. The dark helped me hide.

I really hadn't wanted anyone to know I was back in Orlando. When I'd left for New York, for marriage with X, I'd walked around the lake for what I thought was one last time. And I sang. Out loud. By myself. I thought, *Who cares, I'll never be here again.* I think I sang "Any Major Dude Will Tell You," Steely Dan, or maybe something else happy, something goodbye to this place of sadness and invisibility, the closed houses. Goodbye to hearing that a friend who lived on the lake said he felt sorry for me walking alone all the time.

A disappointed woman should try to construct happiness out of a set of materials within her reach. Okay, okay.

*

Guillermo Kuitca's theater painting, *Plano del Teatro Colón,* could be a spine, with all the white bones. One October in Florida, when I nervously asked Guillermo a question, he stood. Held his hand to my shoulder as if to both balance and comfort. His theaters are seen from the stage. When I worked for the opera, sometimes I'd stand on the stage before a performance, look out at the empty seats, waiting. Dizzy, as if I might fly. Or transform.

After the lights dimmed, Janean and I would leave the high seats to get on the floor, somehow her darkness made me invisible. I didn't like the first opera I'd seen years earlier with Frank and Nikki. But after I was hired, they did *Faust* again.

Backstage the little boy who played the part of the dead baby recognized me. He left the curtain. Came toward me before he came back from the dead. After the performance one night, an old man thought I was Marguerite. He complimented my singing when I hadn't sung. Marguerite cornsilk beautiful, unhinged, everything lost. Then she sang as if climbing the ladder of my body, rungs flooded. Heaven is in the balcony. Night after night, I watch her son come down in white. The sheet to show he's a ghost, but really it's that he shines. As if her song—not sheets of rain, but rolling waves, white caps that rise until there's nothing else—calls him back to her.

That first time I'd seen Faust, I'd gone with Frank and Nikki. At his house on Hillcrest, Frank had shown me the room at the top of stairs, and I'd wondered *how did he get the body down?* His partner, Patrick, had died up there. Then Nikki died from AIDS too. Her sisters came to Orlando, made a circle around me in the health food store where I worked. I was always surprised that her beauty went so unremarked upon, really unseen or mis-seen, a co-worker casting some unkind remark as Nikki went out the door, and I'd thought, *Can you really not see her?* Her red hair cut short and spiky like a crown, small-featured as a little girl. Tiny. A high voice. Stomach swollen.

Kuitca's theater painting could be the image the dead leave on cloth burning their way out, cloudy phosphorescence of fish in dark water. Or it could be a place to land with space for everyone numbered in a red sea. Nikki left us in the balcony, saying, *I can't be this far away from the music.* Short like Janean, her red hair a small fire moving down the aisle toward the stage.

So sick by then she looked pregnant. And though I'd only listened to Frank talk about Nikki coming over Sundays to watch the opera at the Met on his TV. Heard how she'd fall backwards on his couch from the music. Had only rung up her groceries and gone with her that one night to the theater. After she'd spent all day sewing her black dress. Her hair glued in little arrows like a broken crown, and we got caught in a storm, shoes rainy. After she died, when her sisters came into the store looking for food, I said to them, *I knew her.* They circled me then, and the sisters said Nikki had been swimming. She'd gotten tired and had to lie down. In Boston, I told Frank, who had left Florida, that Nikki had died. His cats slept under the blankets with me on the floor. Each named when his lover was still alive, Patrick asleep at the top of the stairs the night we all went to the theater.

*

In the Santa Cruz mountains, a hummingbird will fly over my head in the near dark. L sends me an essay: *Consider for a moment those hummingbirds who did not open their eyes again today...a brilliant music stilled.*

STONE BABY

An eighty-two-year-old Colombian woman discovered she had a forty-year-old baby inside. Calcified, stone fist to stone mouth. It's not the first time. The first sign is an ache. In the x-ray the baby is ghostly as we all are in that light, death foretold. Skull visible. The woman's pelvis—house also a grave—dark holes where her limbs go. A sea on which her bones, translucent stingray wings, glide. The baby so many kinds of white and nothingness: one shoulderbone snow-capped, invisible eyes, a floating milky circle could be an ear. Once it was the color of mourning. The dark around the baby, and his mother's bones more night than body. A constellation we can name.

*

I flew to Boston for a writing conference. For the first time, I'd walked to the place my son died. *Cab?* the bellman asked near the lobby's glass door. He'd come toward me in uniform as I approached. Guardian of the door. Chandelier light so warm it's orange, almost a fire in the air. Early March in Boston, still cold. I wanted my feet on the ground, to find my way. Instead of being transported, taken.

I'll walk. Open space around us like a plaza. People line

up for coffee. Woosh of the revolving door, little breaths of chilly air on both our faces.

My son died in this city in 1982. May 27. Five-thirty p.m. I'd been washing my hair, ironing a dress to wear in Cocoa Beach, Florida, where I would listen to a band whose name I don't remember. No one told me my son had just died in Boston, Massachusetts. No one told me he was in the hospital. I just walked out the door. The immediate cause of his death was in two parts: Acute Myelomonocytic Leukemia. Then, Respiratory Arrest. Which lasted for one minute. Until he died. Lungs still white birds. Could I put my hand on his chest, cover them?

*

Take a left out the door, left on Huntington, right on Boylston, the bellman says. Slowly names the many horizontal streets I'll cross, counts as if walking himself. Start at Dartmouth, arrive Washington. Out the door, I turn, wind inside my plastic coat. City so close to where I was born and lived as a child, but it's always a mystery. Lean in toward the voices, accents of strangers as if they're family. As if I've been returned, but no one recognizes me.

It's stopped snowing. Clear gray air. Streets once water and tidal marsh until filled with gravel. Weirs in the underbody. Travel bag heavy on my shoulder. Too-big snow boots shuffle. A garden. Headstones in snow. Music before I arrived at the trees and the snow, the dead, stones sunk low. Arlington Church beside me, earth brown, high spired to help people look up. Slate stones a vertical walkway. Dark doorways, blue-gray windows—sky inside. Sunday. *It's in Chinatown,* the bellman said.

When I hear music, people on the sidewalk come toward

me. Light changes, cars turn. No way to hide my eyes in the bare air. Only the song knows where I'm going. *I shall possess within the veil/ A life of joy and peace. The hour I first believed.*

Leafless trees. Garden sign says I may sit on the grass, but there's no grass. Everything white. Snow ground, white sky. Black limbs. Something hung from the center trees, like a veil of pollen. Yellow. Then brown. A kind of ghost, transparent swoon over trees. When the word was made in Middle English, it was a sail. It was a bridal veil. A screen. The song carried there. Veils sway like hair. Maybe the remnants of something living. Two men on the sidewalk, one seethes. Tries to persuade the other: *You have to.* Spine bent like a carapace, he dances back and forth jabbing around the other man. Veils inside our bodies, vellum, soft palate that helps us swallow, make consonants. Inside, a chambered blue velvet coat, shine of deer antlers.

*

I walk Dartmouth, Clarendon, Berkeley, Arlington, Charles, Tremont. Reach Washington in Chinatown. Clusters of men near the corner of Washington and Boylston. Right or left? Most people go right. Can't read store signs. People walk fast with plastic bags shushing.

The old Combat Zone. Alive when he died here—round saffron streetlamps; syllabic merge of XXX; elm tree carved in the third floor tannic above Movies Nude Photos; bands of windows, some boarded; Pilgrim Theater open all night. Old red light images in a meat-brown past—the muted clothing a dollar gray-green shimmer. Air metallic, everything coins. One street's dark lilac buildings face bare trees. Someone in an argyle sweater got out of a wet aqua Pontiac with a white roof. Everyone a lantern. The mica flecks of sailors, goldbeater's skin. Five hundred million years ago, a garden of trilobites. Now the nineteenth century's in tall old buildings on either side—rough brownstone, sandstone, brick—embedded in the air. Like walking between pillars.

One tall man from the corner seems to follow me with purpose. I turn again to lose him, to nowhere I know. Another man stands in an alcove with white Styrofoam in one hand. Chews. Heat rises from the square container held below his chin. *Do you know where the hospital is?*

He lowers the Styrofoam to chest-level, says, *No, I'm sorry. I'm not the one to ask.* Accent English.

Okay, I say. He steps out of his hollow toward me. I turn back toward Washington. The Englishman still walks toward me.

Maybe that way, he says, pointing left. *I saw a red cross.*

One minute of respiratory arrest. Lungs not contracting. He lost consciousness. A kind of cloak but also pilgrimage, wandering. What I was told: he died in my uncle's arms. So then, they let him go here.

At first it doesn't even look like a cross. Center building painted red with windows lining five floors. White cross at the very top right. Flanked by buildings the color of deer or desert, with much smaller windows. The right building has a sign, "Tufts Medical Center." Below is a dark blue sign with white lettering, "Floating Hospital For Children." An American flag rose behind. To the right, cobalt awning over a doorway, "Floating Hospital" in white again. The medical ward arcs in a half-circle, hull of a ship.

When Nana was in another hospital in Massachusetts, and I was a child, I sat on the grass outside her window. She looked out to see me, waved. I could wave if I knew where he'd been. Some windows half open, some closed. A few blinds shut. Snow cleared, piled to the left of the doorway.

Thought of what to say if a staff person inside asks, *Can I help you?* If I tell the truth—*My son died here years ago, and I wasn't here*—they might call security. Might think I'm dangerous. I pull the black handle, but it doesn't open. Pull again. Locked. Inside the glass door, orange traffic cones block entry. Have they just mopped the floor, and it's still wet? No one inside. How can a hospital be closed? Where are the sick children?

Inside, a whale or dolphin high on the wall, a red fin painted "57." Blue and yellow fish swam beneath it. Two sea creatures with dark swirling bodies. One curves his head to face me with his white eyes. A dark bird flies like a knife over them. Below, an EXIT sign, red lit. Cluster of white lights like an unhinged chandelier. In the center, the outside is reflected—tan building opposite, white sky brighter than reality. Later, I thought I'd seen a sign that said, "Pediatric." Thought I saw "Oncology." But the light of outside obscured words, the arrows point to wings. *Wing* a replacement for *feather.*

*

Inside the Floating Hospital, almost lost in the reflected whiteness, is a red stairway. I can't see where it leads. Did Tommy see the blue fish, the whale? It was early summer. When he died, how did he leave? One of these windows? Did he pass where I stand now? A kind of wind against someone's face.

Behind me, three people walk up the stairs to the right, into a deserted concrete plaza half-hidden in shadow. I follow the trio to look for another door. One man shambles behind, but their conversation is a tight warp. Even though they don't notice me, it feels like company. The only door a blood bank. Inside, a woman unrolls her sleeve. A sign thanks me for my blood. Behind the desk, a woman in an orange Dreamsicle outfit walks toward me. I could sign up, give blood. But once my blood was so slow coming out, it got stuck. Needle in my arm. I got fainter and fainter. My head leaned on the technician's chest. Then I was flat on a white table. Drank orange juice while the technician said, *Your blood won't flow if you don't drink something.* Don't want to faint here, needle stuck in my arm. *I'm looking for the entrance to The Floating Hospital,* I say. *The door I found was locked.*

It's downstairs, the woman behind the desk says.

No, that door's locked. Is there another? She asks a man, shoulders bent at a task. His hair thinning, scalp visible between black curls. Damp with oil or sweat. He raises his head, eyes heavy. Looks left toward where I've been. *No, no.* I say. *There's no other entrance?*

No, the Dreamsicle woman says. I walk into the plaza again, turn the corner of the building. Just a sign high on the wall, "Boston Blood Donation Center." Plaza behind me deserted. Take the blood street instead. At a crossing, a tall building to my right, Tufts Dental School. Silvery white like a tooth. I could walk there, ask how to enter the Floating Hospital. But the airport shuttle will arrive at my hotel in an hour, and I am still far away.

Make my way to the garden street again, walk past the Arlington Church. A woman with her eyes lined in black, paper cup in her hands, asks, *Can you help me?* She asks, *Are those your real eyes?* Beyond Arlington, I hear music again. It comes from the Old South Church. Poster behind glass:

"Lent" with three rectangular gold boxes. Jesus in the desert for forty days. Thin gold lines ran from top to bottom, like paint or tears. The church originally on Washington Street in 1669. Where I'd come from. Where Tommy died.

The Old South Church door is an alcove. Three waves of coming in, then the inset dark brown door, tall window-panes. A museum? But when I walk inside a woman waits. Like the ushers in my childhood churches. There must have been an usher in the church I entered in Florida after Tommy died. When I was to pretend not to be his mother. Though no one told me this.

The flowers on the altar in memory of my father's "neph-ew," not grandson. Those words disguising me as my son's cousin. Altar covered with flowers. I'd rarely been to the church in Florida. When I was old enough to stop going, I mostly stopped. Avoided the frequent fights to hurry up and get in the car. Or to wear a slip under my dress—polyester layer instantly sticky in Orlando's steam bath air. Church-goers my parents' friends. My dad sang in the choir. I stood to sing, invisible, unable to make any sound. If I connected to the soft palate, the vellum, the veil inside, I would never stop crying. I would have to be carried out of the church. So, I moved my mouth, pretended to sing. My mother and I shared a hymnal. Her voice high and airy, a girl's. There must have been ushers in that Florida church, but I can't see them.

The usher in Copley Square is a woman with a stack of programs. She smiles, so I walk toward her. The singing comes from the right. Pews and then a choir in robes at the front of the church. Many people inside. Glass stained with the burn of breath. Bright with the body's ornaments, scar-let-purple-blue clasps, corded jumprope. All the white bones.

The woman holds out a program. I take it. Walk to the far left of the pews, find an open place in the second to last pew. Hard to stop crying because they keep singing. Take off my black parka, fake fur hood behind my neck like an animal at rest. A man stands to speak at the podium about a lost child. A Baptism either before I arrive or after. The child's name is Margaret Ann.

One: *How will she know that she is a child of God, made in God's image?*

Many: *We will give her our love. She belongs to us as well.*

I could have stayed there with the kindness, the warm light. All the people around me rose with hymnals in their hands. Black book to my right on the pew, gold lettering. So much room there for me. I could reach for the songs, stand up, sing. But my time's almost up, plane leaving. I rise, leave the pews. A man in the entryway looks disappointed. The woman usher looks disappointed. To the right, a staircase to the women's room. Nice to walk up the white stairs, past empty offices. To be inside as if I live there, am home again. Open the bathroom door, and a little boy stands in the entry. I hold the door for him, and he rushes out. His mother behind, yells his name. I forgot about stairs down the hallway, forgot what a small child needs.

I'm sorry.

It's okay, the mother says, straightening a thin shawl, veil around her shoulders. How will I know what to do? All this singing is for him too.

*

When doctors took a teaspoon of blood from a pregnant woman, they found hundreds of cells from her baby, though mother and child were thought to keep their cells to them-

75

selves, placenta a wall. Not only did the baby cells reach the mother, they weren't attacked—you would expect them to be cleared within hours, if not days. Instead, they stayed for decades, essentially forever, floating inside the mother. Even if the baby dies.

This is something they are absolutely sure of. *Even a sixty-year-old mother or seventy? Yes,* the researchers said. *Even eighty, perhaps ninety-year-old women.* At first doctors thought the cells might cause autoimmune disorders in some mothers. Then they found sheets of cells in damaged mothers, whole areas where the baby cells had gathered in unison to protect the mother from harm: hepatitis, ovarian cancer, cervical, endometrial. A liver made whole. Over and over and over and over. Protecting her for the rest of her life.

All this time, I thought he was gone.

GALA

When I was sixteen, I took a bus into the Sierra Nevada Mountains in Granada, Spain, with my parents, brother. To a ski resort. *Did I want to learn to ski? No, no,* I said, afraid of falling, unused to snow. But in the Alhambra, I'd curled into a high open window of the palace, at ease, the tiled pattern of my blouse blending in. The blue sky held me. In the very cold dark Nevada nights, my bus from Reno reaches the top of these Sierras. I'm here to teach creative writing for the year. Living in North Lake Tahoe. A 10,000-foot pass through unfamiliar mountains I ride through, down to the lake I live beside. When we reach the pass, tired, steel icy beneath gloves, I see the constellation that has always matched the freckles on my thigh. Anywhere the night is clear—the beach in New Smyrna, Wellfleet, hills of Virginia, and here. My body a reflection of that stretch of sky. A mirror. I feel the stars inside like stone themselves. Their invisible almost glitter.

*

A galaxy, any galaxy, calms me. Sky of darkness full of light. Stars inside us. Gala's from a party robe, not milk. My shoes were not soft, but glittered. The ladies in the Presbyterian Thrift Store approved. Dress bright blue. Gold apples on gold chains swung from my ear lobes when I spoke. A girl ironed my hair. June was late, having her hair curled at the foot of the mountain. Black eyelashes glued to her eyelashes, one by one.

She picked me up at my condo, drove to the fancy restaurant on the lake. A person in an eagle costume greeted us, the mascot. I looked into his eyes but they were drawn on. Maybe slits were cut in the eagle's face, or his eyes were in his always open mouth. Inside the Lone Eagle room, June led the way to the bar.

As in Spain, I feel sixteen again, alone in a new place. I'd seen June lean toward the art professor as we stood at the bar. And then he was beside me at dinner. I imagined June had arranged it. Kindly. Someone for me to talk to.

At dinner, the art professor told me about the oldest tree in the world, a bristlecone pine with green needles like a bottle-brush. Which made me think of bottlenose dolphins, the photo I saw of our brains a similar size. The bottlenose I found on the deserted national seashore in Florida. Sometimes when a turtle died there, a ranger would come and spray paint a red cross on its shell. Dead. But the dolphins were left to the turkey vultures.

I'd seen a seabird stand guard over its own dead in protection. To stave off, or maybe, just *goodbye goodbye*. Hunched black wings of turkey vultures announced the dead on the beach. They hovered in twos over each body, like surgeons about to operate, conferring. When I've approached, they've sauntered in nervous circles, glancing over their shoulders. Afraid I'll steal their meal: a giant tortoise, seagull whose ice-cube eyes have melted to black pinpricks, and a bottle-nose dolphin so still, I thought he must be gray driftwood from the hurricanes, a piece of boat or porch. But the vultures waited nearby on a caved-in roof. The tail folded like a newspaper, flukes calm as hands resting into one another. Beak a crumpled bottle, so I guessed the name, but what's a name when something has opened your insides, pulled intestines into the sand, like wet laundry still in knots, dull pink, even the blowhole tired, dry, no more clouds. One vulture spread his wings to show me how big he is, how he and the others will cover the dolphin. But the chemical makeup of my body is indistinguishable from the ocean, so I stood beside. At night the sea came up, took him back.

The art professor said one man had convinced those in charge to let him cut sections from the oldest of the oldest trees. Not too far away, in an uninhabited place. Location of the trees kept secret. Cut, the tree died. His friend had been collecting photos of the tree from across time. His friend almost ready to make a sculpture from the photos to resurrect the tree. *But he's dying of leukemia.* The art professor spoke slowly, stopped himself from telling side stories. He tried to stay on track, but it seemed like a struggle. He seemed to have a lot he'd like to tell someone.

I looked up The Oldest Tree, which I think he may have actually called The Oldest Living Thing. And there it was: the bristlecone tree, 4,841 years old. It had a name: Methuselah, "the oldest non-clonal organism on earth." "Located in the White Mountains of California in Inyo National Forest." Its exact location kept a close secret to protect it from the public. "An older specimen named Prometheus, which was more than 5,000 years old, was cut down by a U.S. Forest

Service graduate student in 1964." You could visit the grove where Methuselah grows, but they won't tell you which tree it is. The Mother Nature Network showed a photo of a tree, asked, "Could this one be it?" Swirly, magical tree, like the trees at Green Lakes near Syracuse, place of the enchanted trees, the lake I'd thought to drown in. The spring of 2002 which felt like winter.

Our town in Nevada only five miles from California. That night, June said she was going to punt, asked the art professor if he would take me home. His van was a Volkswagen converted to a Subaru, at least it said Subaru on the back. Tires so high I had to grab a handhold from inside the door, pull myself up to sit on the tire rim, then hoist myself up into the seat. I didn't mind. Though it was twenty degrees outside, and my nylons, glimmer shoes were for other weather. The cold in the van metallic, just over the edge of bearable. You could live in this van, a stove behind me, bed back there somewhere. He asked if I'd like to go to the bar.

Later, someone at the bar asked how the art professor could get lost. *He comes here every Friday.* In the van, he'd said. *If I get distracted, or if I'm talking to someone, doing something, and you want to leave, just tell me. I can take you home whenever you want to go.* Polite. Then we are surrounded by very tall trees like hundreds of cathedrals. *I don't know where I am,* the art professor says. Really lost. And he's lived here seventeen years. Or taught here, living down the mountain.

At the bar, I order water and realize I'd brought no money. My mouth stuck, as if I've been out in the cold a long time, much colder than this. Cold enough to freeze my mouth. A girl dances by herself, in graceful, closed-eyes, sliding. Another girl touches my bright blue knee as I sat on a barstool watching the pool players. *Pretty,* she says. *I wish I could wear a pretty dress. Why don't you?* I ask, but she's too far away by then. One of the other art professors invites me to play blow-job shuffleboard. Blow the puck across the salty board.

A light-haired man asks me to play "hit-the-ceiling-first-with-the-ping-pong-ball," and "around-the-world-ping-pong." It takes five people running around the table together to keep the ball in motion. My shoes unstable. The ping pong ball lands in the crook of my arm. When K from the office leaves, I get a ride. As we leave, S says it will get really crazy around 3 a.m. I ask, *They're still open? There's no last call in Nevada.* One woman keeps slapping her ass with her hand in time to the music. A foot or two away from her, I am like a piece of a boat.

The next day, I'll throw the second-hand, tinsel shoes away. The cold outside like metal, and K says, *It feels good.*

LAW OF SIMILARITY

Appearance equals reality. *It's one bit of very old wiring,* Daniel Gardner said. The Law of Similarity. If it looks like a dandelion, it's a dandelion. Gardner's wallet is stolen. Because the wallet has photos of his children in it, he puts himself in danger. Wanders for hours after midnight with strangers looking for the wallet. Someone tells him he could get his throat cut. He realizes he feels he's lost, not photos, but his children, that he can't abandon them.

Here in the Santa Cruz Mountains for a month, I have my son's photo in my suitcase, traveling with me. Greengold frame. *Doesn't it make you sad?* Sue Anne had asked me years before, seeing the photo on my bookshelf in Orlando. After that, I moved his photo to my bedroom when someone visited. Does the cavewoman in me think she's keeping Tommy safe in my suitcase? Carrying him with me? I also have the open locket with Tommy's photo—a gift from his adoptive mother, my aunt. It's in a small white box of jewelry. Today I couldn't store the box under socks in a drawer because I had the terrible feeling of him being buried under the socks. Tommy, who died in 1982. I'm in Woodside, California, where I'm grateful to stay in a brand-new studio overlooking hills that lead to the blue line of the Pacific. Another ocean. So much sky. Even here and this late, I need to keep Tommy safe.

Do I mistake an image for the person, the image attached to a worry of danger—Example Rule. The image of the person in my mind is not the person. Just a thought. What else do I have?

The law of similarity is not the law of simultaneity: *instant of actuality of appearing coinciding with the instant of appearing.* Not the law of the archive: shelter and forget. Terri placed an imaginary object in her pocket, then waved it from memory with her hand.

*

The book of fear says the brain has System One (Feeling) and System Two (Reason). All the uneasy is some old feeling and *you won't know why.* System One is unconscious. Example Rule is one of its reflexes. *System One's rule of thumb: If examples of something can be recalled easily, that thing must be common.* If I can think of a woman reclining on a sofa who I saw in the flash of changing channels on the TV. Can recall the wine bottle an intruder smashed into her face, ruining her mascara, her corneas, dissecting her forehead. If I can hear her acted scream, remember the feeling that her face is over, she is over. And none of this shopping matters, none of the flavored coffees or sauces. Then my prehistoric mind thinks this is common. Maybe not this murder, but violence. If I consciously tell her to go, can I reduce my feeling of risk?

*

When my father calls me in California and says *bladder cancer* and *aggressive,* when he says, *Kel* in the tone of voice he's used since 1961. A tone of love that lifts part of my body up and back to when I was carried in his arms, and the years between, will I remember the word *leukemia?* Will I see the stone that sits in the grass above my son's body? Or can I recall the doctor's words to my father, *Someone is looking out for you.* As the tumor is on the outside, removed, and the tissue underneath not reached. A wash will be used for six weeks to flood away anything that might remain. There will be a test to see if this is effective. It has a 66 percent chance of being effective. If not, another wash.

Why is my stomach still tight? What does my unconscious hear? It is the cheer in my father's voice, his asking what I'm doing, his laugh that is almost a deep cry when I say I've been to the beach. Ignoring it only creates a fist in my torso.

I'm here in California, in part because Carl Djerassi, the inventor of the birth control pill, created a place in the mountains as a memorial to his daughter who died by suicide here. My one-room studio with a wall of windows was named for his wife, Diane Middlebrook, who wrote about Anne Sexton and Sylvia Plath. In her memory. Deer come to my window. I'm alone here, separate from the rest of the artists who live up a hill in the main house. All I see are green hills, trees so tall they seem to be from the beginning of time, ocean, fog, stars. This big and patient sky. It's so quiet, I can hear everything living. Have I ever felt so safe? It's a wilderness I'd never have entered, but I'm here in the middle of it.

Years ago, my friend Terry in Orlando had come west, brought back a smooth black stone. Gave it to me with a note, *So you'll know there's another ocean.* Here it is. The way in and out a one-way road on the side of a cliff, deep canyon below. Neil Young's house nearby. Many nights, fog comes towards me, cooling. I can sit in the wooden chair on my hill and let it envelope me. As if the ocean missed me, knows there's no way over those hills. Carl Djerassi's daughter's name was Pami. The text below a framed portrait in the main house said that she was an artist, a poet, loved animals. In the black and white photo, she's very beautiful. Long blond hair. A California girl.

Her husband had been at Stanford studying to be a surgeon, and she was alone in her house here with the ocean in the distance. All this land around her. I know that in 1978, she took horse tranquilizers. I know she drove so far out in the hills that it took two days to find her body. She was twenty-eight years old. I'm here in part because of her. I would not be here if not for her. I imagine all these studios gone, the barn, main house, all of us dispersed to other places on the map. In 1978, I was seventeen years old, in my first year of college in Massachusetts, alcoholic and suicidal. I didn't know how to live either. Hungover, I walked to Friendly's. Too scared to kill myself, I hitchhiked so someone else could do it. Isn't that how girls died? Disappeared? But the boys who picked me up were just town boys, lonely for their girlfriends.

Margot, the director of the Djerassi residency, drives me down the mountain, and a woman from Russia paints my hair yellow. She says it makes me look younger. *Like a California girl!* she says. Margot agrees. With her brush in my hair, I feel like a painting. Twenty-eight. I wish I could walk into the hills and find her, bring her back.

*

In the old barn alone at dusk I watch a bobcat walk by the wall of windows, his shoulders moving coolly as a body builder's. Now Janice is here, connecting two mannequin heads together. They face each other, a loose piece of red thread between them. Pacific a flat, far-off blue, like an airmail envelope. Impassable hills in between. Only the fog reaches all the way in, up here on this mountain. Closer and closer until my wooden chair in the grass is enveloped. My glass house. Me.

I can't remember where the red thread meets in the mannequins. Do they each hold a thread end on their invisible tongues? Roped around their necks? Or does it just stop at the edge of their faces? While she was in Japan, Janice learned about the red threads that connect each person to his/her soulmate. The word "soulmate" embarrasses me, makes me feel fifteen. She thinks the story comes from China. *I like to imagine seeing it from above,* she says. From the sky. *All these red threads connecting people.*

A grid. Even if they don't know they're connected. Invisible thread is tied around the ankles of those who are to meet, to help each other in some way. The red thread isn't broken by time or place. Even if you don't know that anyone is there.

*

A dancer takes me for a hike in the hills. I'm afraid of snakes on the more distant paths, but her presence calms me. We cross a bridge so shaded by ancient redwoods, it feels like we're entering a fairy tale. An abandoned building is slatted with verticals of light, but inside it's silver. *My dad has cancer,* I'd told her earlier, unable to stop crying. She helped me find a place to rest in. Breathe. We walk the yellow path in July. The hills are steep climbs. I really have to use my legs, my lungs. I have to try. On another night, all eight of us will walk another path, even further out, and the dancer will find a concave bed in the woods, curve herself into an egg.

I read about a road almost two thousand years old found in a Greek city during excavations for a subway. Children's board games etched into some of the stones. Another road beneath this one, another five hundred years old. Men in hard hats look down. The thousand-year-old children seem younger than the men on the bridge. The place where they played keeping their childhood.

The one-way road to Djerassi is bordered by a very deep ravine, but I sit up front when we take the van down the mountain to sleek Palo Alto for groceries, or to the driftwood-heavy beach of San Gregorio in a valley. Ten miles south of Half-Moon Bay. Sandstone cliffs. I find logs jigsawed into a hut large enough to sit in. Surrounded by driftwood, wild-haired in the ashy sand, cool sun, I look like the sole survivor of a shipwreck. On our trips, the driver of the van is always calm. I follow his lead, lean back in my seat.

A playwright wants to do a reading of two scenes after dinner in the main house. She offers me a part. Normally, I'd be too shy about acting, being scrutinized. But I'm just reading, and like that the playwright thinks I can do it. I'm a daughter in conversation with her mother in a restaurant. We're both having a conversation, but not with each other. Non-sequiturs arrowing off. It turns out that the daughter/ me is pregnant and trying to tell her mother. I feel it then, sitting at this table with a mother who can't hear me, I feel that swelling, a life inside.

*

Manuela, the composer here, went hiking alone last night in the mountains. She said the branches looked like snakes. And then she encountered two real snakes in the grass: a long green one uncoiling away, but the striped one not budging. Terrifying herself with the imaginary, and then the real thing appeared. She'd gone into the high grass to escape. Afraid it too was filled with unseen snakes. Frantic, Manuela prayed, *Oh, if I get out of this alive.*

*

That last October, I'd seen the horse. In the dark. Panic of not knowing if I had the twelve photographs of Tommy with me. I'd packed my things into a storage unit in Florida over a year before and kept moving. East to west. One photo of Tommy always with me, in the greengold frame. But where is the horse? Where is my son and his horse?

Years earlier, when his adoptive father, my uncle, gave me twelve pictures, I felt observed. Didn't want to show the photos to anyone else. Afraid the viewer wouldn't see him, would only see a beautiful boy, would say that: Oh, what a beautiful boy. And I did hear that eventually, and felt their not knowing. How alone we are.

I don't have the horse here. That photo is in Florida, in my storage unit. But your blue eyes. I see you on the big Snoopy wearing a railroad cap. I see you. That night you were on the horse, and your eyes were very very blue. Starting to get sick. Confusion in your eyes. I knew you needed me. Even though you had died, even though the date was late 1981 Christmas coming and tree now forever in the basement, I'd have to find a way to cross that distance for you. Blue of your sleeper in my hand when you were four days old, your foot, almost your whole leg fit in my other hand. Your sleeper blue when you're eight months, nine months, on Snoopy. Christmas decorations behind you. Huge stocking with your name. Happy in so many of these photographs. But I can see I have to come to you.

How do I do it? Become the person who can cross that distance? Maybe I don't have to become someone. I just have to walk toward you. We're in the same room. I can see you. You can see me. Just cross the darkness.

THE CARTOGRAPHER'S ASSISTANT

ORLANDO, FLORIDA
1998

What is the fear of being lost? Mazeophobia. My first memory of being lost: inside the mirrored funhouse rooms at the fair in Hyannis, Massachusetts, unable to get out. All I could see was myself. Near the way out that I didn't know was near, I broke down. Stood still and screamed until someone found me. Brought me back into the world. Still terrified at being lost, unable to find my way back.

I've never had a sense of direction. Each new place appears like an island. There's a seahorse of memory and navigation tucked in the brain's bed. But, for me, north is straight up in the sky and a cold climate. South below. Only on a beach can I find east with confidence, sun rising. West, by sunset. Hippocampus cells in the seahorse misfired or unborn.

Hippos is horses, *kampos* sea monsters. In Olaus Magnus' *Carta Marina* of 1539, sea monsters take up two-thirds of the map. The Sea Monster Key identifies a red sea snake forty feet long. Horned creature whose eye is twenty feet around. Polypus, a lobster big as Norway. Sea unicorn. A green-backed monster imitates an island. Unaware, doomed sailors anchor there and appear in her body, like bones in an X-ray. Monsters like mountains all on attack. When a place was unexplored, maps warned, *Here Be Monsters. Here Be Dragons.* The first map of America looks like a womb. As if a map is a body.

In seventh grade, my geography teacher sent us outside to measure the Florida sky. Assigned each of us a partner one afternoon. Unsmiling, with his flower-petal mouth and dark, angled bangs, my teacher looked like a sturdier Jackson Browne. Too severely pretty to approach and explain I'd been deserted by my partner. Left staring at concrete, a sharp edge. Sky bright blue. Measureless.

Another student, Frank Eidson, a boy in a blond corduroy jacket that matched his hair, took pity. Frank pointed, said a few words, compass points of kindness. The only geography I learned was plate tectonics, which felt solid, knowable. The ground beneath my feet. When in fact it was what moved, shifted. How the world is remade again and again. I need to know how to get around above ground. *The key unlocks the meaning of the map. The legend implies something that has to be read, a story.*

One fall, I was out of work. No phone. Regular eviction notices scotch-taped to the peeling blood-red door of my $385-a-month apartment. Panel of yellow migraine light overhead. Roach colored kitchen cabinets. Pilled gray carpet.

That semester, I'd taught a creative class at the university across the street, one night a week, $400 a month. Stretched my unemployment. One month, I receive a food stamp card. December and classes over. That winter, my unemployment ends. I sneak into the English Department to call a temp agency. Instead of temp work, I could have taught a couple of composition classes as an adjunct. But the ones I'm offered are midday, during the work week. How would I get another job around those hours? Teaching two classes meant I'd only make $200 a week for the semester.

Jodie, a graduate student, had been my assistant at a bookstore. She'd done temp work. How bad could it be? I call, make an appointment. A series of tests, the employees all women in neat pastel suits. Triangle collars of lightweight button-downs peek over blazers.

During the computer program tests, I guess a lot. Aim to answer everything. I don't understand electronic file folders. Or Excel. Have no real computer of my own, just a clunky old PC the size of an oven that had belonged to my brother's kids. They'd used it to play games. It came with a dot matrix printer that prints ghost-like type on paper with perforated margins. I mainly use an electric typewriter. But on the temp agency's computer tests, I score high enough to be assigned a several-week-long job at the bus company. Did the job pay eight dollars an hour? Seven dollars?

The agency hadn't told me anything about my actual job, just the computer skills I'd need. Drive downtown to the bus company tower. A bright voiced woman had given me an address. *Long-term,* she chirped. Several weeks. *You'll get to use your Excel skills.* Worry about finding the place. Luckily, the building is very tall.

The logo is a four-toed fuchsia paw print. Thick, round-edged toes, more mitt and Flintstone phalanges than claw and talon, ungula. Office tower the Disney-blue of Cinderella's Castle at night. Punch the button for a parking ticket, the white gate lifts like a hand. Jagged teeth underneath and a sign warns, "Don't Back Up." I know to keep moving forward. Across the parking lot is a man-made pool where the water flings itself down in celebration. I'll spend my lunch breaks here breathing the unairconditioned air.

Inside the tower, I sign in at reception. *You'll get to use your Excel skills.* I don't remember my guide, just our walk between rows and rows of cubicles, a field of them in the open space of our high floor. In one, a man bent over a miniature city as if playing. But his face is serious, concentrated. Shouldn't a man who can build a city have an office? We're all separated by our half and full walls. Everyone's cubicle missing a door.

We walk toward the far wall. To the left, all glass. To the right, offices. The guide said, *We're here.* The plate on the door: "Mapping Department." Inside a woman with shiny blond hair sits behind a desk. A lemon colored suit. Pink lipstick. Not too much. She stood, *Hello.* At ease with herself. Powdered and poreless and seamless. Like a Tic Tac.

The guide evaporates and my boss, who runs the Mapping Department, walks me to my cubicle. Inside, the gray carpeted walls are thumbtacked with maps of Orlando and surrounding areas. My boss explains my job. I'm to help people moving from welfare to work. Find them on a map. Their house. Their place of employment. Then, weigh their transportation options, select the best, and get each person transported to work and back home. It's just before the turn of the century. Pre-GPS, Google Maps. But, I have a computer with a special program to help me find them.

The wall maps surrounding me are dizzying. At my cubicle desk, the phone rings. A man said he needs a ride to work. I type his name and address into my special program. The list of options to try includes bus, carpool, shared van. The last option is a cab. But he doesn't live near the bus line or near another client or on the van route. I call him a cab.

Why don't we just buy each person a car? I asked my boss. I'd bought cars for $500, but I don't think she had.

That's interesting, my boss had said in a coffee philosophy way. My idea went nowhere. Not part of this federal grant funded plan. Each person allotted $800 transportation dollars. It was often $40 to take a round-trip cab to get to a job at McDonald's or Trader Vic's. The day's work probably didn't pay that or much more. When the $800 were used up, then what?

In my cubicle, I felt a level of boredom I'd never felt before. The air conditioner hummed like a cold hive. Cubicle silence unchanging. Drag drag drag of time. My boss sat in her office wearing new outfits. She said she bought new clothes each season. What did she do with the old clothes? Her laugh flung out like a filmy scarf when one of the other male managers stop by her office. I don't know what she does in there. *Mapping,* her door said. A cartographer.

She never looks at me directly, a temp. I'm seen as a kind of temporary human being. The Cartographer's gaze above my head, or glancing by my cheek. There's a cost to not being seen for hours, days, weeks on end—as if I'm another species—the others around me seen, recognized. I begin to feel less human, less real.

*

Years before, I'd once tried to ride the bus while living in Winter Park, a suburb of Orlando. Car broken down, I had to get to work. Stood on the wrong side of the road for an hour, watched my bus pass by. Crossed the street, sweating through my blouse. Another hour in the heat. No bus. The main routes are downtown, not here on the outskirts. Dirty white glare, exhaust charcoaling my skin, lining my lungs. Blurred yells from passing drivers. Waiting waiting waiting.

When the bus company brought me in, they'd recently received funding to help implement the welfare-to-work program. Personal Responsibility and Work Opportunity Reconciliation Act of 1996 (PRWORA). It promoted short-term help and work by doling out block grants to the states. Replaced Aid to Families with Dependent Children (AFDC). States were encouraged to be creative in their welfare reform efforts.

Sometimes, the Cartographer hands me a manila folder of documents to photocopy. The path to the copy machine is through the expanse of mostly empty cubicles to a vast corner of carpet. Glass wall at the opposite end, Cinderella Castle blue outside, Disney gleam. I'd think of pitching myself through it. Crashing the glass into the unairconditioned air where I would just float, unreal as I was. Cloudy and bloody, full of sharp things.

Instead, I walk on carpet cushy as a giant slipper to the machine where I place paper on glass. Press *Copy*. Sometimes another person waits nearby for me to finish, hushed.

But people still need to get to work, and it's my job to find them. Find their workplace, find the best mode of transportation to get them there. Open my computer map, type in a street address. Voila. Here is a person. Here is McDonald's. In a few weeks, my temp job will end as I'll be offered a full-time job at the Orlando Opera, to make $21,000 a year. Frank Eidson, who I haven't seen since seventh grade, will have a wife who will sign up to come to a dress rehearsal,

Of Mice & Men at the Bob Carr. I'll be in charge of greeting her and other donors. Too shy to ever say I went to school with Frank, and he'd been kind to me. A rich, private school my parents sent me to one year because they thought I was too young and sheltered for junior high in public school. A world I crashed, my own self never quite real among them. Frank's wife blond and nice, polite as the Cartographer. Frank had become a lawyer for accident claims.

I wonder why so many people going off welfare worked at Trader Vic's restaurant. *Home of the Original Mai Tai.* They had a Tiki Bar. The carpooling options I tried never worked for anyone. Rarely, van pooling panned out. No one lived near anyone else. Or near the bus lines. It was almost always a cab I called for a round trip. Almost always $40. I didn't tell the caller I was worried. Didn't ask how much a person could make in a day at McDonald's. Trader Vic's. But how much did I make here at my temp job in an eight-hour day? Fifty-six dollars a day before taxes? Sixty-four dollars? How would anyone get to work when the transportation dollars ran out? No one worked eight hours at the restaurants, shifts shorter.

Clinton was President when they dreamed up the welfare to work program. Seeking re-election, he promised to lower welfare rolls. With Temporary Assistance to Needy Families (TANF) taking the place of AFDC, recipients had to be employed within two years of receiving assistance. A lifetime cap on funds. It was popular. Even Democrats who didn't agree with the TANF changes kept quiet because they wanted Bill back in office.

Peter Edelman, Assistant Secretary of Health and Human Services, resigned in protest when the welfare reform bill was signed into law. *Now six million people have incomes composed only of food stamps.* Today, Edelman says that the problem is low-wage jobs. That half the country's jobs pay less than $34,000. *And a quarter don't pay even up to the poverty line for a family of four, $23,000.* And Edelman notes that from 2009 to 2011, the income of the top 1 percent went up by 11 percent.

Many of the people who call me are dealing with spatial mismatch. Geographers first described it in the 1950s—people don't live near employment and services. When PRWORA was implemented, emphasizing "work first," it was estimated that 93 percent of TANF participants didn't own a car. But they weren't near the bus line either. This is the same year the U. S. Census Bureau estimates nearly 37 million people or 14 percent of the population live below the poverty level. What about those who needed day care, were caretakers of elderly parents, a disabled person, someone who cared for a person with a disability?

In 1997, Edelman said that TANF wasn't welfare reform, that it does not promote work effectively, and that the bill would move 2.6 million people, including 1.1 million children, into poverty. The month I receive food stamps, I don't know that there's been another cut limiting food stamps to three months out of every three years for unemployed adults under age fifty who are not raising children.

I never see any of the people who call me, just voices on the phone. Pick up, drop off.

Each time I call a cab, I feel another $40 fall away. Twenty round trips. That's what $800 buys.

I learn to find each person on the map like a ring I'd lost, scouring square inches. With no sense of direction, I get everybody home. On my carpet walls are the suburbs of Casselberry, Altamonte Springs, Ocala forest, rural Chuluota,

Christmas, Sanford, Oviedo. Orlando is blue with lakes and springs and creeks. Narcissus Ave and Hughey Street, Red Bug, and Snow Hill, Sand Lake, West Lester, Belle Isle, Pine Castle, Conway. Each voice on the phone is somewhere on a yellow street. I look closer. See how one thing can hide another. Behind that electronic push pin is the electronic drawing of a house in Florida. Inside, it is December 1999, and a woman needs a ride to work. My voice a flicker on a wire. True north is the direction across the earth, to the North Pole. Polaris, the brightest star in Ursa Minor, is the closest star to the North Pole. The Guiding Star. The magnet in a compass is drawn to the North Pole, so with a compass, you can always find North. Maybe my geography teacher should have given us a compass. The earth's magnetic field calls the magnet in the needle. The needle has no choice.

Just before my temp job ends, a flyer arrives in my cubicle announcing that the bus company is hiring. The opening is a full-time position for the job I've been doing. The Cartographer said, *You could apply.* Salary, benefits. I don't apply, but I'd learned to find other people, the places they need to go. *Just spin me around twice,* I thought. *Ask me to point north. I'll be free.*

SECOND LANGUAGE

ORLANDO, FLORIDA
1998/2000

It was always sunny unless it was pouring rain. Sometimes both, a bucket dumped from the sky. Either way, the weather was drenching. Our skin shining, hydrated. When M arrived at the international language school in Orlando, I wasn't her main teacher. She was in the Beginners course. I taught Low-Advanced. But all of the faculty also taught electives for students at other levels. The students in their late teens, early twenties. They came from Belgium, Bosnia, Croatia, Finland, France, Germany, Italy, Spain, Switzerland, Japan. The students had had a joke: *What do you call someone who speaks only one language? An American.* We were housed in a series of portable classrooms at the back of a hot, sprawling campus. Still a graduate student, it was my first full-time teaching job.

When M took a seat in my Idioms class for Beginners, her red soft shoes swung beneath the desk. Her feet never seemed to reach the floor. She spoke in a high voice. I barely knew her. I spoke too fast for students at Beginners level, frustrating them. They sat in a circle around me, quizzical, brows furrowed.

Frightened of teaching, disliking attention, I used creative writing and theater exercises. We put on plays—*The Odd Couple,* taking turns playing parts, wearing clothes I'd brought from home. The students only here for nine months. We were supposed to be learning "Business." But beyond a series of videos and workbook scenarios featuring American businesses, and Business English vocabulary work, my only real skill was teaching them to speak, read, and write English. In class, we'd have collective dreams—sequential really. In a circle, I'd ask Jane, *What would you like to dream?* We'd start dreaming together. Each student found her way into the on-going dream. *Ma mére, ma soeur,* they called me. Forgiving me for only knowing what I knew. Verbs made me sweat—the progressive, perfect, the past and future perfect progressive. Grammar like math. My training was in poetry. We wrote poems.

Eventually, all of the faculty without M.A degrees in Linguistics would be fired by a new director from England. We'd then be invited to rejoin the faculty as part-time adjuncts, on a haphazard schedule and a much-reduced salary. I would decline, joining adjunct faculty at various community colleges, and the university, teaching Creative Writing and English. I taught a beginning Linguistics class for journalism majors who had failed their entry exams. I taught Reading to older students who were in retraining programs—one man had asbestos poisoning from his old job. The classes were full. Reading took place at night in an auditorium.

In one class I also taught students how to use computers because our classroom had each student seated at one. But I did not know how to use a computer myself. At home, I had an electric typewriter. I relied on handouts I found in the hallway, students who did know how to use a computer to mentor both other students and me. We learned together. Exhausted driving my $500 burnt orange Mercury all over the greater Orlando area, from 8 a.m. to 8 p.m. on Monday, Wednesday, Friday, but grateful for the kindness of those students. Eventually I would leave to work for an opera company.

But after I'd quit the international language school to adjunct at those five different Central Florida campuses, my past colleague, Frank, who taught Advanced level, decided to move to Italy. *If I stay in Orlando, I'll just watch movies for the rest of my life,* he said. So, Frank moved to Rome, got a teaching job at the English Institute, Via Cosi, met a woman on a bus, married her, and had six children. Baby after baby. Before he left, Frank said he needed someone to take over tutoring M. It paid $20 an hour, much more than adjuncting. I said, *Yes.*

M's family was wealthy. Embarrassed for her to see my place in the old Haystacks apartments, on Hoskins Holler, across from campus. Student housing for decades. Two low-ceilinged hobbit-like rooms. Slough of dirt-colored carpet. I'd bought Frank's nice wicker dining table for $50, and two days a week, M and I sat here to review her work. In Japan, she'd trained as an engineer. She'd already graduated from the language school, and was attending the local community college with native speakers. M and I didn't have much small talk. She had a red car that she drove very fast. There had been more than one accident, but she always seemed fine afterwards.

Then M missed a whole week of tutoring. She phoned after the first missed session, from a locked ward. *What happened?*

I have to stay twenty-four hours, she said. Voice high, empty. Tiny bell in a big room. *I can't call my parents.*

M, what happened?

I swallowed too many of my sleeping pills.

Are you okay?

Yes, I just want to go home. Said she'd see me Tuesday.

Why can't you call your parents? For some reason they couldn't know. All a secret.

On Tuesday, M knocked on my peeling, blood-red door. Sat on the very edge of my orange velour couch. I was on the edge of the matching love seat. The furniture a gift from an office assistant at one of the schools. It looked as if we were both getting ready to jump or dive. Coffee table between us. *What happened?*

She told me. Before she came to the U.S., to my class, she'd been in love with someone in Japan, engaged. But her fiancé died in a car accident. She thought she would never love again. But she did. Got engaged again. M had been standing in front of a restaurant with her second fiancé. *When he got into his car, I had a bad feeling,* she said.

The second fiancé died in a car accident too. It was bizarre. Two fiancés, both killed in car accidents? M had collapsed, lost her mind. Outside my ground-floor apartment, it was getting dark, frogs croaked in the retention pond. I leaned toward her. M said, *I'm bad luck.* She had to be institutionalized in Japan. Her doctor said her only chance for recovery was to go to a place where she would have to learn everything all over again. A place where she didn't know the language or the customs or the people. She'd come here, to the language school.

Someone in M's community college class befriended her, and M confessed her engineering background. But she told her friend that she wanted her study group members to learn things for themselves. *Don't mention it,* she'd said. Her new friend told the other students. The study group took M's side, and ostracized the other student for betraying her secret. M turned the whole class against her, like a rock in her hand. A few days later, the ostracized student was in a car accident. The accident was announced in class. M collapsed, sure her bad luck had caused it. As if a person could think another ill. Cause them harm. Like a witch. Voodoo. An ambulance came. But M convinced the EMT that she was okay, that it was just a shock. Then went home, and swallowed all the pills in the house. Pills kept on hand to help her sleep. M might have died, but her roommate came home early and found her unmoving. Fine. She'd told the EMT, *I'm fine.*

Stomach pumped. Baker acted. Under the Florida Mental Health Act, commonly referred to as the Baker Act, which allows for involuntary commitment if a person is in danger of harming herself. Couldn't call her parents. She'd called me. So calm. At first, I assumed the overdose had been an accident. *Why didn't you call me when you were upset,* I asked. Though who was I? That's what I'd thought. Detaching.

But I wasn't peripheral; I was her teacher. I was the one she'd invited to her house for dinner. M lived in one of those old Florida houses with a sunroom. We sat at a little table, and she gave me a plate of food like jewels, a tiny painting. I could have reciprocated. Invited her to dinner. Maybe then, she might have called when she needed help. Thought of me as a friend. I might have been her friend. I corrected her grammar, proofed her papers, took her money. Even smiling, I felt opaque. Who did she have? Who could have been her family here? Not Frank in Italy. The roommate who saved her. Her classmates. I could have stepped in. I could have tried. I don't think I even hugged her to welcome her back into the world. I could only reach toward someone who reached toward me. What about the person in the dark who can't reach? M took every pill in the house. She thought she was bad luck. Found herself in a room she couldn't get out of. And still I stayed on my love seat. As if I were behind glass. But M had trusted me, told me the truth. I trusted no one.

After our tutoring ended, we lost touch. A couple of years later, I got the job at the Orlando Opera Company. My office once underwater. A storage tank for the town, now drained, furnished. Singers on one side of the concrete building, ballet dancers on the other. A round performance space in between for practice and small productions. Lake across the street, and my new pink 1940s apartment high on a hill. Lake where I will think to drown in 1999. Where, instead, I will go to a recovery meeting, and then to a friend's house for two days because I cannot be alone. I will not tell anyone about the drowning idea. Instead, I will write a poem, my first book, *Underwater City,* and hide the drowning deep inside.

I could walk to work from my pink apartment. The opera had high tiny windows, three stories, turrets. A fortress. It's near the dog park where Frank and I used to walk. The windows high because no one looked out. Room underwater for decades. On the floor had been limestone spheres. Somehow, all that ancient, condensed life made the water pure. Ground down into nothingness. Calcified and shaped into these balls that made the water drinkable.

One night, I was handing out programs in the circular space, performance about to start. I was greeting people when I heard my name spoken with joy, surprise. M stood there with a friend. Shoulder-length black hair shining. She'd graduated with her B.A., was leaving town in a few days for another state. Graduate school. Had never been to the opera before. It was luck she'd come. I was trying to find the surface. Seeing her, even underwater, I felt more myself.

I went toward M. The highness of her voice reminded me of the singing inside. No one else carried her whole story of trying to die, of coming back. It was as if I'd known her since she was born. I hugged her. She was showing me what it looked like to go forward. To keep going. Her only chance had been to learn everything all over again. Learn to ask for a glass of water. Learn the names for birds, flowers. Food. A new word for everything. Like a strange fairy tale—the accidents and bad luck. The bravery. *Go to a new land. Where no one knows you. Where you don't speak the language. Ask for everything you need.*

There is a story in which the narrator is afraid of a person who is homeless. Not afraid of the person himself, but afraid of how thin the line is separating her from him, from being homeless herself.

I'd thought there was a line separating me and M. I'd thought I was on the other side.

AT SEA

CAPE COD, MASSACHUSETTS
SUMMER 2012

In Ezra Baker Elementary School in Dennis, Massachusetts, I sat at a desk in a classroom dimmed with rain. Lit with yellow overhead that buzzed like bees just waking up from darkness. In a town built on a fingertip of land dipped into water. I'd asked my mother *when was I born?—the time of day*. And that day in class, I watched for it. Turned around to see the clock, breath streaming. No one had wanted to stop it, no one held a lit cigarette to skin, like a painting of skin or snow, and you would have to touch her to know this is a real girl. Even with the straight red cut on her chin from a fall in play. The second hand ticked fast, closer to a secret. Surrounded by children on almost every side—another clock inside her chest and she's here, but still there too. The classroom quieted by cold, a patient and electric girl watching the clock, waiting to be born.

*

I'm back on the Cape, back home for the summer. Visiting my grandfather's sister Taimi in a convalescent home. *I'm at sea,* Taimi said. My grandfather's sister. She had a small stroke a few days ago. Early afternoon Cape light calming through her upper floor window. The sky I know, the trees. Voices.

I've come from California, the Santa Cruz mountains. On my way to Lake Tahoe to teach for a year. In between, I come home to the Cape, Wellfleet.

*

Panphobia is the fear of everything. Or, *constant fear of an unknown cause.* Also known as omniphobia, pantophobia, and panophobia. *A vague and persistent dread of some unknown evil.*

Taimi's husband died two years ago. She's ninety. O of her mouth when she sees me and my parents enter her shared room at the rehab center. Her chest rises, makes her a little taller. Her body shaken. Mom and Dad in front, so I'm a little hidden. Seatbelt on her wheelchair like a rope keeping a doll body upright. Dark hair a tower I remember from childhood.

I don't know the facts of Taimi's life that well, but almost no one knows me better. We've sat in rooms together since I was born, all my life. In her parents' house in Centerville, where her sister Mary stayed on after they died. Then Mary died in the house. Walk inside, you're in the kitchen, a table to your right. Keep going into the living room where I sat on my great-grandmother's lap, Empi. They came from Finland, strangers here. But now nowhere else is home. A secret staircase goes upstairs. Emil my great-grandfather is big—stretch of his shirt like cloth across a table. His belt below his belly, loops. Light straight hair soft as a baby points in different directions. Empi's eyes wide and happy to be holding a baby girl, me. Her body thin and boyish like my mom's. My eyes wide to see everything. Yellow light, dark walls, cush of the couch. Emil to my left, his back to where the house ends.

I hide behind my parents' rush toward Taimi, my face I

can't control crying like a baby to see her tied to a chair. But that's no good. Breathe breathe, swallow. Even now she holds herself with elegance, composure. Not a mask to remember, but who she is. I wish I could remember her young.

Lean down, hug her. The thick belt like a man's. *You're a grown girl,* she says, surprised. Kisses my cheek. Before I sit down on her bed's red blanket, she says, *Mary? Where's Mary?* Her sister. Mary of the violet eyes.

And then she lowers her head a little, says, *Mary's dead.* And my mom says, *Yes. Everything is going so fast now,* Taimi says. Turns to my mom. *Is it going fast for you?* Mom says, *Yes.* When Mary died, they sold the house. I could go there now, get down on my knees and beg to be let in. Why did I never save money, buy the house? I've still never been upstairs.

Where do you swim? Taimi asks me. The aide makes her eat at a white table with two other patients in white. One woman is wearing a white cloak. *You can all sit together at a table,* the cloaked woman says to us. She's alone. She's had a stroke. Everyone old. We are the visitors. I'm afraid to kiss people on the cheek, afraid they'll move, that my aim will be off. But I kiss Taimi when she sits at the table with the cloaked woman. She stays still. My kiss reaches her.

*

In her room, Taimi had been sitting by a table with many paper cups scattered. A man in his seventies had the job of "Visitor." He wore a white name badge. He stayed in the room with her at all times, for hours and hours, even while she slept. Even at midnight. Someone would break him at some point, and he would go down to the cafeteria for a meal. He stood the entire time we were in the room. Though all the seats (two) were taken by my parents, every so often, Taimi would ask the Visitor, *Would you like to sit down?* She kept noticing him, forgetting him.

When we'd walked into her room, my parents ahead of me, I'd been surprised and panicked by the momentum of tears. The way the belt held her. The surprise on her face to see us. While my parents embraced her, I'd pushed the sadness down. I didn't want to confuse Taimi even more. *I did my best,* my father says in the elevator. All his joking, his warmth—of course it was best. But even for him, a man who sings as he pays a bill at the register, it was a hard push. What is next for her? Her life in this chair, being wheeled. Her glance all affection....*This is my family,* she says to the Visitor. She sees me. I never saw her alive again.

*

In a Worcester library, the previous April, I'd found a book with a photo of West Yarmouth school children from 1928. The caption says they were some of the last students to be taught in the schoolhouse. Three rows of kids who look between six and nine years old. Her name appeared: Taimi Halunen.

She's in the second row, though I can't be sure which girl. The children don't stand in even rows. I think she's one of three girls. I think she has straight hair. Probably the tallest girl with bangs or shadow hiding her eyes. Her parents spoke Finnish. In Florida, I have the photo in which I am younger than Taimi and sit in her mother's lap. We're the color of ether, clothes tannic. Taimi's school is white. Children in the yard. Boys in the front row, each down on one knee. The photographer must have told the boys how to pose. Many of the children squint into the sun, eyebrows scrunched. Four open windows behind, black inside, though a flowering branch appears to come out of two. One branch has a bright white flower. Two windows have flowered curtains, pulled open. Eighty-four years ago, these thirty-eight children were here.

*

Who will tell me what it was like on Baxter Ave when Taimi went to the end of the street, to the ocean, to swim? *Where do you swim?* On the Bass River shore, they dug up the bones of the South Yarmouth Wampanoags buried there. The salt works were being built. But someone complained, said the bones could not be built upon. They needed to be moved. My 5th great-grandfather Thomas Greenough, the last of the South Yarmouth Wampanoags, still alive then. Those bones buried again on Indian Memorial Drive. Here the slope rises to trees my mother ran through as a girl, down to Long Pond. Taimi swam here too, with her sisters. Mary. What was the glint between trees? Is the Recording Angel getting all this down? Gabriel with *the writing case at his side?* Your guardian angel can also be your recording angel.

*

Taimi dies before Christmas. She once placed a yellow smiling face on the seal of her letter to me postmarked Oct 19, 2001. I was almost on my way to X. Feeling grown, loved. To be married. Finally, my life would fall into place. Like the astrologist said, after he'd come into the health food store when I was in my late twenties, offered to do my chart. I never saw it. But he figured it out, said things would be hard for me until I was forty. Then happiness, an arrowing up. *This must be it.*

Taimi placed two LOVE stamps on the envelope. With a red rose climbing the stamp through the sepia faint handwritten words to become the "O" in LOVE. Inside is a Finnish document with the names and dates of my mother's relatives, annotated by her. My great-grandfather, Johan Emil, is here: "synt. 16.9.1891 Phajoella kuoli 24.6.1975 Amerikassa, jonne mennyt 1914." Someone typed this densely filled document.

On the final page: Following "KUOLINILMOITUS," after "Muut tiedot," is my great-grandmother's name (*the "P" almost invisible*): Puoliso Impi Kotila kuollut 1969. The year she died. I thought her name was Empi. Is Puoliso part of her name? This was typed in 1975, stamped with a seal, Finnish words. "New York," at the bottom, alongside an upright, walking creature. Like a lion, with vast regalia on its head. So complicated it obscures the head itself. Yes, here, in Taimi's handwriting on a piece of typing paper she's cut into thirds. On one third my great-grandmother: Empi Saimi Kotilla, born KiviJarvi, Finland 18 (*and in pencil*) 92.

Another sister of my grandfather, Ina, moved to California. So far from Florida and Massachusetts, it could have been Australia. So far away I would forget her name, if she were living or dead. But just this summer I'd been in the Santa Cruz mountains, and she'd been below, in a nursing home. I didn't rent a car in San Francisco. Too scared to drive the one-way cliffside road up and down, I never found her. Never asked to be taken. When I thought about knocking on her door, I felt behind glass. Like the geisha doll my father gave me. Then she dies too. Ina. Ina was her name. Her husband, Charlie. Taimi the last sister. All gone now. The meaning of early is *in the distant past*. So even early is already gone. Though it's also *the near future*.

But even when I can't act, people will appear. As if life isn't one punishment after another for poor decisions. As if it's something else. Through a woman who worked at a Finnish bakery in West Palm Beach, Florida, my mother found a cousin in Finland, Seija. Seija came to visit my parents in Wellfleet and in Florida. A woman in her seventies who swam naked in a cold lake in Finland until it froze. My parents flew to Helsinki, and the newly found relatives drove them around Finland to meet my mom's family, the famous Finnish composer, even to see the ground where her grandfather Emil's house had stood. She met the children, including Tuuli, Seija's daughter, who miraculously lives just down my mountain in Santa Cruz and up another. She works for Nokia, is here a year with her boyfriend. I email her.

On a trip to town in the residency van, I meet Tuuli for lunch in Palo Alto. Her name means wind, but I think tulips when I see her. I've almost always felt tall, but she is Amazonian, her clothes like flowers, straight blond hair. When she steps out of a cab in a short skirt, her bare legs are like ladders. Her eyes so large, I feel the urge to hide as if her seeing is a more powerful camera. As if she can see something I don't know about myself. A raggedness. But her eyes' wide openness is also familiar, familial. Mine.

Many years before, her father went into his bedroom and didn't come out for seven years. Her mother raised the children, taught school. Her father who had been recognized by the King of Sweden, been given a medal, who taught skiing, who brought my parents into his home and to the family's summer home, who made them so at home, they entered separate saunas, stripped down to sit in that warmth. I wanted to ask her about her father, those seven years. What did he do? Especially, I wanted to ask, how did he come out of the bedroom? How did he do it? Unfreeze. Come back to life. Like Tuuli, her father was a beauty. He has died recently, and I can't ask Tuuli how he'd come back to life. It seems rude to ask Tuuli these questions, her big eyes will know my selfishness, resound with it. Next time. *Depression,* my father said of her father. *He struggled with that.*

But when Tuuli and I meet again for lunch, the restaurant is darker with my hidden questions. My own need to know how to live. So busy obscuring what I want, all I can do is sit across from her radiance. See the strain of keeping her eyes so open, the little lines.

Like a dream I had of myself as a child—this family. Long-lost to Empi and Emil, their daughters, the three sisters swam in Long Pond on the Cape. Glint through the leaves. Their brother is my grandfather who would laughingly call me Daddy Longlegs. The hill of trees nearly hiding the bowl, drop off into lake. A secret. Their spot became private, bought by others, but the girls still went. Ignored the summer people, flung their hair. They jumped in. When I drive by Long Pond in my red rental car, a group of children turn from the trees, water between leaves. They eye me narrowly like a stranger.

BILLINGSGATE

WELLFLEET, MASSACHUSETTS
JULY/AUGUST 2013

> *I am not this body. But I am.*
>
> —Barbara Ess

When I arrived in Lake Tahoe to teach for my second summer residency, opened my suitcase to a mash of wrinkled sweaters, mittens, several half-empty bottles of conditioner—one leaking chalky aqua, one an amber oil, hardcover books, no pants whatsoever, a dozen dresses, I laughed. When I'm dead I'll learn to travel.

I'd started traveling two years earlier, and I am no better at it now. Maybe worse. Here in this Tahoe dorm room are all the boxes and bags I couldn't fit in my jeep when my visiting teaching job ended in May. Winter coats, snow boots, a bag of popcorn fell out of a shopping bag. I'd saved food. June had let me store it under my desk for the summer since no one was using the office until Fall. On arriving a couple days ago, I'd piled it all on a cart. Made a precarious tower, rolled it along the campus sidewalk to the dorm. Hauled it up the elevator. Why so much stuff when I don't live anywhere?

I'd moved from Tahoe in May, to my parents' house in Wellfleet, Massachusetts. I wanted to live there, wanted to stay. Let myself want that. I have an upcoming residency for a couple of months in late fall in Virginia. Then four months in

Connecticut for Spring, just a couple hours from the Cape. Jeep packed to the gills. Impossible to see out the windows, except on the driver and passenger side. Couldn't drive the ten thousand feet down the switchbacks of Mt. Rose in any vehicle, never mind my over-loaded jeep with no rear view. Between me and Massachusetts were states I couldn't fathom—deserts and mountains. Feared I'd die on some outcrop of highway. Tipped over. In my last days in Tahoe, I'd found a man who would take my jeep across the country on a car carrier for a thousand dollars. I flew to Boston, bus to Wellfleet.

My mom couldn't make sense of all my Tahoe boxes on her porch. Why didn't I live anywhere? Why didn't I have a job? Behind their condo, a field for all the units. The complex, Billingsgate, named for the island off-shore that sank. Houses floated to land. At a certain time of day, you can still sail out to where the island was, a little land appears. You can go ashore. Have a meal. Forget what it's like to disappear.

Their backyard field full of bunnies, until the foxes came. We loved the bunnies. Now, a small fox comes out of the woods to watch me hang laundry on the line. We sleep together at night, separated by the light wire screen. Foxes in the yard, me in a blue blow-up bed where I roll as if on waves. Dream of a black bar. The kind you'd push to select a song on a jukebox—long, thin, Kit Kat length. If you push the bar, instead of a song, you get me. I'm a selection. But when the bar is pushed, what comes out is the cry of the fox. All alarm, transistor scream. There is no jukebox; I wake with the scream in my own throat.

I sit up, look out into the dark screen. It's all black. A breeze cools my face. *Body everywhere* tonight in the yard that runs the length of this house and beyond, yard that backs into woods.

The next day, in the Provincetown library, I find a seat by a window. Strangers keep stopping one by one to look out the glass, hand on yellow casement. White hair held up, eyes on the clustered boats, white-blue water coming in so fast, the little waves. From the street below, a man holds a small black camera, covers his eyes. Takes a picture of the window where I sit invisible. Walks away. What's on his film? A shadow? My plaid thrift store shirt? I was listening to the mermaid parade. I was ready to give up my clothes.

Yesterday I walked between water and water. When I left the harbor, I walked toward a darkness at the water's edge. I have never seen wings like that. Black body of a bird still rising with a little air. I would have stayed, but the tower of me was no comfort. I walked away so that he/she wouldn't die in fear of me, catapulting fear.

In the library, a woman stands beside me in pink shoes with holes in them, looks out the window. Her camera clicks. Clicks again. Again. From here I can see where the current carried me yesterday through pools into the ocean. Or maybe not, maybe that harbor is behind me. Another white light-house.

I'm never sure what profane means. Sacred or its opposite? *Profanity,* a woman said.

Maybe that's your problem, my friend said. *In general? Yes.*

It means outside the temple. When the black bar is pushed, what you get is me. Nuar asked, *What is the black bar?* It's for a song on a jukebox that isn't there. Black bar pushed—I don't know by whom. And the fox—male or vixen—outside the screen of my window on the porch where I sleep, screams, alarming the yard.

But the scream comes out of my chest.

The small Wellfleet house tense with fear. My mother's childhood friend comes to visit. *Don't embarrass your mother,* my father says, eyeing my stacked boxes of books and clothes. I tidy the porch, put my shoes away. I don't have a closet, hide them under a table. But it's my mother who announces, *Kelle has nowhere to live.* Her voice rising in disbelief. As if saying it will make sense of it.

I want to stay in Provincetown. Dangerous to let myself want that. Want anything.

What chance did I have? No job, little income, no home, no plan. But I let myself want it. When I sleep, I see a woman with the vixen's face. I've met her in the yard too. Hanging my bathing suit on the line to dry, or taking out the trash, one or both foxes will appear. As if I've entered their realm, come to visit.

The woman with the vixen's face has bars of light across her eyes as she rushes window to window, gold light across her eyes. Her light in the shape of the black box you could press for me—"what I am." It reveals me. Her eyes see me as the foxes see me in the yard. Band over the vixen different. When she came out of the woods to watch me, I got a good look at her curving mask, lighter brown coat. The woman's gold bar of light over her eyes is a kind of treasure. More like my own bar, though gold moon-bright instead of black. Still a mask. She's keeping her eyes on me.

I can hear the tide come in. The male fox sings to me, sees me. His call when the vixen ran in front of me along the edge of yard and woods. It came from behind. I turned from the laundry line to see him right there. Solid and calling to me in the open grass. Light brown, long tail. This intensity a diversion, protection for her. He loves her. What would it be like to be loved like this, unmistakably? In a practical manner, body a fence.

When I photograph the foxes in the green yard, a bright white light emanates from the center of every picture. In one, they both appear, jumping. Frolicking. The yard is theirs. Then they disappear into one body. My father looks out the glass, says, *Maybe they are making love.* Not mating. *Making love.* As if the foxes create love, making it over and over.

When the woman with the vixen's gold band leapt window to window, I was in a long house, long room like the porch, but not. We were back in time, and it was more like a meeting house, Quaker house. Her eyes of such intensity like a fire in which the body is abandoned. Window to window—my porch a series of open screened windows too, a glass door, but we weren't in the present. She won't let me hide. She's not sure I can be trusted. Maybe I don't know what is sacred. In myself. In anyone. This giving up—no job, little money, no housing. Turning to stone. Giving up on a life in my body.

Some nights, when I don't dream of foxes, I dream of opening my mouth deep underwater in the weedy pond. Wonder if I can get to the surface before my throat opens. Worry if I can trust myself not to drown. I hope I always wake before the water comes in.

I don't know what the fox calls mean. Someone recorded the calls, defined them. I can push a button and listen. I can know what the fox wants.

...because in this space between spaces/ where nothing speaks,/ I am what it says.

The black bar pushed and the fox in the dark comes out of me, is me. Why am I making this sound? Why is it coming out of my chest, throat, mouth? The fox is in my throat. Here, when I sleep, the foxes come inside.

SUNFLOWER HOUSE

The sunflowers are as tall as people. Bright round faces, yellow hair waving. They line the brick walk to the front door. Happy sentinels, courtiers. The tallest sunflower on record is twenty-seven feet tall in Kaarst, Germany. The sunflowers at the entry to my house are ten feet. It's not the door I use, but when I look outside at the ocean, the sunflowers line up below. Show me the way out, into the bay, to Long Point. Lighthouse there. Beyond into the Atlantic.

In New Smyrna Beach, Marie Ponsot had written, *to Kelle, daughter of the Atlantic* in my copy of her book. She'd climbed the stairs of my old beach house. Her round yellow button worn every day: STILL AGAINST THE WAR. All the little pinholes in her clothes. We sat in the living room, several writers who reached for books on shelves. Heads bent reading as if in prayer with all the windows open, salt breeze. Here in Provincetown, outside my high window I can see the land end. Mornings, I see the sun light the top of water. Rise up. Nights very dark outside my ten windows, except for one flickering streetlight.

I don't rent the sunflower house. I'd been living on my parents' porch in Wellfleet, two towns up the Cape. My two suitcases overflowed on a fold-out table in the corner. Boxes stacked from my last teaching job out west. Plastic totes filled with folded clothes I planned to stash in a corner of this summer house. Until I found a new place, new job.

You can put those boxes in the attic, my father said. *No, no,* my mom said, *there's insulation up there. Fiberglass. It'll get in your clothes.* In the end, the attic argument moot. The neighbors next door had a party. Invited my father. My father who used to run marathons, and had run the Wellfleet Road Race every year, who had played tennis daily when his knees could no longer handle daily runs, my father who was diagnosed with bladder cancer a year ago, caught early, in remission, but still requiring preventive care. Now, a hip replacement, and an infection he hadn't been able to shake. My father said, *They don't want some old guy at their party.* He loves parties, people.

The party was for the daughter of his friend next door. She rode a standing board all the way down the Cape. *She's been practicing for weeks,* my dad said. He was so proud of her, as if she were his own child. And so he went to the party.

It was two days later when I learned a man at the party said, *I'd like to buy your house. Make me an offer,* my dad said. And he did. My parents sold the house. I'd hoped in a magical thinking way that my parents who had never let me or anyone stay in their place without them, I'd hoped they might see their way to change. Say, *Hey, you could stay here for the winter.* Instead, they sold it to a man who bought it for his daughter. What to do with all my winter clothes, books? Totes almost to the ceiling. *Ship them to your brother's in Virginia,* my dad said. *He's got room.* My brother said yes, so I sent almost everything to his house. Figured I'd stop there while in residence in Virginia, pick up warm clothes for winter in Connecticut.

It was the end of August, and I was jobless, homeless, income-less, the lesses building. My friend Beth sent me an email. I'd been writing on the third floor of the Province-town library, chair in front of window. Computer on my lap. Tourists flitting around me, clicking photos from the window onto the street. From the street, tourists aimed cameras at the windows.

I don't know why I didn't think of it before, Beth wrote. *We're going back to New York. You can stay in our place.* I was standing in the library parking lot, and felt like I could breathe again. Like air had enough oxygen.

I've been trying to get back to the Cape since I was eight years old, and we moved away. As a kid, we came back almost every summer, stayed a month. We came home. But then my grandparents' house sold, and we had no place of our own here. Until the Wellfleet house, rented for several years, then bought eighteen years ago. Few weeks ago, the final papers signed. It's empty now.

Though it's in the new owners' hands, they won't use it until next summer. Bought all the contents too—couch, tiny rocker, blue fold-out with a middle back-breaking bar, easy chair, kitchen table, three TVs, coffee maker, all the dishes, towels, sheets, framed cover photos from the Wellfleet town magazine published every summer—a wall of summers. Stomach sick with thinking what is left. The life left there. My goddaughter beside me on the blue couch, holding the imaginary cat I've given her. *That's a cheap gift,* my dad said, laughing.

In the week before the house was sold, I'd go to Provincetown every day for a recovery meeting and to swim at Herring Cove. Before my friends left for the summer, we went to the beach one last time. We were going to the little pools, but it was rainy cold, early evening. Time getting short. Ocean waves high and wild, opaque gray-blue. In Wellfleet, I'd been smashed to the shore a couple of times, came out scraped and bleeding. It surprised me, as if the shore was a wall built too close. I'd watch where swimmers swam, saw to get out past the break. That to be in the break was to get slammed, thrown down.

I'd swum here every day, at the end of Herring Cove. Yet, this time, when I walk toward the water, I hesitate at the size of the waves, their number. In my hesitation to go under the wave, I'm in the break. Slammed and slammed. Even as I head for shore, I only go sideways and down. Swallowing water, bleeding. Later Nuar said, *The kids were scared when they saw you.* Nuar had been further back, didn't know for sure if I was playing or distressed. But the children saw my face, how I couldn't get out. The waves could make sand of me. I don't know how I got out. Swallowed as much air as I could to hold each time I went under. And then, I was released.

When I'd arrived in Wellfleet mid-summer, I'd had that dream of drowning: *Dark green water, almost black. I'm under the surface. Nothing but murk of weedy water, and my mouth is open. Throat a door still closed. If I take a breath—I can feel it, the need to take a breath, verge of automatic action. If I take a gulp and water comes in, I'll choke underwater. How will I find up? Air? I have to find it now before the door of my throat opens. I have to rise, now.* I could be screaming when I wake up, I could be holding my breath—there is a lot of noise (water in my ears, blood in my brain). But when I wake, I haven't yet made it to the surface unless the surface is waking up. Gasping in the blue blow-up bed on the porch. Outside the screen, sun warms the field, the foxes.

On the shore, the children in a little group watching. I'm relieved, but stung that the ocean attacked me, confused me. Nick waves to us, waves high around him. *You needed to go under the wave,* he says later on shore. *I know, but I was afraid. Well, okay,* he says, *be afraid, but you've still got to do it.*

HANS HOFMANN HOUSE

PROVINCETOWN, MASSACHUSETTS
SEPTEMBER 2013

In Lake Tahoe, I learned I was acrophobic (from the Greek *akron* meaning peak, summit edge and *phobos*, fear). In normal people, when they travel higher, their visual cues recede, and they maintain equilibrium in other ways. Acrophobics continue to rely on visual cues, overload the cortex.

Driving along the side of a cliff, I felt gravity weakened. As if my old green jeep might just sail off toward the red rocks into the canyon that could swallow cities, into the river below. My problem was with balance and spatial orientation—semicircular canals, otolithic organs in bluish purple pouches, sacs and fluids of the labyrinth of the inner ear.

It wasn't vertigo. Acrophobia: "an extreme or irrational fear of heights in a category of space and motion discomfort." With vertigo, one spins. An acrophobic has panic attacks in high places. The sufferer can become so upset, she can't get down. "As height increases, visual cues recede and balance becomes poorer even in normal people. An acrophobic continues to over-rely on visual signs." Locomotion at a high elevation requires more than normal visual processing. That's exactly how I felt. I couldn't get down.

In Tahoe, everything came at me at once—mountains,

stone, sky, clouds, light itself too sharp, the road, other cars, the sun—like mega 3D, like 50D. Some proponents of the alternative view of acrophobia warn that it may be ill-advised to encourage acrophobics to expose themselves to height without first resolving the vestibular issues. Ill-advised! Vestibular issues.

I've often felt ungrounded in space, even with my feet on the ground. Trying to see where I am on a map's flat page, what surrounds me. After nine months in the Sierra Nevadas when my annual check-up showed decreased oxygen levels in my blood, I knew my body had never acclimated. Asked where I wanted to live next, I said, *Sea-level*. What I meant was home.

I'd headed back to the east coast, to my parents' place in Wellfleet. Beth and Kiki, generously and miraculously, offered me this place in Provincetown. Some mornings, overwhelmed, I freeze up in fear. Unable to move. But then the light—bright or dim—comes in all the windows on the bay. I hear the tide. The whole world—the one I'd known from the beginning—comes toward me until I can breathe again. Walk into it. I think of Hans Hofmann painting here when I was three, four, five years old, living up the Cape in a red or white house. Kiki mentioned other writers who stayed here. Connected to others, I feel less precarious.

There's a lot of good energy in the house, Kiki said. I feel it.

*

In September 1926, Henry Beston came to his two-room cottage on the Cape to spend two weeks. It was only a vacation house for him. He wrote, "The fortnight ending, I lingered on, and as the year lengthened into autumn, the beauty and mystery of this earth and outer sea so possessed and held me that I could not go."

It's September 2013. I have two more weeks, and I still don't know how I'll leave the Cape. Thomas Merton is slanted on a shelf over the kitchen sink, under the eave that shields the whole house. I pull the book down, read in *A Body of Broken Bones*, "The plainest summary of all the natural law is: to treat other men as if they were men. Not to act as if I alone were a man, and every other human were an animal or a piece of furniture."

I feel held here. I used to get lost leaving Provincetown at night, and always wound up somewhere I didn't know—a small strip of land and dark wind with ocean all around. The feeling of driving under tree limbs, everything blowing fast and moving. And me on the road in between, beside water. Thrilled there, lost, just driving until the road led me out. And though I didn't know where I was, it was always the same place of darkness and ocean where I'd get lost and lifted up. Where I'd let the road show me where to go.

This borrowed loft at the top of a house is near the very end of Provincetown. On the west end shore road of Commercial, harbor out my window. Boats. A painter's studio made into a home. End of the world, ocean all around. Tomorrow I visit Larry to hear about his ruby glass photographs, see his many tintypes. He befriended me, owns an antiques store.

Nana gave this book to me too, Beston's, *The Outermost House*. With Mary Oliver's poems. She gave this place to me, the Cape. With no house here now, I'll have to find my own. Find a way to stay. Stay or come back. Leaving has always felt like the wrong direction. A wall of glass windows toward the harbor and street, glass door out to a deck, and another wall of glass windows on the opposite side of the room. It's one big room. A window at each end too, and through all this glass, the few voices on the street carry up to me clearly. They feel close. Up here at night, it's like the dark road near the ocean where for years I'd get lost trying to leave Provincetown. Where I was lost and thrilled and carried.

At the top of the house, I'm already turning to stone. Silver blazes through all the windows overlooking the water. How can I not get up? Still, making coffee I think, drink it in the white curtained gauzy bed, hide away from the many windows on both sides of this room—hide even from the sun.

It's brewing, one window open, sun on the blue, and all I think is *morning*. Next to last Sunday here. Hear the tide coming in, and open the screen door, climb a few stairs to the deck. Street quiet, and a man stops to stare at me in my just woken braless in old bright blue shirt state. Contacts not in, but I can see him, slim dark hair glasses, staring at me as I take a photo of the bay in case I forget what beauty I had. As I seemed to be already forgetting as I stood before it. I don't know how to leave.

The man waves his arm like a surprising oar in my morning. I raise my hand, arm. Surprised before to be seen up here because I thought I was too high, far away. *Hello,* he said. All the little birds flying in the garden outside. *I'm doing the cover of a book on Hans Hofmann whose house this is.* There's something lovely in his voice, as if he carries what he's seen in his tone. As if he has paintings inside.

I know, I say, though how would I know such a thing. I mean, I know this borrowed loft, a large attic, was Hofmann's painting studio. Perhaps he thinks I'm the mad woman in the attic—my hair is everywhere.

May I take a picture of the house? He's almost leaning his chest into the green hedge fencing the front yard, except for the brick walk lined with the ten-foot-tall sunflowers. Like bright sunny people with yellow petalled hair lined up to greet you. An abstract expressionist, Hofmann's paintings beat with color—the sunflower yellow, my blue shirt are in his "Pastorale" from 1958 with a block of purple I could eat.

It's his "Maiden Dance" from 1964 burst apart with thin rust that I can't turn away from, all the white space in between. "The whole world comes to us," Hofmann said, "in the mystic realm of color." He bought this house in 1945. In a photo he and his wife Miz stand by the hedge below me, smiling. Array of small windows in the loft at the top of the house where I sit, looking though glass at the sea.

When I was five years old, Hofmann died. I try to see him walking the floor, behind me at the kitchen table. The loft is thirty-four of my feet long, window to window, and twenty-four across. White painted beams over kitchen and bedroom. Wide floor planks golden, like the beginning of a fire. *It's not mine,* I say to the man on the sidewalk. Morning still so quiet, I don't even have to yell—our voices carry. *But, yes.*

I'm not sure where to look. At him, the camera? Smile? I'm startled again to be seen and with such kindness. Wipe my eyes, lean on the gray wood railing. I choose the sea. So now an image exists of Hans Hofmann and me—his house in any case, but in the record of his life, I now appear. Here where Hans Hofmann may have also stepped out of his painting studio to climb the deck, old widow's walk, to lean and look out at the bay and boats to see this world come in.

Biked to Herring Cove and back home, tired, pushing up the big hill. A couple came out of a hotel, terraced place, and the curly haired woman said, *Good job* as I pushed my way up. Embarrassed to be seen trying so hard, but the woman buoyed me, her cheer. Her husband laughed a little as if embarrassed. I came so close to them, everything so close to everything else in this town.

Could I just stay here all fall, into winter? Until my residency in Connecticut? Virginia residency approaching, but I worry about driving the jeep that far. Will it even make it? How make it back north to Connecticut? I don't want to leave. Could I stay until late January? The possibility opens the world in front of me. A horizon instead of tunnel. I ask Beth and Kiki, *Could I stay?*

Yes.

Yes. Everything lightens. My body settles down. Underground plates shift into place. I can stay. Be home.

An enormous gift. The loft is listed. If someone rents, I have to leave. Unlikely someone will rent late fall or winter. When Beth, Kiki, and their daughter, Lula, come for the holidays, I'll fly to my brother's in Virginia for a visit. But I can stay here all fall, come back in January until I leave for Connecticut. *No one has spent the winter there in a long time,* Kiki says.

YOU GROW IN A MEADOW

PROVINCETOWN, MASSACHUSETTS
OCTOBER 2013

The Salt Marsh sign has photos and accompanying code breaker: "8" is raccoon, "2" is cordgrass. "5" is hay. A girl stands beside me, sniffles. She's come from a bus of girls that just arrived. One girl with dreadlocks and a Tufts sweatshirt has skin so glowing she seems unreal. I forget that people can still look like that. That alive. I move over a little from the girl, *Oh,* she points to one of the code breakers. Another girl arrives, very tall, to stand beside me. The first girl says, *Cordgrass. I'm writing my thesis on this. It grows in a meadow.*

You grow in a meadow, the tall girl says, and they both walk toward the breakwater.

*

The last time I spent the fall on the Cape was 1978. Seventeen years old. Nana took me shopping, bought a warm coat for my first semester at Bridgewater State. This fall, I buy a coat online—puffy, shiny black. A carapace. Nana's favorite place was the marsh.

At the top of the house in this loft, I'm surrounded by windows. Front faces the bay across the street. Early October, already windows from the early 1800s rattle and knock.

131

Two hundred years ago someone lifted the windows I lift, someone with my family's names. Nickerson and Freeman. I won't know this until November when I visit Town Hall to see who owned the house before Hans Hofmann. What sent me there to find out who owned a house I'm visiting? I'm in a room where my ancestors may have lived. Do I pass through their lives like glass on top of glass? Fingerprints and DNA colliding on these windowpanes.

At Bridgewater, a college outside of Boston, I ran through the empty town at night in snow. In Provincetown I can run Commercial Street in front of the house—runners go by this morning—up the street to the hill, water on my left. All fall, winter, until I have to leave, I can run again. All this space and time has opened up for me here. Run to the marsh dead end, and a right turn swerve toward Herring Cove and the ocean. We are on this small arm of land reaching out into the ocean, circling around like a hand. The hand is out my window. This house is in the hand. I can run, wake the stone woman. A man runs by in long turquoise shorts with a thick black stripe on the side, his knee lifts slowly, almost slow motion. Sun comes out. I don't have to be afraid of the cold. Don't need to be frozen. Remember Mary said that gratitude is action, action of the body is gratitude for being alive.

*

The painter Mary Hackett's house is across the street, a diagonal line from Hans Hofmann's. The entire living room, is windowed. Through the glass, I see Mary's empty house. I'd found the Building Provincetown website, looked up the houses on my street. It was still night when I found Mary's listed. I looked out the windows and wondered how far away she was.

Morning, I close my door, grab the blue-green bar overhead for balance as I walk down the attic stairs to the long windowed hallway, blue-green floor like the ocean in summer sun. Down the next set of stairs to the entryway shared with the tenants below. Through the garden of green and stone, up the brick stairs into the white shell driveway, onto Nickerson Street. Look at the numbers. Mary's house unnumbered, but all the others around her tell me, this is her house.

A man who worked on Mary's house said, *Everything is crumbling.* When something crumbles, lead dust is released. Then he repairs it. I imagine doorknobs coming off in his hand, corner of mantle dismantling, little puffs of poison like gray dandelion fluff. *She painted everything in the house too,* he said. The doorknobs? What else, what else?

The morning I find the house right here, almost beside me, I wonder if I can look in the windows. No car in her broken shell drive. I lean against the white fence between me and the grass, me and the door. Curtains are pulled to the side of the windows, but from the road, it's dim inside. In the front door's left corner is a strand of red beads from Carnival in August. Were her children here this summer? Her children's children? Did one of them stand on Commercial Street that day in August when I stood there? Did they catch the red beads in the air, leave them by the front door? Or left by a stranger? Or just thrown in the air uncaught, pooling here. Smooth fingernail glass in green scooped into a circle on a step. 5 Nickerson Street. I lean closer. A black cat appears.

I call her, and she comes. Hops on the pointy-but-dull fence posts, and balances her paws on them so I can pet her. Rubs her forehead on my hand. Stays with me, until I think to open the gate. But then two little dogs in the house directly across the street see us. *Barkbarkbarkbark.* The cat and I separate. Caught, I leave. Walk a few steps home to my house, the house Mary painted in 1946: "View down Nickerson Street of Hans Hofmann Emptying His Trash."

The water is so close! How do I live so close to the water and not know it. But then I see the houses that block the bay were not yet built in 1946. I park my green jeep where Hans Hofmann parked his royal blue car. But his trash cans were on the left side of the drive; now they are on the right. His arms bare and brown. Sky white and blue. Roses fall down the white fence across the street from Mary's house. It must be summer. *Hello, hello.*

In her painting, "The Big Me Standing in My Way," from 1950, Mary is in DC. She is foot to foot with herself, but "The Big Me" is more than a head higher, blocking Mary's way. Both Marys wear brown suits and keep their arms to their sides. A bottle rolls behind her, down the bridge. Sometimes my chest feels caverned out. A hole. I think it's a chakra, probably heart. Where light comes from like a sun, and in darkness, caverns. Also fear, another cavern that can open at night, so that I have to hold my hand over it to comfort the place. To un-cavern.

But tonight, after I walked back from Hatches Harbor as the sun was going down, wind cold like water in my face waking me up, my chest felt full. Like a field, swell of puff and sway. So far from empty, sparking on the left of my chest like a necklace. I thought, *Oh, I remember that, that gladness.*

There had been a giant blue coiled boat rope further up the shore, almost in the dunes. At first I worried the jumbled shape might be coyotes. I imagined waving my hands and arms high over head to look bigger. The sun made everything, including me, yellow, then copper, luminescent in the moments that it fell. Everything shone like creatures from another planet. The only other people on the beach, a couple, walked behind me toward the coiled blue, curious. When the rope lay still at their approach, I calmed, wondered what large thing the rope had held in place. Then, freed.

SMALLPOX HOUSE

PROVINCETOWN, MASSACHUSETTS
OCTOBER 2013

the trees / are turning / their own bodies / into pillars / of light

—Mary Oliver

Broad leaves of black oak and locust, lit maple. Beech on either side, a church aisle, as if this visit to find the dead is a kind of funeral. Though it feels more like a wedding with me and Larry who carries white carnations small as a baby's fist, damp and cold. We're on our way to the smallpox cemetery where everyone has a number instead of a name.

From above, it's completely hidden by trees, a green curtain. Wearing my first pair of long underwear since I was a child or maybe since my first year of college at Bridgewater. A couple hours from Provincetown. Remember the bumpy geometry of a thin henley in white or washed pink on my chest, a few white buttons breakable as a child's tooth. In this new pair, black top and bottom, I look like a cat burglar. As summer ends, a stranger in the post office watched me open a box, pull out rain boots with laces. *For winter,* I'd said. As if I knew what would be required.

Long underwear too, she'd said. I nodded. All my winter things from Tahoe packed away in my brother's closet in Virginia. With just summer dresses and bathing suits, I'd moved into Beth and Kiki's loft. Bought a green sweater and black waterproof boots. On this trip to the smallpox cemetery, I'm wearing everything I have that's warm—the long underwear, sweater, boots, black skirt. Thirty-six degrees. October 30, 2013. It's rainy, so Larry and I stop in the church thrift store on Shank Painter. I buy a giant purple raincoat for a couple of dollars. I could sleep in it. Purple is a boundary, one limit of our perception.

Neither one of us knows the way to the cemetery. Before we knew each other, I'd heard Larry talk about a movie in which the dead are remembered. The Civil War dead. Nervous, I'd approached him. *I'd like to see that movie,* I said. We became friends. I'd visit Larry in his antiques shop on Commercial. Look at the ambrotypes, people made of ruby glass. He gave me a documentary about Vietnam, about his return after many years to remember those in his unit who had died. Their bodies hadn't been recovered. I told him about my son, Tommy.

Larry said if I ever felt suicidal, not to tell him. To tell someone. But not him. I hadn't mentioned feeling suicidal. But he'd seen something in me. His father died by suicide. Larry himself took medication. He knew.

When his shop assistant told me about the smallpox cemetery, I asked Larry if he'd go with me to find it. *No, no.* A trek, the directions vague. But a week or so later, when we met at noon near the thrift shop, Larry said, *Let's try to find the cemetery.* It's within the Cape Cod National Seashore's Province Lands. Northwest of Duck Pond. The directions: "The trail that will lead to the cemetery is the first area after Shank Painter Road." Area? Larry and I look for an opening in the woods off six. We see dark in the green. Pull over onto the shoulder. Battery on my phone dying, I read all the directions aloud. Larry said, *You memorize half, and I'll memorize half.* We look for the fire access road. This beech tree lined path of wet leaves must be it. Ground slippery.

We're to walk thirty more feet to "the small area" where the trail branches off in three directions. *This could be it,* I said, counting three possible trails radiating from our bodies. Alone among the quiet trees on either side, leaves like medieval stained glass: wine, ocelot, ermine, crown gold. Air the yellow-green of something being born.

The thing about one wrong turn is that we still guess the next one from our lost place. Guess a small rise might be "a hill" to the right. But it doesn't lead us to "the top" or "a rise." I make another stab at seeing "the small area," the encircling trails. *Maybe that's it,* Larry said, pointing to what is now our left. Doubtful, path overgrown and narrow. Disappearing on the ground, obscured by trees and vines, catbriar. But it is a substantial hill, ridge at the top. Larry climbs.

I follow, worry about ticks from the tree limbs catching like skeletal hands in my hair. I have to grab them in handfuls, push them aside momentarily so I can pass. They swing back like a door. Scratch my hands like fingernails. *Take it slow,* Larry calls from above in his low, steady William Hurt voice. When I reach the top, I see the drop into fallen leaves below, the thin ridge along the edge that leads forward. *The ridge!* We climb the top edge as if we are nervous tightrope walkers. *We follow it to the low point along the trail,* I said, *to a narrow trail that branches right.* Carefully, we shuffle forward on the trail that already seems very narrow.

Only his shop assistant knows we're out here somewhere in the woods. The narrow trail leads down to the base of the hill. After walking the length of the ridge, a bowl opens up before us. No visible path down, hill dark with mud. Earlier rain. Downhill very slippery. Three trees grow from the hill, the last near the base. Evergreens. Pitch pine. They grow in sand and salt where others can't.

We'll go tree to tree, Larry said. *I'll lead.* He wears nice street shoes, jamming his heels in, but still sliding down the hill of wet leaves. He reaches out and grabs the first tree. *I did this in Vietnam,* he said, leading the others. He laughs a little. I laugh a little at the thought of myself as a soldier. Larry skids sideways toward the next tree. *I hope we don't fall,* I said. It's a long way down. Below, the smaller trees, black cherry and shadbush, watch. The destroying angel has twelve wings, is full of eyes.

I take a step or two, reach out my hand and feel thorns in my palm. Hold them in the air, and aim my body toward the tree. Skid, and then hold tree bark in my palms like rough plates of armor. Body resting against the trunk. Tree hugger. Watch Larry move to tree number three. Hope we'll be able to climb back up the hill. Get out. Larry waits for me to make my way to the second tree.

We don't even know if this is it, I said. *Can we get back up from here?* Larry says something, but it's all blur, as just behind him, in the bowl, I see: *Look, look, look!* I point behind him, into the leaves. White stones in a weaving line. Larry turns, smiles. *We found them.* Trees in the bowl in halos of the yellow-green light. Later I said I was surprised we found it. *I thought that we'd find them, didn't you?* he asked. And I did, really. He had a way of questioning me without judgment toward my true answers, the clarity of what I really meant. Larry carries the white miniature carnations he'd bought at the Stop and Shop.

The cashier had said, *Those are nice,* as if imagining the

pleasure of the recipient. I liked how it seemed we were giving them to someone living. That no one would imagine our real intent to place them on the nameless, numbered stones of those who died of smallpox out here in the woods. *Buried deep in a forested glen down a steep hill.* The white petals have the coolness of flesh, a damp silkiness easily torn. But with carnation froth, spiky celebration.

The hill encircles the site behind us and circles around to the left. To the right are wetlands. The Smallpox Cemetery also reachable through lowlands around Duck Pond (bring garden shears to cut through briar "and wear jeans you can afford to sacrifice"). I won't learn this until weeks later. Won't know there is another way out. Fourteen graves here, but only five have visible stones. Where are the other stones? Broken or sunk? *Vandalized maybe,* Larry said.

We lay the white flowers on each stone, and out toward the invisible graves. But we laid no flowers there. Only on those we could see. Try to distribute them evenly, like Christmas presents among children. As we lay the flowers down, we both touch each stone as if touching a cheek, the face of someone ill. Larry walks an overgrown path beyond what I consider the beginning of the stones, the one almost hidden behind a tree, a little separated. Perhaps people were also buried in between. The stones in a semicircle face northwest. Larry walks toward the wetlands. *Here's the house.* He stands in another bowl, the small hole of the cellar. *I'll take your picture,* he said, *get in.* I hesitate, but go down inside the open cellar. Stand in the center. Strange to smile. Seems I stand in the place where fourteen people suffered and died. Climb out quickly.

I don't know what to do here, I said. *What do you normally do in a cemetery?* Larry asked. I kneel by a stone.

When he went back to Vietnam to the valley where his fellow soldiers had died, their bodies never found, he had knelt down. Someone had taken a photo. We're still here. There's no way to photograph the dead. We photograph the living. Those living now. But maybe they are in the white spaces, or their time here is a layer beyond our layer of time. The bowl a reverberation, lives in waves.

I wonder how long it takes smallpox virus to die. The smallpox hospital was built here in 1848, far from where the townspeople lived. One fourteen-by-fourteen-foot room. A pest house. Difficult to find nurses who would live out here with the patients. By 1872, Dr. Newton of the Provincetown Board of Health found the pest house desperately unfit for patients: "The poor afflicted one here entered into what seemed so like a tomb." Later, Larry said, *It hurts me to think of the suffering of those people, as if they were my own family.*

Names aren't on the stones because of the stigma of smallpox. There's no fence here, no marker, nothing to identify this as a cemetery. So many leaves have fallen, we brush them away to see the stones. I keep thinking, maybe we can find the unseen stones too, if we keep kicking away the debris. The surviving oblong, white-gone-gray stones all have "NO" carved at the top, the number below: 5, 6, 9 (bright moss surrounding the stones, greening becoming part of the forest), 10 (moat of bright green moss around it too), and then the broken stones without carved tops. Those missing pieces not even nearby. But maybe the short stones just sunk here in the lowlands. Maybe they aren't broken after all.

Jenner, a country doctor, had announced a smallpox vaccine in England in 1796, but it was a long time before the vaccine was in general use. People recalled the contagion of inoculation, the earlier version of vaccination with smallpox itself (instead of Jenner's non-contagious cowpox). Not only were deaths associated with it, but those who were inoculated were still contagious for a time and went about in public places. Smallpox spread through breath, tiny droplets in the air. Usually from a person no more than six feet away. Though contaminated items could carry it as well. Vaccination was too expensive for the poor. People lived in dread of smallpox. If one caught it and survived, she would be immune. In 1801, Provincetown sought to combat this fear by various decrees. No dogs or cats allowed outside the home, on threat of death to any animal on the loose. Groups of six or more people outlawed, no church services, and school closed.

Apparently, no religious services were held for any of the people who died in the pest house and are buried in the woods, considered "unhallowed ground" by Bonnie Steele McGee, a former Provincetown cemetery commissioner. She said that it should be hallowed. From Old English *halgien,* from Old Norse *helga,* derivative of *helig,* holy. The Norse who some say came here to Provincetown, Thorvald Ericsson, son of Eric the Red, brother of Leif Ericsson—the first European to discover America in the year 1000—Thorvald arriving in 1004, when the keel of his ship broke, forced him to come ashore to fix it.

The ruins of his visit said to be buried under the Norse Wall House on Cottage Street. *Holy.* The *Beowulf* I read drunk at seventeen at Bridgewater State College took place in Sweden. But its beliefs were also Norse, that the only afterlife is in the memory of those left behind. I imagine all those lives, souls of the dead, held aloft like floating balls, because they were remembered. Their lives contained by the memories held, stories told by the living. I feel it. Felt it at seventeen in my classroom at Bridgewater, relaxed in my pressed blond cardboard seat with a morning rum and coke in my veins. *Don't let them disappear,* I'd thought. One of my teachers at Bridgewater liked a Viking comic strip, Hagar the Horrible, and laughed about it in the aisle by my seat. Long rectangle of cleanly cut newspaper fluttering in her laughing hand. One character was Helga.

*

The year before the Pilgrims first landed here in Province-town in 1620, a smallpox epidemic killed many Native Americans in the Massachusetts Bay. So many that the Pilgrims' leader, John Winthrop, thanked God for their deaths as it left the land near empty for the Pilgrims to take. As if the Native Americans weren't even human, but a pestilence to wipe out. It's hard to think of the Pilgrims' work as holy after that. Is a battlefield hallowed? What makes it holy? If it was all holy for the Native Americans, was it desecrated after their deaths? Is my Wampanoag relative buried in an unmarked grave? With other people of color in Ancient Cemetery in South Yarmouth?

Though the gravestones display only numbers, there is a Book of Deaths in which the numbers appear. Larry said, *Someone carved these numbers with care, so beautifully,* the little swirls. Smallpox makes skin a bubble wrap of fluid-filled sores. But it entered through the mouth, infected the mucus membranes first. And when those burst, spilled the virus throughout the body. Maybe in a fever, in pain, there was delirium, a dream to carry them. Fear not stigma drove the people of the town to take victims outside town. Their clothing burned. What were they buried in? Are the bodies naked? In sheets? In 1801 Provincetown, even vaccination with small-pox wasn't widely known. The only treatment, isolation.

We left our flowers. White now in the leaves. We climb the hill along the far left side. Five black feathers crisscross the path. A kind of shelter appears to our right. Rough gray wood, some broken planks, built like a matchstick house. Black rubber tarp inside rolled up at the edges, filled with brown leaves. Walk over. Look inside. Larry nervous. *Let's get out of here. I think someone is, or was, living in it.* Someone might appear. Pest house shut down by Dr. Newton in 1873. Vaccination and isolation used instead. Last case of smallpox worldwide in 1977.

I'd been afraid to enter the woods on my own. Relieved that Larry would accompany me. Though he owned the antiques store, Larry's a painter. And a photographer—his images taken during the Vietnam war. In his studio, he has a black binder with the stories of the dead. Newspaper clippings saved in plastic sleeves.

At Thanksgiving, Larry orders everything I like from the health food store. We'll watch boats from his window. He'll tell me his partner's name, show me his photo from long ago. When Larry and I visited the cemetery, we hadn't known the names of the people who died and were buried there. *But you're going to find out, aren't you?* Larry said. We left the white flowers, still cool inside, the pistils. Touched each stone that we could find. Leaf crunch underfoot. My wild sweeping away of heaps hadn't revealed any other stones. Thought I'd seen a glimpse of broken stone underneath. For a moment, I'd been so sure. Kicking desperately, as if I could find someone alive, save her. Larry had smiled. He knew it wouldn't be that easy.

In the woods, Larry had had trouble breathing. *You memorize half, and I'll memorize half.* In his studio over the post office, he tells me the names of the men who died, how they died. He's painted one man twenty times on marble. There's no way to bring anybody back. At his table, I tell him my son's name. Black binders to our left, human figures in paintings on the wall behind and to our right. In front of us, an open window on the town and tower. The names of our dead in the air like a heaven.

NAUSET HOUSE

Provincetown, Truro, Wellfleet, Eastham. Three towns up
the Cape was Henry Beston's house on Eastham Beach where
he went to spend two weeks in September 1926. My grand-
mother's sister's family had a house near his, in Nauset. As
a kid, the water freezing even in summer. Ever after, Nauset
synonymous with cold. Little gray shingled house a storm
took one year. Maybe the same blizzard of 1978 that took
Henry Beston's house into the sea. I was surprised a home
could be taken by the sea. Just disappear. The place you lived
year after year, rooms full of your life, and nothing left but
sand. As if you'd never owned a thing.

But in 1926, Beston's two-room house was only a year
old, a summer place, he'd thought, until he couldn't leave.
My September ended too. November now. I'm still held here.

When I walk down Commercial to the library or post
office, I stop at Larry's antiques store. Warm inside, calm.
Sit in the chair by the door. Larry behind the glass counter.
His voice very deep and low. He speaks slowly, like a patient
teacher. Today, he tells me that Agnes Martin, the abstract
expressionist, was a real stone woman. If Agnes was in tur-
moil, chaos, she'd just go still. She believed in being solitary,
he says. No partner, friends, or pets. He met her in Taos at

a taco shack. It made sense to me, that whirling down into yourself. A little trance. But Larry says, *No, it wasn't like that. Agnes could become catatonic.* She'd turn to stone. Rigid, stuck in there. Once it happened on a ship at sea, and when they docked in Bombay, she had to be hospitalized for a month. A stupor.

The day before, walking down Bradford Street just before noon, I'd felt like I was in a dream. Houses on the street so old and familiar, the longed-for architecture of my childhood. And further back, as if time was widening around me, arches opening. X used to say, *I'm not where my feet are.* As if he hadn't caught up with his body. Later, I'd stopped by Larry's shop. *I'm not getting anything done here,* he'd said. So, we decided to go to his studio over the post office.

I said, *Maybe I'm in a dream.* It was still light, but now dark came earlier and cold. The next day, I heard there had been a few snow flurries. We'd parked in a lot behind Masonic Place, and walked by the A-House where in the 1800s, the stage coach stopped from out of town. *No, you're not dreaming,* Larry said.

You don't really know me that well, he said, and showed me his baby book recently given to him by his mother. The book lay flat under the shelves of black binders. A necklace of flowers on a plain yellow cover. On the inside, she'd written: *Dear Baby, you are so loved.* In the loopy handwriting of a mother-girl, she writes several messages, all *Dear Baby.* I've never seen anything like it in a baby book—writing to the baby. After a few pages, the entries peter out. *Maybe she got tired,* Larry says. The blankness saddening, but then, three lines on one page. The final in a lighter ink. *What does it say?* There's a date in October.

"First laugh out loud." *I've never read that before,* Larry said, and we laughed. Paintings hung on the walls around us. The Provincetown Tower I'd climbed as a child was out the window to my right. Nana had brought us there on rainy days in summer. *I saw that picture of you with your son,* Larry said. *You were in the hospital, holding him.*

No, I said, *there is no picture of us in the hospital. Yes,* he said. *You were thin. The nurse gave him to you. Yes,* I said. *It happened. That was true in life. But no one else was there. Just me and Tommy. You were smiling really big,* Larry said. Even though there was no picture, I liked that Larry saw me smiling. Tommy in my arms, so he was all I saw. Of course I smiled.

But no one took a photograph, I said. *No one saw. There's only one picture of us together, when he was four days old. In my parents' house. I wore a pink dress with lots of darker flowers.* A dress of tiny flowers, like Ophelia in the river, but pinks and reds.

No, he said. *You were in the hospital, the nurse gave him to you. Yes,* I said. *That happened. No one else was there.*

I saw you. We sat at a table under the window. *Maybe it was a dream,* Larry said.

Agnes told Larry that all her paintings were about happiness. In one painting with yellow, she'd been thinking about a girl from childhood who was the Buttercup Fairy. When I watched Agnes speak in an interview, I thought she said that if we just sit quietly, the feeling that comes is happiness, transcendence. That our happiness is abstract, more than the world. She said, *Their lives are broader than they think.*

THE FIRST HOUSE

PROVINCETOWN, MASSACHUSETTS
AUGUST—DECEMBER, 2013

> *I let the light change also me.*
>
> —James Merrill

In a photo, Henry Beston plays his accordion in the snow. The snow is coming soon. Storm windows in, steaming up today, November 3. In the first house I visited in Provincetown, I wrote at Nick's kitchen table. End of August. Sat there with my small travel computer, journal. Can I sit here and not worry that I am forgetting some impending doom I need to attend to. Can I forget possible calamity?

The second house, Beth and Kiki's, is also the Sunflower House, the Hans Hofmann House. Also a gift. I stayed a week in late August. *Could I come back?* I wondered. *Could I stay into the winter? To late January?* Yes. Every recovery meeting at the same time each day, and every bike ride to the ocean, walk to Hatches Harbor, rocks under my feet, and then the sand and silent pools, had a light that met a light in me. How could I leave?

How are you liking it up there? asked Scott, one of the men who lives in the main house below. I was walking by his antiques store, shy to enter his doorway, say hello. But I did. *I love it,* I said, *but I miss riding my bike, walking the beach.*

You can, Scott said, *you just need to get hardier.* Thirty-seven degrees, little sun, but I had a long flannel scarf, heavy sweater, warm jacket, Wyoming cap, boots for twenty below. I can get hardier.

Myra wrote me a note that night, said, "You're a wonderful mother." Why did she think that? After the meeting, I asked. Myra said that I was with Tommy always, that her own mother was never like that. That I was always turned toward him, I think is what she meant. Whatever she said made me cry. Pushed past a hallway of people to get in the bathroom, cry in private. Karen was in there. Myra followed. Roll of toilet paper in my hand, tore pieces to dry my face.

A baby who had been making high flying baby sounds outside the bathroom now sings behind me in her mom's arms. *I hope you know that every time you talk about your son, that baby appears,* Myra said.

Outside all the black birds lifted and flew.

*

The stadium was shaking, a boy in the airport said to a stranger as we waited for our plane. I'd been on my way to visit a school in Colorado and give a reading. Before I read, a boy introduced me as *one of the strongest women in history.* For the first time, I decided to look at the audience more. Once when I looked up, a girl jumped the way I would jump in an audience with startled happiness to be seen.

In the book signing line, another boy said, *I love your hair too.* I wished that love were an object, something tangible I could hand to him, so he couldn't miss it. In class, he sat in the front row, not talking. Though after I'd read in the auditorium, after he'd stood in line, reached me, the boy had talked and talked. His teacher said he almost never talks.

Their school far from Provincetown. I'd injured myself falling off my bike the night before my flight to Colorado. Knee gash still bleeding without stitches. No time, no health insurance. No bus back to Provincetown when my flight arrived late in Boston. So I spent the night in Newton in a friend's spare bedroom. Remembered the feedlots we'd driven by in Greeley, Colorado.

They'd been moved from the center of town to the outskirts. Cows and sheep stand in their own shit rising around them, eat there, until they're big enough to be slaughtered. We drove by the gray creatures, a living cemetery. Sheep lined up in long rows horizontal and vertical, sheep on both sides of the road. Their whole lives standing one next to the other, fields of gray animals, until they're killed and eaten. Lisa said a nurse works at the slaughterhouse. *A nurse? For cuts?* I asked. I imagined the big knives of slaughtering. Cleavers.

No, Lisa, said, *it's mostly burns from the antibiotics. The workers wear gloves, but it's like acid in the blood when it spills out. Antibiotics burning their arms.* What about the animals who stand there in their burning blood?

When I return to Provincetown, my heels feel dug in the sand. How can I ever leave?

151

WILDERNESS

PROVINCETOWN, MASSACHUSETTS
NOVEMBER 2013

> *We enter solitude, in which also we lose loneliness.*
>
> —Wendell Berry

A month since I'd fallen off my bike. I'd been riding into town for the first time, instead of out, toward the ocean. Already dizzy, rushed by the increase of people as I got closer to the post office, panicked by the cars coming toward me. And then I was arcing to the left to avoid a car, then falling. Near the water, a man with white hair watched me bicycle into traffic. *You looked like you were doing fine.*

Stood over me in the arrowhead gravel that cut open my pants, skin. I didn't see blood or feel the broken finger bone. *I am.* He offered water, a place to sit. Car millimeters from my wheels, pale idle cameos from the coffee shop sidewalk, black kimono crows. In my panic, I forgot how to steer, how to use my arms. As if they weren't mine. *This is not going well,* a voice said, wheel in the gravel turning as if it would make a circle smaller than itself.

Mid-November now. Index finger still with a hard lump from a broken bone. Bruises, knot in right leg healed. Gash sealed shut. Below my knee still swollen. Rain forecast today. I remember what Scott said, *You have to get hardier.* Collect a pile of clothes. Dress in a tank top, two long-sleeved fleece tops, footless tights, corduroy leggings, light rain jacket with a hood, mittens in the pocket, socks, bike helmet.

Unlock my purple men's bike with the bar straight across, carry it up three steps to the broken shell drive. Since the accident, I've been afraid to ride again, but now on the bike I feel steady, strong. Dirt road now covered with shiny new black tar that pills at the corners, collects in egglike clusters. But easily bikeable after weeks of torn-up roads—bumpy stones, uneven dirt, hollowed mud.

A traffic barrier further down that I can barely get around by biking onto an arc of rocks. Then, there's no one, just the road ahead leading to the Pilgrims' First Landing Park. Of their arrival, William Bradford wrote: "Being thus arrived in a good harbor and brought safe to land, they fell upon their knees." But the Pilgrims only stayed five weeks.

Bike past breakwater stones, the marsh's orange and brown light. Turn left toward the ocean. I pass a man near the Bradford Street extension, his dark hair in flat curls like wet seaweed on his forehead, under his cap. He nods at me, smile benevolent. Pass two runners running slow. Turn left onto the beach path in the dunes, down into the parking lot—that whole expanse is mine—cross it. Cross the entrance to Herring Cove, bike past the many empty ocean-fronted parking spots, to the very far end. Lock my bike at the entrance to the trail. Climb the path through the dunes onto the beach. Everyone leaving. Rain coming. Once I'm here, I wonder how I stayed away. Walk toward Hatches Harbor on the slope of sand, as close as I can get to the incoming waves without getting my running shoes wet.

A woman comes toward me. Raise my hand to greet her.

It is so unlike me, but it's just the two of us, and a hooded man behind her. My hood up, and I can't hear her. Walk closer. *A lot of seals out there,* she said. *Playing and jumping. I don't know if they're still there.*

Oh good, I say. I want to say something else. She's not very tall, like Nana, and she has those marks on her face, like Nana's—like mochi dusted with sugar, lines straight across. Not Nana, but I wonder about the sharing of genes—Nana's family here since the beginning, even before the Pilgrims. If it's just one gene between the stranger and me, we're not strangers. *I brought my camera,* I say, patting the pocket with my mittens and phone.

Oh good, she says. I'd dreamed I was far from everyone. A seal watches me walk. We watch each other with our big eyes. When the rain comes, I'm near the far end of the big, fast moving pool. Wind carries cold rain directly into my face. Put my head down and head back, into it. When I reach the path through the dunes, there's no one. To my right, red berries ripe as summer blueberries on low green plants. Not tiny cranberries. Bearberry? Some already blackening unpicked. Yellow-orange leaves like arrowheads carved in filmy gold from some long gone civilization. A gray-green plant has covered itself in white dust, anchored in the sand. Biking home, I pass the front of my house, see all but one or two of the giant sunflowers gone. Yellow-petalled courtiers who'd lined the brick walkway all the way to the front door. Cut down. My face covered in rain, dripping. Water fell from my eyes as if I were crying.

*

Look at this, LuAnne said, handing me the *Banner* at the hair salon. On the front page was a photo of a boat, homeless men sleeping outside in tents on the beach. *You turn over a boat and hope you don't find someone frozen to death.* There are three homeless women on the Outer Cape. There is one woman living in her car. I don't want to be a woman living in my car. There was a hotel where the homeless could stay, but it's being renovated. The article says that the year-round places are harder to find and keep, as they can be sold out from under the renters.

Welcome home, a woman said to me as she left the salon. Afterwards, my neighbor passed me on the darkening, dug-up mud street. He said hello to me as if he were somewhere else. I passed no one else. Not even 5 p.m., and the whole town shut down. Quiet enough that maybe I could hear something.

*

When I sit in the warmth of Larry's antiques store on Commercial, he tells me there was a woman who worked at Wal-Mart, who one day in the store took off all her clothes and climbed into one of the box-like structures they sold. Something that resembled a tiny home. *She had a psychic break,* he said. I wondered if he was gauging my reaction, seeing if I might break too.

Another man said that spiritual hunger drives him to buy stuff. Leads to other hungers because the spirit is ignored. Is that why I have all these clothes, shoes? More than I can carry? *I'm living on cans of soup in a borrowed attic on borrowed time,* I tell Ann. *That's a great line,* she said. Soup cooks so quietly it boils long before I notice. Sometimes the black beans a mass stuck to the bottom of the pan, liquid burned away. December wind blows off the open ocean through glass loose in old panes, as though thick cellophane. *A cave in the snow.* I heat food hot as I can swallow. Try to keep a fire going inside.

Someone contacted Beth and Kiki about renting the borrowed attic. It's part of the deal—if they can rent the place at any time, I have to leave. And I have to leave for the holidays as they spend them here—another couple of weeks. I'd agreed. How could I not agree? They'd never rented before in winter, but the condo was listed in several places. Now, where will I go? The rootedness I'd not really noticed sinking down is disappearing. The feeling of being safe gone.

I called Myra who said, *You won't have to live in your car.* Which made me very nervous. As if that is something I'd consider. It's thirty degrees out, a twenty-five-per-hour wind. Here at the end of the world, this place doesn't belong to me. *We'll keep you in the loop,* Beth says, after she asked if I could leave. *It's just a query right now.*

My hand shakes. My brother calls. *What do you want to do?* he asks. I appreciate that. Not telling me what to do.

I want to stay, I say. He says he'll help. Larry sends me an email, says to call a woman named Wilderness who owns the apartment above his shop. He gives me the names of several people who might have a place, and repeats, *tell them you are a friend of mine.*

*

Learned helplessness was defined in the 1970s when I was learning to be helpless. Martin Seligman found that we learn self-initiated behavior. If it's blocked, the person "begins to feel helpless (that is, that he or she has no influence over his or her environment)." The opposite of this is learned optimism. Seligman wrote a book in which he explains "how to get out of the habit of seeing the direst possible implications in every setback." Have I been set back?

Sinistrophobia or levophobia is a fear of things to the left. This seems terribly specific and encompassing at the same time. But it may just be where the sun rises feels right. Selenophobia is fear of the moon. Who is afraid of the moon? When Terry was a student at Vermont College, she heard a lecture by Mary Ruefle in which at least one astronaut who had once stepped on the moon was now afraid. I don't think the astronaut was afraid of the moon so much as the distance between the moon and earth. More afraid for the earth, for all of us here floating on a circle in darkness. *Years later,* Terry said, *the astronaut said, Wipe my footprints off.*

I imagine that the blackness between me on the moon and earth would have caused me to leap. To try not only to bridge the darkness, but also to get back across that unbearable distance.

Heard Lisa's voice from Colorado in the meeting on Shank Painter today. When a man stretched his long legs out in front of me, and the thigh of the man in the chair beside me touched my jeaned thigh. When there was no room for my black puffy coat with bright gold zippers except in my arms. When on my other side was a woman so tiny I wondered how she could contain everything necessary. When I was late and squished between all of them with my long legs held tight and uncrossed against my chair, I heard Lisa's voice say, *Oh, it's like a herd, you herd together.* Safety, protection. I could breathe again then. Let myself be held among all the other tightly spaced bodies.

My mother is afraid of birds. Ornithophobia. Once a bird flew through a car window, and died at her feet. I don't know if she was afraid before this happened, and this bird's death intensified her fear, or if this bird set everything in motion. Some people are so afraid they can only travel at night. Some are too afraid to even look outside in case something swoops by. Fear of happiness or gaiety is cherophobia. Fear of travel is hodophobia. This can also be a fear of moving.

George of Angel Foods said *hello* to me in the post office, and again when he approached me on his bicycle on the near empty street. Each time he seemed surprised to see me. Hardly anyone on the street now. In the Community Kitchen at the Methodist Church, he'd sat at a back table when I approached with my tray. Hungry, out of money, I was grateful for the meal. George smiled at me, *Welcome to Provincetown.* Last summer, Nick had pointed him out to me for the first time. We'd been walking down the crowded street. *And that's George's son,* he had said of a man on a bike. I'd reached out and touched the arm of George's son to help keep us all in balance.

*

Sometimes when I'd begin to speak, he'd laugh a little, and I wondered if I'd done something strange or funny. His laugh was almost a cough or a choking up. The first time I saw him on the street, I'd been so surprised, I walked past my own street. Didn't know where I was. Spinning in a vortex on Commercial like a space traveler, atoms of my body coalescing. Afraid he'd see me lost on my own street. Afraid he'd think I was looking for him. That I would be a conversational burden. *I didn't mean to startle you,* he'd said the next time we met. November, almost no one out walking.

No, no, I was just surprised. But glad to see you, I said. The last time we'd passed on the nearly empty street, he'd worn a black winter cap.

I almost didn't recognize you, I said. *It's a good disguise,* he said smiling. And then today, as I passed him, having entered frayed with the fear of not living anywhere, he looked younger. He said, *I'm always glad to see you on the street.* How nice that we can just tell each other the truth.

Me too, I said, *I'm always glad.* And as I left felt I lived here. The renters who would have displaced me from the borrowed loft didn't rent after all. Noise of the torn-up road, ongoing construction dissuaded them.

Larry told me that someone from town killed themselves a few months ago. He was losing a house. *Lose the house,* Larry said to me. He said, *I've been thinking about what you said.* Larry laughed a little, like the man on the street did when I spoke. Almost like a cough or choking. *I always think a lot about what you've said.* A woman who had been without teeth for several days touched my arm in a compassionate way.

This morning I stood beside the storm window in the kitchen, so close to the glass I was warm in the sun coming through. Below freezing outside, but it felt like a summer sun across the bay on my skin. Everything goes on without us—the sun, gravel road, grass—unless I'm wrong, and we're not separated. In the afternoon, Larry leaned over boxes of books in a hallway of the church. So many donated books. It looked like someone's library. *Like someone died,* he said. *I can see my own books here. No, no,* he said. Later, as we left the health food store, Larry said, *He's so beautiful.*

Who? I asked, and he nodded toward the front window of the store. A boy about to pass by. He looked sleepy to me, but beautiful in the way that everyone is beautiful now.

A woman from Wheeling, West Virginia, said she'd been afraid to buy a book because it would be blasphemous. She was afraid of what God would do to her. I said *hmm*. But I'd been terrified by something not a dream. Just words as I woke, words that said my mother died. And all day long, all night I've been pressing one finger to another in tiny desperate maniacal prayers. As if God would let her go if my words stopped. If my fingers did not touch each other. As if God made up these rules instead of me terrified of losing everyone I love.

If it isn't constant prayer that's required of me, what is it I'm supposed to do? Or is constant prayer a different thing. Something not fear. *Since before time you have been free,* Thich Nhat Hanh said. He said, *When we understand that we cannot be destroyed, we are liberated from fear.*

Further down the shore, Marconi sent his radio signals, thought they could be used to reach the dead. Larry said for years, he couldn't find his father's grave. Every time he went to the cemetery, to the place where his father had been buried, he was gone. Year after year. He asked his brother, *Can you find the grave?* No, his brother couldn't either. Twenty years went by. He asked the caretaker to check the records, direct him to the grave. Maybe he had the wrong place all this time? But when he followed the caretaker's directions, there was no grave. Finally the caretaker accompanied him to the spot, and a workman arrived with a kind of spear he drove into the grass over and over. Larry was horrified, wondered if he was trying to strike the coffin.

Then, the worker, said, *Here it is.* He'd hit the stone marker. Sunk in the ground, grass grown over. This could happen after rain, after time. So each time Larry went to visit his father's grave, and left feeling he'd lost him, he'd found him without knowing it. *That would make a good story,* Larry said. All I hear at night is the wind.

*

Around midnight, rain falls sideways on all the little windows that front my attic on the sea. Falls as if dropped, something being emptied. Wind loud as a living thing shakes the house, me in bed. Touch my face, but my hand shakes, can't keep its place. In Florida hurricanes, I learned to shelter in a windowless space. Crouch in a hallway with doors on three sides shut around me. Here, the walls are windows. *We're out in the middle of the ocean,* Larry said. *Like a boat.*

Roof rattles as if someone might remove it, a white wooden beam in the kitchen shakes. I hide in my gauze curtained bed, under the eave. If the roof came off, what could I do but look up? When I'd climbed to the deck a couple of days before, another wind turned the bay dark blue. Surprised how tightly I'd had to hang on to the wooden railing. How little it would take to lift me up.

I understood why my ancestor's almshouse on Cape Cod was built on the water, why those with money chose to live inland. This house protects the one behind it. Before the rain, a neighbor on the street asked, *Are you okay up there?* Could this all be swept away? Glass broken, flying through the small room like little daggers.

This is nothing, Larry said. *Just wait.*

The bay out my window is protected. But at Race Point, behind me, it's open sea. Race Point is 3.9 miles away. Herring Cove, the in-between, past the bay and before the open sea is 1.1 miles away. Bay across the street. This house looks down on a boating school, no protection for my attic.

A woman just drowned out there, Larry said. *Walking at Race Point.* Her partner's glasses fell in the ocean. She went in after them. I know what it's like out there. A woman wades in, footing lost. Swept up. *I don't like that beach,* Larry said. Big drop-off, and the shore is like a shelf. It's hard to get back out. This summer, my last day in the water, I was too afraid to go under a big wave, and it battered me. Gulped air between each gray wave pulling me under, afraid I'd drown. Near dusk then.

Van Gogh could paint rain, Larry said. I watch rain fall on a wheat field painted in November 1889. An invisible sky. Rain streaks like chalk or the fingernail scratches of ghosts. As if I know what a ghost is. What their touch is like, or color. Though the wind has died down, it's cold on my face inside the attic, through the storm glass. The original windows, installed in the early 1800s. Someone then was in this room, felt the wind on her face. Floor heater on, but wind comes in from all sides.

Against the blue-purple sky with yellow-white light, the rain is a see-through curtain. Rain in the seams and folds. On my face it washes like headlights of an approaching car. The base of wheat is *kweid*—to gleam, bright. The rain is a curtain on the curtain of sky, and what is behind that? Van Gogh's light reflected on me 124 years later. He shot himself soon after painting another rain. In the summer of 1890, in Auvers.

The best part of hearing the old music in a cathedral, a woman said, *is seeing the faces of those listening.* Van Gogh wrote what he saw: "The immense plain with wheat fields against the hills, boundless as a sea." Violet rain is heavier, threads shot down into the fields, connecting it to the sky. *It's a prayer* someone said. Van Gogh was thirty-seven years old.

The lighthouse keeper reported seeing a person in the surf near Hatches Harbor. It was the woman, floating. When she'd been caught, winds were twenty miles an hour, gusts of thirty. Maybe wind caught the glasses. After the 911 call, a ranger was there in five minutes, but couldn't see her. Coast Guard, police, and firemen looked for her all along northern Race Point beach. But she'd been carried away, near the little pools where I'd floated this summer and fall. Where I walk now, dunes to my right. Her body out there earlier, a woman floating in the icy water as if at ease. Had I gone earlier, I might have seen her. Might have thought her brave out there, some kind of Amazon, until I'd notice it was the ocean moving her body. Somewhere out there she'd had to let go.

What separates me from the next world, seeing it, could be violet rain, an off-white sky. Passage through that country. Passport from the French for vision. As if we are on a carriage with facing seats. Why do I think we might be able to hear the same music, some of it anyway? You on your side of things, me on mine.

A SAILBOAT ON A TINY SEA

The person who had the antibody could be used to cure the afflicted on the science fiction show I watched as a child. A serum could be made from the blood of the person with the antibody. The body which had fought off the disease. A person could be a cure.

Bodies bent over other bodies, drawing blood from one into a tiny glass tube. Concocting the serum. Injecting it in others who slumped and then revitalized. Young again. The person with the antibody immunized. I am the person immunized. When I lived in Orlando and was just getting sober, my boyfriend's brother arrived one night, said, *He doesn't like to be reminded that he used to shoot up.* My boyfriend smiles/grimaces. Doesn't meet my eye. At least a year of unprotected sex. But I don't know about hepatitis yet. And yet, my drinking was blackout for years, so maybe it wasn't him.

Still, when Alice told me she'd been through the year-long treatment, and I told her I'd tested positive, she'd asked, *Did you shoot up?* Terrified of needles, queasy at the word "vein," fainting when blood is drawn, even "blood" dizzying, *No, I didn't.* The positive terrifying, and so the liver doctor, the deeper DNA test showing that I don't have the hepatitis

C virus, but I was exposed to it, and have the antibody. My body's army inside surrounding and attacking the invader. Saving me.

I am a cure, I thought. Imagined the science fiction men in their tight-fitting polyblends surrounding me on an alien planet—a violet moon—the inhabitants children living in caves or blond sylphs in bubbles. Strapping a rubber band around my arm, piercing my vein, drawing my blood to immunize the others. For once, not fainting, for once strong, because my body after all had been just that, fighting back. Winning the fight.

Marconi down the road, famous for transatlantic communication. But he also wanted to use wireless technology to talk to the dead. The first transatlantic wireless communication on Marconi beach in 1903. He'd heard something "anomalous" through his radio receivers. "In wireless contact distilled spirits and not bodies communicate." Marconi's first wireless was "a small and fragile glass tube about the thickness of a thermometer, and two inches long."

Thich Nhat Hanh said that simply because we don't have the television or radio on, doesn't mean the waves aren't there, all the messages being sent. Though we don't have means to receive. "We have not come from anywhere, we shall not go anywhere. When conditions are sufficient, we manifest. When conditions are no longer sufficient, we no longer manifest. It does not mean that we do not exist. Like radio waves without a radio, we do not manifest."

Hanh said this to help us not fear death anymore. There are parts of ourselves that aren't our bodies. There was a spark. Waves. A key held down. Fine nickel dust in a slit. A current passed through the slit. Later, there were towers that fell into the sea. Or were dismantled. The messages sent across the sea came from a cliff. Each year, the sea took three feet back. Marconi used a simple telephone. "It provided a dimension in which the unheard (and who is less heard than the dead) was combined with a second frequency that could transform it into audibility."

*

The Anxiety and Phobia Workbook is dedicated "to anyone who has struggled with anxiety or an incomprehensible fear." There are several specific anxiety disorders: panic disorder, agoraphobia, social phobia, generalized anxiety disorder, obsessive-compulsive disorder, and post-traumatic stress disorder. It is unnerving to see that of these, I may have something of five of the six. It is also a relief to see things named. Fear has two pathways, fear/anxiety circuit is fast and focused on the amygdala, sending us running; the OCD circuit requires the orbital frontal cortex (slower interpretation that judges the danger). They involve different neurological circuits.

Genetics also play a part. "One particular gene, the serotonin transfer gene on chromosome 17, has a short and long form. If you're born with the short form, you're prone to twice the level of amygdala activation as people born with the long form. You are more vulnerable to life stressors, more likely to develop an anxiety or mood disorder."

The book says my fears of others coming to harm, those thoughts, are just "random noise." I find this hard to believe, but I want to. I worry it's like a telegraph, and I'm its only interpreter, the only one who can understand the signals. The idea that what I fear—though it feels very organized, repeated over and over—is random, is noise. Is inconsequential. Nothing to be corrected, stopped, erased. Nothing at all. It's like a metal belt around my waist came loose. Like something used to hold a condemned person in the electric chair. Undone. What if I could let loose this fear?

*

Larry said Agnes Martin drove around in her jeep for two years, lived in it, before she settled in Taos. He talked to me about hue and intensity, how light blankets all of us. Paint that—from some place in time—and it will tell us something. Something else can only be seen in black and white. Abstract expressionism connected to the Surrealists, the psyche. Seeing the artist's hand. I could sleep in an Agnes Martin painting. I could eat a sherbet. I could think clearly. She called her catatonic states a trance. Trance so close to dance, but the body's still. She slept in her jeep in those years. Larry asked if I slept in mine. I need to be indoors. My safety needs require walls, roof, door, lock, key. Preferably high above the ground where no one can reach me.

*

The electronic symbol for ground looks like a sailboat on a tiny sea. The semaphore has an alphabet of two flags. Before Marconi's wireless, to talk to people far away, one could beat a drum, blow smoke, wave flags or oil lamps. Hit the ground and someone else can lay his ear to hear it. Sound waves work in the river too. The telegraph sent signals across cable.

You could reach anyone with wire. A children's book advised learning the code by heart. Dot-dash click click click click. *The letter "a" would be bz (pause) bzzzzz.* There are also instructions for making my own telephone with a cell from an old burglar alarm. For fun and to save on phone bills. The glass envelope is sealed. For radio waves, one wire is air, the other is the ground. To receive the waves, you need an antenna. If I receive the waves, am I an antenna? No, I am not a wire. Be careful with amplification, no one wants screeching. I only understood Earth Science, the naming of rocks on the tables. Surprised when my teacher in El Paso chose me out of all the students to attend the Earth Science Fair. They all seemed broken off. One rock was pink. Many glittered. I remember a white hall, like a blank mall, wandering. Rough ridged fossil bodies like touching the waves of the past, reaching through them to the indentations of a small creature. To receive a radio license from the FCC, you must know Morse Code. *Then the world will be at your fingertips.*

*

Thich Nhat Hanh said, "The space in the room is full of signals." He said, "Just because we do not perceive something, it is not correct to say it does not exist." The father who thought his son burned to death, held a bag of ashes, and couldn't let go of that belief when his son came back to him. Knocked at his door. He never opened it. Am I holding a bag of ashes? Am I caught in one idea? Hanh said that if we don't manifest, it doesn't mean we don't exist. He said that if we ask a flame where it came from and where it's going, the flame will reply by "its presence." He said this is the same of flowers. "If there is a baby who is lost, we should not be sad. It is because there were not sufficient causes and conditions for it to arrive at that time. It will come again." "It" makes it sound like the baby is unborn. What if the baby is born? Will he come again too? Hanh said, *Practice like a wave.* Like a wave whose true nature is water.

*

In the cereal aisle of the Stop and Shop, Larry told me that Susan Sontag bought photos from him in New York. Beautiful men naked or half-dressed. Big annual antiques show. In the toothpaste aisle, I told him about Lacy's book. How her therapist said she has PTSD as a result of her kidnapping and rape. I'd thought about my own abduction, the unopenable door, the three men, rape, suffocation and death. Shock of not being able to save myself. Having to let go of myself, life. *Could I have PTSD?* We moved into the larger aisle that circled the store. Paper towels in rows behind us. Deli ahead.

My isolation. Keeping close to the door out. Never wanting to live on the ground floor as too easy to kill. Fear of crowds, cities. Hyperalertness. Need to protect/save everyone. Jumpy. When Lacy wrote about the times something would shift, and she could no longer bear the touch of her children, bear touch, I thought, *Oh.* It seemed so strange in me, with my physical loneliness. But sometimes I go cold. People don't even try to hug me as there is some vibe of *No*.

I don't know how it happens, that shutting off. I'm not a soldier, and it was long ago—the abduction and rape, and the other rapes. *You'll try to deny, minimize it,* Larry said. *Early on, they found that rape victims and war veterans had similar symptoms.*

In his painting studio over the post office, Larry shows me more news clippings about the men he went to war with, the ones who died. Gives me a book on PTSD by the clinical coordinator for the Vietnam Veterans' outreach center in Silver Spring, Maryland. *PTSD is an entirely normal reaction to an abnormal amount of stress. A single life-or-death incident lasting as little as a few seconds can be enough to traumatize you. In those few moments, your emotions, identity, and sense of the world as an orderly, secure place can be severely shaken, or shattered.* Matsakis says I could have behavior now that might have helped protect me then, but now those survival mechanisms are not useful.

Facing it is the emergency stage, and Matsakis gives a list of cautions. The book says that if I am truly frightened, I can try touching a physical object or petting the cat. I don't have a cat. PTSD develops in 35 to 92 percent of those who are raped. This seems a broad range. I fill out the questionnaire. According to DSM-IV criteria, I have either PTSD or partial PTSD. More of some criteria, less of others. I don't see images or have trouble sleeping, am ready to discount the diagnosis, minimize my symptoms.

Under Criterion B, I don't have dreams or nightmares that replay the attack. Though the Criterion says it's possible to simply have dreams that you're under attack, for example, drowning. *These are not rape dreams, but they capture the feelings of helplessness, fear, anger, and anxiety you most likely experienced during the rape.*

I have many dreams of being under attack, of war, of drowning, torture, abduction, mutilation, tornados, plane crash. All dead. Matsakis mentions a name I'd recently come across, Martin Seligman, discoverer of learned helplessness syndrome. Under *"When Stress is Prolonged,"* Matsakis describes Seligman's 1975 experiments in which he gave animals electric shocks. No matter what the animals did, they couldn't escape the pain. *At first the animals fought, tried to get away, and uttered cries of pain or anger.* Then, they gave up. So that when another test was administered, this time with a lever to stop the pain, the animals didn't even try to press it. Their neurotransmitters may have been depleted from the constant adrenal secretion and/or the animals were just completely beaten down. Without hope.

Seligman said this helplessness is also true of people who have been traumatized. Matsakis says I can learn to make my own choices instead of the ghosts of trauma. Didn't I have a kind of learned helplessness even as a child? Does trauma compound it? Last summer in Wellfleet, I dreamed of drowning. Careful in the dark green, almost black lake where I swam alone every day. I stayed near the lake edge where the water wasn't over my head. But in that dream, three men wanted dark water in my mouth. The men would first take one of my arms, then a foot, fingernails, last ovary. Dismantle me, ribs in a neat pile. Waking is how I escape.

JOURNALS IN ICE

One day I entered this room and was not afraid of ghosts.

I'm living in James Merrill's house in Stonington, Connecticut for four months. A town geographically similar to Provincetown: the end point of a finger of land surrounded on three sides by water. I entered the Ouija board room where James Merrill called the spirits, and for the first time, was not afraid.

It was after a friend phoned, spoke in a register that calmed me. But tonight, opening the yellow door with its gold metal sun, there's a knitting-up in me. As if a spider lives in my throat, wove a web inside my chest. Inner bodice of silk he runs up, pulls. *On a pound-for-pound basis spider silk is stronger than steel.* Remember that Ivy said the scarlet room always felt *occupied*.

Switch on the table lamp, round the corner. Scarlet room to my left, darkness ahead. Fingers tremble to switch on the large lamp before the ceiling-high thickly gilded mirror. I'm nervous and I'd run back out, but I want the *Timetables of History,* left on the table upstairs. Breathe, say a little prayer. If there are ghosts I think it best, as with bears, not to take them by surprise.

I haven't been in here for a few days and, if there are ghosts, they may have forgotten I'm familiar. A neighbor. Somehow I feel safer next door, as if ghosts can't walk through doors. Still, I don't feel them in the apartment across the hall, or even much on the fourth floor or deck. As if ghosts haunt only one place.

I'd arrived at 107 Water Street in the heavy snow of January. Writer-in-residence in the house of James Merrill, a leading (and much lauded) American poet. The son of investment banker, Charles E. Merrill, co-founder of the Merrill Lynch brokerage firm, James Merrill had been rich his whole life. He created the Ingram Merrill Foundation to support writers and painters. His will named writer after writer to whom he bequeathed money. And on his death in 1995, he gave this house to the town of Stonington, to do with as they wished. The Stonington Village Improvement Association created a writer-in-residence program. Kept everything in the apartment as Merrill had left it, and the first writer arrived later that same year.

The house, a late-Victorian, is where Merrill and his partner, the writer David Jackson, lived for forty years. He and David contacted spirits at the round, milk glass table in the scarlet-pink room in the Merrill apartment. Here, he wrote the 17,000-line epic, *The Changing Light at Sandover* from séances with the Ouija board. He transcribed these sessions with otherworldly spirits, creating a 560-page trilogy of poems. Merrill called the spirits to this room for decades.

The Merrill apartment is at the top of a steep, narrow staircase, on the third floor. I sleep and cook in David Jackson's apartment, across the hall. Merrill's barber has a shop on the ground floor, and there are two residential apartments on the second. Merrill and Jackson added the fourth floor, an open room of sun with black-and-white checkerboard floor, windows on all sides, and a deck with 180-degree views.

I love reading up here on the hard turquoise couch in the sun. A large painting of James Merrill, David Jackson, and four friends in the 1950s—titled "The Surly Temple"—to my left. In the painting, Merrill sits on a curved couch much like the one where I recline to read. On the orange coffee table, books I've pulled from shelves. To my right, a concrete *chiminea,* like a miniature spaceship. His grand piano under the eaves behind me.

A sliding glass door opens onto Stonington Harbor to the right, Rhode Island's Little Narragansett Bay to the left. Straight ahead is Long Island Sound, Fisher's Island, Montauk. Stonington a one hundred and seventy-acre peninsula at the far eastern edge of Long Island Sound. When I'd arrived, parking on the snowy street in front of Merrill's deep sapphire front door, it was Merrill's barber who greeted me. *You're the poet.*

*

When I enter the Merrill apartment, it feels like another world. The sitting room not visible at first, blocked by the massive gilt Venetian pier glass that barely clears the ceiling. To the left, on a whiteboard in the kitchen, are Merrill's instructions to guests from twenty years ago. Straight ahead and left again is Merrill's bedroom with an electric green wooden floor.

Rounding the mirror, a kind of glass throne, his sitting

room is wallpapered blue with bats and clouds. Ouija room to the left, Merrill's study and library hidden behind the sliding bookcases to my right. A telephone room and floor-to-ceiling record collection divides the sitting room and secret study. Just before the bookcases is a staircase, leading up to the black-and-white checkerboard of the fourth floor.

Of course it's not James Merrill who scares me—he was so generous. If he is here, I can't imagine he'd mind me. Doing much the same as him: reading, writing things down, watching water out the window. Listening to a truck go by. From the beginning, I felt James Merrill's benevolence, and was intensely grateful for the space he'd made for me. For the depth of kindness that allows a man to give a house to a town. When I read his words, "I let the light change also me," I'd thought, *Yes, I want that too.*

No, it's the dead dead who worry me, those who never lived in this house alive, but were called afterwards. How do the spirits know not to come back? Even when Merrill thought he was done, the spirits had disagreed. Ordered him to write two more volumes. They had minds of their own. Once, on a walk in the mountains, I'd seen that bear on the wooded road. I knew I couldn't reason with the bear. Plead. We didn't share a language. But what about ghosts? Can we talk?

Matthew Zapruder, who lived here one winter, wrote a poem (and book), *Come on All You Ghosts,* in which he mentions this place: "(house/of the great ornate wooden frame/ holding the mirror the dead/saw us in whenever/we walked past)." Sometimes the writers-in-residence come in twos: Cate with her baby, Sandra with her husband. They *slept* in here, in James Merrill's bed. And Matthew, in his poem mentions an "us," a "we." So he had company too. Having another person here would make things feel more normal. But I'm here for months on end, snowed-in, just me and the ghosts. I'm glad, but jittery.

On that one day, my friend's voice on the phone had calmed me. He'd reminded me of my real dead. I thought of my son who had died of leukemia as a baby, fourteen months old, in a Boston hospital. Who I would do anything to find. I was reminded of my own death. How if I came to haunt a room, my loneliness, already strung in every cell, would be without even those cells. How after my grandfather had died, he'd come to me and cried, had to lean down so far to rest his head on my shoulder. Crying for my grandmother whom he couldn't find.

How without this body which I do love, I might be made of solitude with no hope of even a cashier's hand in mine to give me change. No hand. I wouldn't want the living to be afraid of me. We're all so close, little line of here and gone. Matthew says it too: "how we will someday / (right now!) be together." A matter of time which now seems to move so fast I barely see the ones I love and surely would do all I could to find them.

*

If you cannot release your /self into a quick blaze
then how can you let go / of all your despair?

—Farid ud-Din Attar, translated by Sholeh Wolpé

Dark blue water rushing out to sea so fast I can feel it. Snow on the opposite shore. Here a dock, snow, a house across the street, brick chimney in my window. At the first event to welcome me, a tall man who'd lived in England said, *Your hair is a poem!* He had one in mind, sent it to me, Yeats's "For Anne Gregory":

"I heard an old religious man / But yesternight declare / That he had found a text to prove / That only God, my dear, / Could love you for yourself alone / And not your yellow hair."

Everyone solicitous in this small seaside village, the Borough they call it. For four months, I have the house on Water Street where Merrill invited spirits in the scarlet round room. He was called one of the "strangest and most unnerving poets." All his important papers are no longer in the house. They're at Washington University's Library in St. Louis and Yale's Beinecke Library. In the Merrill Apartment, I find a bunch of cancelled checks in a desk drawer. Photos in a cabinet. Box of flowers so dried they're almost dust. One drawer stuck. Knife the stuck drawer open, wanting something secret. It's full of books.

*

I love Merrill's study hidden behind the sliding bookcase. On his desk beside me is the Attar of Nishapur's *The Conference of the Birds,* a Persian fable of birds who travel seven valleys to see in a lake that God is the world. The birds had been seeking Simurgh, a mythical flying creature, to be their leader. But, "in the reflection of each other's faces these thirty birds ...did not know if they were still themselves or if they had become the Simurgh."

In the bathroom, on the bottom shelf of a dark brown wood cabinet is a tall glass. Cherry red candle inside. Label reads: "The Most Powerful Hand" and a palm is raised with a cloud balanced on the fingertips on which four men and a baby (or another very small man) stand in robes with haloed heads. Wax slightly cracked, but I can't tell if the candle has ever been lit. Maybe just used to prop the shelf above.

In the telephone room, the floor to ceiling bookcases are filled with record albums, mostly classical. I've been listening to music on headphones for so many years, not wanting to disturb anyone, to keep the music close and private, I've forgotten how it feels when music fills a room.

Above the records is a sculpture of two human feet in different colors, buff and tan, unattached beside an old bronze box decorated with leaves or green bats. Or the feet are small mountains. I take Dvořák's *Stabat Mater* out of the paper sleeve, play it. Speakers crackle static, music from past. Walk through the sitting room where there had once been a leak in the ceiling. It had dripped onto one flying bat on the blue wallpaper, clouds his aqua eyes.

Into the scarlet room, the gateau room, and for the first time, I sit at the Ouija board table. I want to do what scares me. James Merrill and David Jackson contacted spirits at this table, which slides a little, whoa, under my laptop. A white round tabletop on top of another round white tabletop on top of a round wood tabletop on top of another. I type on four tabletops. A kind of insulation?

The room bright with sun coming in from the harbor, setting in an hour or so. Windows hung with crystals, and one from the chandelier. They are the width of three fingers. But heavy, you could knock someone out. One of the four windows doesn't have a crystal hung from the pane. That crystal lies on the sill. That window has a stained glass yellow-green bird. Above the bird's head: "Dum spectas fugio" which I hope is not a kind of spirit-calling tool. It translates: "While you watch I fly."

Even the word "occult" makes me anxious. Since I was a kid, I've been afraid if I let my guard down, something—diabolical, paranormal—will swoop in. Afraid I won't be strong enough to protect myself. Looking down, I see that around the round table, just beyond my chair (and the other three), another circle surrounds us. The circle made as everything within it is lighter-colored wood, gold within and without. Throughout the rest of the house, the floor is dark. What made the circle of the table light? As if the sun had shown just here for many years? No skylight, just the palatial dome, ceiling for a king and queen. Versailles cake. Conch-like swirls and wreaths and crests and leaves, adornment within adornment, within each row all identical.

In the center of the table, a bird or dragon, old gold, with silver circles all over. Like nail heads. Nose or beak broken, and more damage between the eyes, a hole slightly to the right exposing rust inside. Elaborate tail or feathers—like lace made of gold. Not lace. Fire. The bird is made of fire. Its feet wooden or clay. I don't want to touch it.

Stabat Mater is a large-scale choral work. The text a thirteenth-century Latin poem. Rhymed terzines. Dvořák was "too realistic...to allow his sacred works to become abstract, mystical, set apart from life in this world and from his own life and feelings." The *Stabat Mater* poem describes Mary's anguish standing at the cross. All three of Dvořák's children died, and it was five months after the first child's death that Dvořák started writing this piece. He returned to it after the deaths of his other two children.

Beside the record player, there are ten messages on James Merrill's phone. The light blinks. It gets darker. I never stay past dark in the Merrill apartment. I've always returned to David Jackson's, until now. Light in the window across the street, on the slung telephone wire, on snow on the roof. Chimney bottom metallic gold with the sun leaving, sky edge yellow-white.

A nearly life-size, terracotta woman bows her head behind me, white mask over her hand held to her breast. She's barefoot, delicate. Swirls in the hem of her robe. On a pedestal, she wears a tiara. There's a kind of whiteness splashed on her earth-colored body. Even in her eyes, the elbow I held to feel what she is made of, as if escorting her somewhere. Her elbow has a deeper white wound, uneven.

The first movement has a long, orchestral introduction, instruments cry out. I turn on Merrill's purple lamp with fluted flower opening, gold edged. I can stay a little longer. For a few moments, all I hear is static, and then a man starts to sing.

A small insect, nearly invisible, flies by. I hope it is not a spirit. All windows closed. It's twenty-eight degrees. How did it get in? More snow on the way. The heat under the Ouija board makes a low, quick gong. Change the record to the other side, hear the calm hope. It helps to have a chorus. Light so dim, for a moment I can't tell if I'm trying to read German or English liner notes. It's German. So many languages I don't know. *In the alto solo,* a voice is flying. Snow shovel scrape outside. One voice but she is like birds.

Oh! hush thee, my baby, the night is behind us, / And black are the waters that sparkled so green.

—Rudyard Kipling, "Seal Lullaby"

"Convergence" is torn in my red dictionary, the act of coming together. Every day I flip the pages in mine, or in James Merrill's deep blue dictionary open on a wooden stand by his study window. Place my finger on a word. See what it is. This morning I woke early in Jackson's apartment with the sun coming in through bamboo shades on one window. Sheer white cloth on the other in my bedroom. Walk to the kitchen in old fur-lined slippers, slippers I wore when snow fell on my Tahoe deck, and I wanted snow on my hair, face. To be snowed on. Pour water from a jug into a turquoise coffee cup, set it on my nightstand. Let the bed hold me like a night sky I don't fall through.

Voices from the three-hour dinner the night before with the residency director, her husband, and a few of their friends. We ate salt cod, once a plank of fish that kept people alive in winter. We had it for the difficult novelty. It required a forty-eight hour soak in a gallon of milk that had to be thrown out.

I leave the house. Walk by the harbor, on the dark dirt path by the dock, until the concrete begins. No one around. Just windows of big empty waterfront houses on my left—clapboard and shingle—dock and harbor to my right. I'd walk down the sliding bridge to the dock, but the air's so cold, I could die in the water if anything gave way. If I slipped. Climb steps to the wall overlooking the water, stone barrier.

Pass the new condos under construction, half-covered with a white tarp, hammering inside. Still no one.

Walk to the Point, turn right. Pass the old, shut maritime homes. Near the closed stone lighthouse, closer to the tip of the peninsula, water on all sides. Then, I see the white seal. She's on a big stone on the right side of the peninsula, small, young. Toddler size. If it were warm, I could climb down the boulders into the water, swim over. Though of course I wouldn't, am worried even my looking may make the seal nervous. Dark eyes conscious of me watching. I've never seen a white seal. Sea navy in the cold, but the sun's warm, consistent. No clouds. A couple in a car. And a thin, older man on a bike behind me. *She's been there all day,* he said. *Since 10 a.m.* I nod. *You think she'd be hungry, get in the water.*

Tide's already come in. We both turn our faces to look at the seal. *I'll freeze if I stay any longer,* the thin man says. Bikes away. A photographer is far down on the rocks crouched over, concentrating. Forehead dry white with light ragged lines, like concrete just applied, raked with a nail. Eyes too gray to see inside. I stand on a slab above him. *He's been there all day,* a stranger beside me says. He's late fifties, early sixties. Brown coat.

Could he be sick? I ask. *You see them here sometimes,* he says. *A man from Stonington discovered Antarctica, and they used to go there to club seals. Bring the furs back to sell.* I look into the dark pools of the seal's eyes as she keeps looking around, watchful, nervous almost.

What is she scared of? I ask. *Sharks maybe, but we don't have many here. Is she afraid of us? Who would be scared of you?* the man says, laughs. *There used to be whales here too.* The seal is a blond white, stretched out. Petroleum killed the whaling industry, he tells me. But Stonington wasn't really a whaling town. They made ships here.

Whale oil was used for lamps, he says. *It gave a white light.* Expensive, so only the rich used it. He tells me that most people used beef fat, but it gave a yellow light, smoky. I nod. My hands are very cold. Hair pulled back in ponytail, ears red. *But then kerosene was invented, and you could just pour that,* he says. I imagine a flask of yellow oil. Everyone else has left. I try to walk away from the man, but he keeps talking. I head toward a boulder smooth as a slate sidewalk to walk away on, toward the peninsula, and then away from here, him. Back home.

But the man cuts me off, sticks out his hand. *We've met before?* He laughs. *Your hands are so cold. Here, take my gloves.* Tries to hand me a thick, brown work glove. *No, no, I have pockets.* Jam my hands in. He asks where I live.

So cold a tear falls from his eye. His nose runs. *I'll have to walk you back,* he says. The implication that he's keeping me safe. When a car comes toward us, he says, *You need to move onto the sidewalk. I like your body whole, not in pieces.* I ignore this, look out at the water through trees, aware that I need to keep my eye on him. Like the seal. We're barely up the street when he turns into a walkway, toward a house on our right. He says, *Hey, C'mon, come in here. C'mon.* Walks to the blue doorway and looks for the key.

I stand unmoving on sidewalk. Rooted. Go inside a house with him? *No,* I say. *I have to work.* His face goes blank, as if erased. Was this some kind of fantasy? Pick up a lone woman in a parka, and win her with tales of whale oil and kerosene? When I refuse, we walk a bit more toward my place.

Well here you are, he says. Something is over now. We

shake hands again. In the eighteenth century, Stonington got rich on the sealing trade. *You're safe,* the man had said to the white seal. *He looks sad,* he'd said, *but seals always look like that.* Later I read that if a seal looks you in the eyes, to back away. People can seem like predators, cause stress. The seal had looked over her shoulder, over and over, in a jerky motion as if startled. She stayed on the rock all day, just changed direction. As we'd walked away, she flipped her body up and down on the stone to face into Narragansett Bay. Toward sea.

*

Someone who cared about me once suggested I watch a movie in which seals became people, shapeshifted. There was a little boy who disappeared, was gone. And then he appears again on an island. In a boat that is a cradle.

I'm the mother of a boy who died long ago, disappeared. I've been looking everywhere. I'll need the supernatural to find him. I don't know how to live. Moving place to place. No plan. But that's not true. The plan has always been to write. I worry that in places where no one knows me—everywhere now—I can't keep myself safe. But I can. When the stranger tried to get me to enter that door, my feet were stone. My body strong in ways I could not imagine. As when my son was put into my arms when I was weak, bleeding, dizzy. Afraid I'd fall, drop him. But once I held him, I was solid. His touch glued me together. On the sidewalk today, some strength rose from my feet up. I felt not boundaryless, not like fog, but grounded in my body.

What is the bird on Water Street whose song sounds like a construction worker's whistle cut short? I think it's a red bird, I saw one for a moment at the top of a tree, like an ornament. What is the tree that looks like palms held in a prayer of branches? It's near the miniscule marsh, beside the old high school in the Second Empire style. Some days, the only voices I hear are birds. The red bird could be a Northern Cardinal. The leafless prayer tree, a Paper Birch. Or Yellow Atlantic White Cedar, Striped Maple, Pin Cherry, Quaking Aspen, Eastern Hop Hornbeam, Pin Oak—they all look like hands to me.

My neighbors are going to sleep soon. I hear their muffled voices in bed beneath my floor, even over the music. They keep talking back and forth, words unclear but each falls back into a hollow, funnels of sound. It makes me want to open the door, go out into the night where none are below me. So many houses have a plaque with the name of a man who taught dance or practiced law, captained a boat. *Prominent Ship-builder.* All of this so long ago, three hundred years. Somehow I imagine there would be someone among them I could talk to about the whistle and the trees.

A girl once tried to ride the elevator out of the Jackson apartment but it got stuck. The elevator at the end of the apartment's long center room. A desk in front of it now. The girl's parents were poets, living in the Merrill apartment. The girl, their daughter, lived in the Jackson apartment, my apartment, next door. Before that night, she'd left undetected. Where to go in the dark? Just the harbor of sleeping birds. Even the tide quiet here. The elevator is in the wall behind my desk, a bronze plaque surrounds the yellowed button. It seems you could still press it and go somewhere, but no, I've tried. Maybe she just wanted not to be kept inside.

I'm trying to remember what it was like to dance even with people living below. It's been so long since I closed my eyes and fell into someone's voice as if it were the ocean or a bed. Danced until my arms ached, until I had to catch my breath, sweating in a room with every light off. Skin close to burning. Saturn is beating a moon to death before it can rise into the sky, or maybe it's another being born. Hard to tell yet what's appearing or disappearing.

*

Winter has moved off / somewhere, writing its journals / in ice
—Larry Levis, "Rhododendrons"

Snow heavy again last night, roofs outside my windows white. In Jackson's apartment, I fill the borrowed silver kettle, light the blue flame. Saucer of roses with a tiny drop of blood underneath, turquoise mug. Listen for the boiling like someone arriving. Bergamot from oranges doesn't taste like anything orange, so bitter I barely let it steep. I want to see flowers again, the way they rest against each other, awake or slumbering, as if this life will never end.

In one of Merrill's books of photographs, east of Nairobi, the Tree of Life appears to be the only shade for miles. Thirty-six thousand elephants once lived here. Animal tracks spin out from the acacia in orange, like landing strips, or striations converging on the iris, little crypts. Thick paprika circling the tree which from the air looks like a broccoli sprig.

In Jackson's yellow sitting room, on TV, is a man who came back from war and found everyone he knew had been killed. He carved each missing person from wood, the shoemaker, the flames. His room's white walls lined with shelves that hold the people of his town. Someone translates for him—so many languages I don't know. He brought the dead back as best he could.

I hardly speak to anyone lately, snowbound in the house.

But when I leave the Jackson apartment, cross the hall to Merrill's, unlock the door, step in, I feel like I'm visiting him. Especially in his hidden study behind the bookcase, reading on his red blanketed daybed. His writing desk in the far corner. A small oak stand-up desk near the doorway has a top that lifts completely like my desk in elementary school. Six small drawers empty except for the paper clipped cancelled checks. The drawers fit back in so squarely, it reminds me of a church in Ireland made entirely of stones that fit one on top of another. The hollow below holds many envelopes with this address at Water Street, waiting to be sent. His bank statement, a twenty cent postcard stamp, along with several dozen postcards.

All these postcards he'll never send: Here is Georges de La Tour in Merrill's desk (Jimmy is what they call him): candle, and Christ sleeping sitting in a chair, bent at the shoulders, neck. Head almost perpendicular to flame, brow lined tight. Struggling or pained even in sleep, mouth slightly open. Robe fallen off one shoulder, arms crossed one on top of the other. I want to lift one arm, give my shoulder without waking, help him to bed. Wrap the robe over his chest. I forgot how young Christ was.

Maybe Jimmy sent these postcards to me, for now. Another time, for whomever opens this desktop next. Here, Joseph Cornell sits in a corner room of a house in Flushing, 1969, with a book held upside down beside his face: *The Bestiary*. His head leans forward, eyes toward the planked floor, dark bruise under his right eye. Storage system of shelves and bags in the foreground—records and tissue paper, *No Smoking* bumper sticker on the narrow door. A mirror behind his chair shows the back of his head. There are too many flowers on the wall. I want to open the door but it seems too skinny for walking in and out. Perhaps it is a closet. I want to turn, find the door.

Each night the seabirds fly in, always saying the same thing. It sounds like *Wake up*. I first see them at dusk. In the hidden study, I stand at the window. Hundreds nearly cover the long dock, still more arriving. No idea so many gathered here. A bird hotel. After dark, they quiet, sleep unafraid in the harbor. Each body like a boat.

*

You said the only cure / For anxiety was fear.
Now solitude undoes loneliness / Like a ribbon from your hair.

—James Galvin

The painter across the table says, *You wouldn't want Van Gogh here for dinner*. When no one agrees, the painter insists, *You wouldn't want him sitting at this table*. As if wounding a painting. A dinner party to introduce me to people in town. In my living room, one of the paintings is slashed. A diagonal through a woman's face, James Merrill's sister. Painting repaired so that you have to know the damage is there. First the cut in the light bottom right corner lifts up, then the cut through the dark upper left, then her face marked forever.

From my roof here in Stonington, I can see New York and Rhode Island. Little Narragansett Bay, Long Island Sound. Water and land rising, though I don't know what's what. I need an arrow that points to the Atlantic, broad way out. I've seen two houses made entirely of stone blocks. The man beside me wants to keep talking about the royal family. He says that Prince Harry doesn't look like his father, that Charles is a *faux pas.*

Some things that go are gone. In my office in Florida, for years, I read a poem by A.R. Ammons every day or every other day. To remind myself to live my life. To get up from my chair and walk out the door. I've walked out the door. Harbor outside. Snow on top of snow. Today the sky was white, like a screen. Looking out the window, I had an eerie feeling the world had turned into a blank movie while I wasn't looking.

Just after I move in, an open house is held. One of the visitors explains several pieces of furniture to me. *They burned the wood,* he said. Of the Eames chair that is too frail to sit on, he said it started with a war, splints and stretchers made of plywood. Whole warehouses filled.

Entering the Ouija board room, he says, *I never realized this was a round room.* A rotunda. I hadn't realized it either. The castle-like tower on the street is this room, where I live. *It's not my taste though,* he says, *a gateau room.* The ceiling is like a cake, white criss-crossed frosting. Clear scarlet walls. Of the living room, he says it's European because it contains an Oriental rug, the huge gold mirror, Eames chair—*The mix of things* he said, *makes you feel comfortable. Most people stay with one style.*

After a dark-haired man comes down from the deck overlooking the harbor, I say, *Goodbye.* He heads toward the front door, but comes back around the big, gold mirror.

The last time I was here was sixty years ago. I was sixteen. Jimmy Merrill's partner, David, tried to kiss me. I was appalled, he says, laughing, flattered. It was before this man came out. It was his first kiss, a try. His hair dark black at seventy-six, wanting his beauty. *Is David still alive?* he asks. Did he wonder that as he walked up the narrow old staircases? To this open yellow door with a gold metal sun. A Van Gogh door. Almost leaving without asking me.

I find a yellow door from Merrill's apartment opens behind the bookshelves at the back of the hallway to David's door. I've been afraid of ghosts in the dark, but it's quieter in the Merrill apartment. I've lived in a shared house before that had little insulation between floors. Listened to the couple below my bed fight and have sex that sounded nothing like sex, more like blood being drawn, needle puncturing the vein all the way through, purple embolism filling an elbow. But in Merrill's apartment, I can't hear either of the two neighbors below. As if I'm in another place.

*

We were surprised you have a basketball, Kiki said on the phone. We were doing math, trying to figure what I owed for heat in Provincetown this winter. *I love basketball,* I said, I can't throw the ball away, give it away. All these years in my car, the orange ball lets me see the orange-robed monks who I didn't see, but heard had played at the basketball court down the road from Atlantic Center in New Smyrna Beach where I came to work after the monks had gone. The monks played basketball in the days they made the sand mandala, before they blew it away.

In Florida, the days and months blur, divisions small— but in Stonington and in Provincetown, I look at one moment, and then, a moment later it's gone.

*

I heard Roy died. After I'd left Orlando for New Smyrna Beach, for these years of travel. I realized that when I'd passed him in meetings, before the rows of seats, trying to find mine, he hadn't judged me in those early days of sobriety. Hadn't found me wanting. He'd woken up in prison after killing someone while drunk. He spent a long time there—ten years, twenty. I can't recall, time blurring. Roy muscled, his hair the black of undersea ink or oil. Voice low. There's a doorway to the left behind him. He sees me. Right now, Roy sees me. I might be twenty-two or twenty-five and sober. I might be twenty-one and about to go back out. About to die and come back. I'd thought Roy looked down on me for not being good enough. He smiles. I'm welcome here. The last time I saw him, he was walking away from this little house under the oak trees where we'd gathered, talking to someone young, new. Heads bent toward each other as if both intent on seeing the same small thing. The last thing I saw him do was help another person. I remember gladness in his face seeing me. How can he have died? It feels as if he must be there somewhere in Orlando. That if I walked into enough rooms, I'd see him again.

*

In Massachusetts, in the late 1960s, I remember singing with my hand over my heart in a lit room. I stood toward the back, to the right. Near the door. Do you remember your childhood? I'm afraid I lost mine when I died. But maybe it's there somewhere, waiting for me. I read Philip Levine's poem with his six-year-old son in kindergarten at 9 a.m., standing beside his desk. "Pledge your flag and sing / slightly out of tune / 'for spacious fields of grain.'" A poem I found in his second poetry collection, *Not This Pig,* on my way to David Jackson's kitchen for a cup of coffee on my first Saturday morning in Stonington.

This morning, with the bedroom windows open on the winter morning because of the woman smoking in the apartment below, smoke filling my apartment through the floor. Because of the open window, I hear all of the birds calling to each other in the trees, some like zippers being pulled open and shut swiftly, some sweet high note with silence on either side—listening—most a chirp chaos, everyone talking at once. A dog barks three times. But before the birds and dogs, Levine's words brought me back to South Dennis, Massachusetts, hand on my heart, my sixth year.

*

WHEN I WAS THE RIVER

> *When I was the stream, when I was the forest, when I was still the field,*
> —Meister Eckhart

A girl stood in the river, on Barn Island, Connecticut. One boot on. The other in her hands, emptying water. Her sock red. Though we're the only people on the trail, she focuses on the boot as on a prayer, water pour, as if baptizing the air. Appraises me from a distance, walking the sand road with round rocks underneath. Ocean to my right, marsh and yellow meadow to the left, forest beyond I'm heading toward. In between, May blue river and girl. She lifts her head like a deer.

Moon almost full. The stars aren't going to last forever after all. Fire keeps them going, expanding until a star uses up its supply of everything. Just iron at the core. Which contracts instead of expanding, pulls the whole star inward until it explodes. Iron in my blood made the moment a star died. Everything in me made from dead stars. At some point, every single star will die, a woman says. The universe will go dark until *the end of time. Whatever that means,* she says. The screen goes black to show how everything will look. She says, *but it's Eden now.* Now we live in this world lit by the sun. We are dead stars looking at living stars. This is Eden.

To find the river, drive a winding road past a white shingled house with a suit of armor flashing in a tall, dark window at the top of the house. The armor looks inhabited. Hardwoods to the left of the house—a little forest—dotted with miniature houses painted blue, red, green. Birdhouses? Does someone place seeds in all the houses? Some so high, a person would need a ladder. Some, you'd have to climb the tree.

Before the river, take the opposite path to Little Narragansett Bay. A skull lies just off the path, in the grass. White, small sharp teeth, long head, large almond eyes, part of the animal still being eaten, a mashed darkness below where the neck would be, flies. A deer? Coyote? A sign says hunting is allowed. A little beach in the marsh, your feet sink. One swan in the cove. In Orlando, there were swan boats in the lake. The swan is not a boat. As I approach, her orange bill opens, a low croakiness. Walk past to show I am mild. A goose once chased me beside another lake in Orlando, protecting his mate. I wonder if this swan might rush me. No escape. Can't go forward—the marsh turns to watery reeds, then just water. No path. Only way out is back, past the swan and skull.

I don't yet know that mute swans are the attacking kind. Or that here by Rhode Island, where I'm walking, is where the mute swans live. Cygnus olor. From Europe and Asia, imported in the late nineteenth century as status symbols for the rich on New York estates. But swans escaped. Became wild. Mute swans not all together silent—hissing, grunting, and snoring. Fierce when protecting their young. Eggs laid late-March to mid-April. Hatching in thirty-two to thirty-five days. May 13 when I arrive, cygnets hatching any moment from eggs in the grass.

Mute swans usually don't kill, but try to smash the human with the burrs on its six-foot wings. Break bones. In East Hampton Village, a proposed New York plan would have the mute swans "eradicated in the wild by 2025." A swan hunting season is being considered. White feathers flying. Swans exploding like stars. The swan lets me pass.

Before this, it's Mother's Day, and I hide out. Think of Jeannette who worked with me in the health food store, not so long after my son had died. Jeannette who was unafraid of my sadness and gave me a Happy Mother's Day card because she knew that day was happy, Tommy's birth. Later that day, I read Marie Howe's words: *In the game, someone has to touch you to free you / then you're human again.*

*

LIVING ROOM

MARCUS WHITE LIVING ROOM,
CENTRAL CONNECTICUT STATE COLLEGE, NEW BRITAIN

After months of snow, I visit a school to give a reading. Seating a mix of leather brown couches and rows of folding chairs. Voice far down inside, my frenzied hair uncalmable. But each person reaches out a hand. My papers wet and salty from living by the sea, already yellowing.

I want to make them laugh, tell about an opera singer come back from the dead to go to the dollar movie with the man she loved. No one laughed. I had to tell them about the day you were born.

Sinking and rising of my body after. One boy asked if writing helped me to speak. I said, *Yes*. I meant, the parts I can't corral in person. This intercoastal between the ribs of the body, and those no longer breathing. His smile easily wide as if his mouth were still being made.

A student's mother raised her hand, said it's hard to know how to tell her story of the orphanage. Her grandmother would visit, take her out for ice cream, bring her back. When it was over, I made my way down the aisle. As I never did marrying or after the funeral of my son. Following the coffin a thousand miles away from other parents who couldn't explain me. No goodbye. Plastic black coat on my arm.

Another boy I hadn't seen before. Face an oval locket. Dark hair. Dignity in how he stands eye to eye with me. We're alone—everyone else heading in the direction of food. He says, *I'm adopted.*

In the close space of the aisle I ask, *Have you met your birthmother?* I don't think I've ever said that word before. It feels fake, as if I'm on a talk show.

He said, *Yes. Before I shipped out to Iraq.*

That's amazing, I say, the house of my brain lakelike. I mean, *You are so alive.*

Yes, he says. He's written his first poem, *But they didn't take it,* he says.

Write another, I said. He's turning away. Down the yellow aisle toward the others, coffee, orange cubes of cheese in pyramids. He turns back.

Half faces me. He says, *I'd be glad if you were my mother.* Or, he said, *I'd want you to be my mother.*

The most beautiful sentence, and I can't remember the exact words. My body propelled back. As if a great gift had been placed in my arms. As if I were carrying an invisible child. I would like to at least get his eyes right, a darkness that saw me whole. And also, his hand which he waved toward the podium: *This. What you're doing.* He's silent a moment, nods. *It's good.* Hearing what it's like to be his mother, to belong to him.

*

MYSTIC

On my son's birthday, I lit a candle for him in the yellow room. Orange cathedral, flame melt spires. Fire high and steady near the twelve glass windows of my door on the harbor. Years ago I had a butterfly candle someone gave me, and I'd light it for him. Blue wings burn away each time.

The town clock chimed midnight. In the early evening, at a church in Mystic, a woman losing her hearing made me laugh. Threw her dark hair back with her hands at her temples. Skin flushed from chin to just below her eyes, as if she'd been running hard in snow. She keeps touching one finger to her ear trying to hear better, everything now not sounding like itself. But she's never heard my voice before, doesn't know what I sound like other than this waviness.

The candle flame shimmers on either side with an energy like rain. The older men in this church work days. Several reach their hands out to me, hold mine. I see a birdstone. Smooth as a casing that might crack, reveal the bird inside.

*

A TENANCY

JANUARY—MAY 2014

> *Look to the rock you were hewn from,*
> *To the quarry you were dug from.*
> —Isaiah 51:1

While Nana did come back twice that I know of clearly, I was surprised it wasn't more often. But I had the sense she had a life, in death. She'd come back to a little house in a field whose steps I'd climbed. Leaned over me in the bed in New York—*wake up, wake up.* When I was so relieved she was alive, her death a mistake. Sun on my face with her over me. Safe, thought I could sleep for a long time. Thought we had time. She was gone when I woke.

I'd had the sense she'd had to move through the gravity of two worlds to come back to me. That it wasn't natural. That she needed her life there now. As if even the house in the field—a place I've never seen before—had to be constructed just for our visit.

Nana's own son died at seven years old in the sledding accident, hit a tree. Gramp carried him home in his arms. Jeffrey her late life baby, my uncle, though I was three or four. A beautiful boy. She's missed him all this time, taken away by surprise. She never got to say goodbye. As I never said goodbye to my son.

197

Jeffrey's name was misspelled on his gravestone in Ancient Cemetery. He died in the late 1960s. A couple of years older than me. My grandmother in her forties when she had him. So unusual at the time to have a late-in-life baby. I remember Jeffrey's striped shirt, the curve of his back as he played. His eyes. He was seven when he died. He'd seemed much older, kind. I sat on a split rail fence with him, swung my feet in the air. We had a small round swimming pool we splashed in. One of the first people I ever knew, ever loved. Winter and someone pushed his sled off, down a hill. Jeffrey hit a tree and died. I have no memory of that. Just Jeffrey and then the absence of him. My uncle. Thirty years or more before we noticed his name spelled wrong on the stone. "Jeffry Halunen" My mom surprised. The kind of grief that makes it impossible to read a headstone for three decades. No one noticed, not his parents, no one, until my mom saw it one day.

*

On TV, a woman wears a white satin Fallopian tubes dress, backed with wings of white net. I've lived in James Merrill's house three months, and all of a sudden tonight the bed shakes. Stops, shakes again, stops. Gently, side to side. A train? Tracks far away, down Elm.

The end of Stonington Borough is called the Point, but the whole thing really is. Protected in a harbor, an arrowhead of land jutting out with water on three sides. During the day, I've been playing James Merrill's records again, depressed the LOUD button, so the static popping underneath the songs is less. Graham Nash's *Songs for Beginners* from 1971 sounds like the radio when I was nine or ten years old. Like the triangle that anyone could play—you just hit it and it rings.

In the poem, "A Tenancy" in *Water Street,* Merrill wrote,

"I did not even feel the time expire." Was he only thirty-six when he wrote that? The book published in 1962, Merrill born 1926. Was he already feeling old when I was being born? "If I am host at last / it is of little more than my own past. / May others be at home in it." Under the red lounge in the hidden study, I find an old copy of *Poetry* with one of e.e. cummings's last poems. (Or at least one of his last poems submitted to the magazine, two months before he died unexpectedly) The poem has a kiss in it. When the editor wrote to thank him, he sent back a postcard and wrote in red and blue ink, *Thank you.* One color for each word. When the poem was published, he was already gone.

*

In Mystic, in one of the old houses, the guide explains to a group of schoolchildren the chamber pot that sits like a covered casserole dish at the foot of the bed. And the trundle that pulls out from underneath like a sidecar bed. Then, he tells them that Rhode Island is the hub of all vampire activity in the U.S. Says Bram Stoker took his story from that of a Rhode Island girl who'd been dug up and stabbed in the heart. *Cool,* a kid says. They head down to the kitchen where a woman serves them apple squares and asks who chops the wood. Who carries the water? Dried comfrey hangs in front of the fireplace.

In another building, down a flight of stairs, I'm startled to see a room of ships' figureheads, all with their heads and breasts raised. Looking at the black ceiling, but not really. The women, turbaned man, Seminole, eagle head, sisters, all communing with something, completely focused elsewhere. Attentive. Each the spirit of ship. Ocean in their wood.

Onboard a boat at closing time, I'm the only visitor.

We're anchored in the Mystic River. A guide says, *You can go below deck.* Hard to take in the captain's quarters, whale blubber room, and I seem to completely miss the kitchen as I'm rushing to get out. My breath had tightened as I'd walked down the stairs, had the odd thought that it's just a hatch up there. It could be closed. Shut me in. And what would I do? Who would hear me? I don't want to be impolite by not looking around, I just want out. This claustrophobia isn't normal. A family of three comes on board, as I come up the stairs. *Go below, if you like,* the nice guide says.

*

May is still not warm after the long winter. Rain all the next day. Fog. I walk on board the world's last wooden whaleship, built in 1841, undergoing restoration before it sails up the coast to Provincetown. To a place where whalewatch boats go. Just to hang out. Not open to the public. *Some whales live to one hundred and fifty, two hundred years old,* the guide says. *They might remember this ship.*

Whalers didn't hunt blue whales because they'd sink to the bottom. You couldn't haul them back shipside to unpeel them like an orange. Blubber removed in blankets they'd cut up below deck. The whale rolled as the fat came free. Then, they cut it up even smaller, into "Bible books," feed it into the brick house near the bow, where it was rendered. I walk down below, and I'm okay here. Lots of people working on restoration. The boat leaves in a week for New London. Then she sets sail. Two men at a table discuss paint color.

The Captain's Quarters includes a living room under the bow, a curved couch. Bedroom has a closet. Bed gimbaled to stay steady when the ship rolled. Table out front where the men sit. Skylights. Giant crystals sunk in open spaces. To the left, first mate's cabin, second mate's. Further in, bunks for the cook and two others. In the center, the Blubber Room. Dark wood shining, finger-thick nails. Blankets of fat lowered down where I stand, where they were cut into "horse pieces" about four feet long, six inches wide. Then they were "minced" into the books. How did they breathe down here? It's fine now, aired out.

The guide says more whales were killed in the last four decades, up to the 1900s, than in all the time before. Frenzy of whale killing. The whale had three things people wanted: baleen, the vertical blinds inside that trapped food for the whale, but let sea water out (called whale bone though more like cartilage, bendable, like plastic, used for corsets), spermaciti in the sperm whale's head for oil to make candles, and blubber. Scrimshaw done on the teeth of whales. Teeth used for piano keys, chess pieces.

In the nautical building, a guide talks to a young German couple. *Losing one second doesn't sound like a lot,* the young man says. *No, but using celestial navigation, losing one second means being off by fifteen miles,* the guide says. The guide says three clocks are used to not lose time.

Mid-conversation in the cooper's building, the cooper tells the same German couple (tourists few this rainy day) that he didn't know why a Japanese visitor had rubbed whale oil on her cheek and smiled. I wonder where she got the whale oil. All I see are the makings of barrels. Later, another Japanese tourist told the cooper her mother used to rub whale oil on her skin.

I ask why one barrel doesn't look like a barrel, how I'd seen one on the Charles Morgan and wondered how could it hold anything. The cooper and another man laughed. *It can't, it's just the staves.* Men on board would put the barrels together from the staves and the hoops around it, and the barrel tops. There are so many ropes on the ships, I wonder how the sailors keep track. I couldn't even tell a barrel from the makings of a barrel. In the rope-making building, the ropewalk is another multiple strands process, as is the loom in someone's home.

I lack the spatial awareness to do the work of the past. What would I have been good for? So much practical skill needed as an everyday thing. The dock isn't roped off, and it wouldn't take much, a little spacing out, not watching where I was going, and I'd be overboard in that cold water. In the underpopulated early May Mystic River. Would I sink like a blue whale? Rise up again, feet kicking, arms clearing a way upwards to the surface before I breathed and swallowed water, began to drown. Would anyone notice? Maybe I should have left a note on the door: Went to Mystic River. Be back soon. My days are numbered in Connecticut. Sixteen more.

In the pharmacy, the guide says, *I spend 40 to 50 percent of my time talking about leeches.* There's a white cookie jar behind her labeled LEECHES in black caps. That might be the conversation starter. She wants to talk about Nervine, a bromide that relaxes. She reads the label: *Safe in all doses. It reacts with a bromide in the body, so that in large doses you'd be...* She imitates a Gumby doll slowly moving all limbs at once as if underwater. *It could lead to hallucinations and coma: "The Bromide Sleep." And Miltown was another one, Mother's Little Helper,* she said. *Now, leeches are back. Medical leeches, raised just to suck the blood out so wounds can close. For skin graft.* She's got what looks like a glass jar of yellowish clear water that she moves from hand to hand like a relaxation ball.

She sets the jar on the counter. Dizzy from her constant rush of information, the lack of breaks to inspect the displays, just constant eye contact. I don't understand at first why she's handling a jar of water. Then I get it. *There are leeches in there?* I ask. They float on the side of the jar she's tipped, like wiggly black olive slices. *When they're used to suck blood, the leeches get full. They can only suck so much blood—maybe thirty minutes—then, they'll fall off, if a nurse doesn't take them off. Replace with fresh ones.*

The pharmacist also made insecticide. A label on three bottles the size of A-1 Steak Sauce reads: *DESTROY.* They're corked. Another finger-sized tube bottle label says: *Safe Pills.* George's Carminative. Dickinson's Witch Hazel, a brand name product I use myself. Granules of Gelsemium is a beautiful dark blue glass with brown label. White Poison Vine, White Jessamine, Wild Woodbine are other names for the flower. All control of limbs is lost, eyelids droop. *Death seems imminent.* But patients recovered. Loss of motor function seems the primary effect.

A lot of these were alcohol, she said, *opiates.* The pharmacist would make his own medicines from the herbs in jars, but if pressured by customers, might carry some patent medicine too. Patents not disclosing secret ingredients. Atwoods La Grippe Specific a large lightly rootbeerish bottle. Dysentery Syrup covered by the tan label, except where torn, top lifted. How did anyone survive? So many ways to go wrong. Madame Dagar's Elixir. Dr. Miles Nervine. On the whaling ship about to sail for the first time in eighty years, the guide takes my picture at the wheel of the boat. My hand on the smooth wood, turning it slightly, as if steering.

*

In a diner in Mystic, Gillian tells me she rode a bus in rain on the way to the Isle of Sheppey off the northern coast of Kent, in the Thames estuary. Everything gray, and then she saw the field of rape. *Blinding yellow,* she said. It was the 1980s, and she was an extra in a music video with a London band, Shriekback. Everyone wore red and white and brought something to throw into the fire. Out the windows, the rape field in flower. Shriekback from Kentish Town, a post punk band. *Dirgelike,* Gillian said. This weekend, she'd been to see her son who she'd given away. Two days of looking at him. I look at Gillian across the booth in Mystic, comforted to see her skin intact.

The Stonington map to the thrift store said, *Walk down Elm Street until you come to stairs. Climb.* How can stairs appear on a street? Houses on both sides, road winding. Then, rackety metal stairs appear at the end of the road. Lead up to a fenced-in walkway. Over rusty train tracks going somewhere I can't see. At a meeting the night before, one man shook off my hand as fast as he could, another held it like a book he was reading.

A brown bird looks like wood carved on a lintel. But then he turns his head, dark circle in his eye moves sideways. At the end of the Velvet Mill road, I sat on a granite slab balanced on three stones in a meadow with robins. The word I'd opened to in the dictionary is *luminary,* a light-giving body. Illuminations betokening rejoicing: luminaria. Lumen plural lumina is light, an opening. Three white-flowered trees in the meadow, browned at the edges by April frost. Night snow falling just after the eclipse.

What flowers are these? Buds held in fur as if these are animals. Some bloom, some buds so full and near to opening, I feel the desire in my own body to be born, new. Once open, I count eighteen petals on one flower. Green windowed Velvet Mill across the street, all brick, with dark granite window sills uneven as dirt.

I pass the home of Dr. Silas Holmes, shingles white-gray. He drowned returning from an errand of mercy on Block Island in 1791. Boat capsized in a thunderstorm. The Island 15 miles from Watch Hill, Rhode Island which I can see from the Point at Stonington.

James Merrill's house is a 1901 Queen Anne/Colonial Revival. Turreted like a castle. William Terret's House from 1787 is around the corner. White clapboard with two windows close together above the front door, two windows to the left, one to the right. A black tree has wound around it, limbs smooth as human arms coiling. High branches reach for a top window with a curtain sheer amethyst. Dark slit open and white whirlpools in it like a soul. The lower window has the white bones, vertebrae of a being leaning on the window sill. In profile, the head and shoulders almost sickle-like, cut from glass but also a kind of fume. A figure in the door. Me in the glass: red suede leggings, quilted white jacket with bright orange zipper. Camera to my eyes, the mail slot right across my hips. Dark green shutters.

A chalky white tree with red grainy flowers on the way to the wetlands where I stand on a high boulder overlooking Little Narragansett Bay. A boy appears from behind me. Voices though I only see him, children here in privacy. He leaves now, no eye contact so I think it must be drugs or sex

I've interrupted. Granite wall on the water broken through in a V as if by a giant sledgehammer. Leads down into a slope of boulders where you'd be unseen on these rocks except by someone across the water in the big white house on Rhode Island, a state away.

The Northern Hemisphere in the first world map in 1538 looks like a rounded heart or wings, an apple halved but tan and bronze. Earth via satellite so deeply blue-greened, land red and white, as if it is the cell of a larger animal under a microscope. How are we all held here? A third alone is the Pacific. When a boy rings up my old Atlas in the Westerly, Rhode Island bookstore, he flips through it. *To see if Czecho-slovakia is there.*

I like it for the geology, I say.

Totally. That doesn't change, he says.

*

(MOTHER'S RESCUE)

Three women come to see me at the Stonington library. They'd read about me in the newspaper. In the front row, they smile so warmly each time I glance their way. As if I could do nothing wrong. The woman with blond and purple hair tells me she works at a treatment center in Groton for mothers with addiction. Most of the clients young. *Mostly heroin,* she says. Asks me to sign two books. *I want to read to them from your books. You know how one thing can give a person hope. You never know what it'll be.* She says, *Most of these women don't know they can have a voice.*

When I tell Gillian, she says, *Oh, that's Mother's Rescue. But there's no twelve-step step there.* It's what the caseworker tells me after my library reading, when I'd ask if they have recovery meetings. *We used to, but not anymore.* I look it up—it's Mother's Retreat. Maybe I misheard. No website. I tell Gillian, I'd like to go, bring a meeting in. *Will you come with me?* Gillian says, *Yes.*

*

WHO BY FIRE

> *And who in her lonely slip, who by barbiturate,*
> *Who in these realms of love, who by something blunt,*
>
> —Leonard Cohen

T had a sweet bird flying in her hand, on the lined paper. *I have another poem* she says. Sits beside me on the carpet in a circle of mothers. Family night in this double-decker tan house. Eight women and their children live here. A substance abuse treatment center, mostly narcotics, mostly heroin. I'm a guest. All I know of Groton is the frozen fish commercial, yellow slicker of the Groton fisherman on his boat, rocked by the waves.

Driving Route 1, I don't see the ocean. Groton borders Long Island Sound, is between two rivers: Thames and Mystic. The names, early seventeenth-century founding. At seventeen, I saw the Thames in London, beside the Tower. Ran my hands over the stones to touch the fingerprints of the condemned.

Morning of my visit to Mother's Rescue, I wake exhausted. By afternoon, I just want to lie down. Sleep in the yellow room with windows open. Cool air holding rain, sleep through the afternoon, night. Mary McCarthy spent her honeymoon in this apartment, bedroom. Light coming in these windows. It was her fourth husband, after Edmund Wilson, as James Merrill and David Jackson didn't buy this building until 1956. So it was James West, a diplomat, she married in 1961. The year I was born. Mary was forty-nine. How will I talk in public in this sleepy haze? Feeling drugged, I drink coffee cold from breakfast.

In Groton, Melanie, the case manager, leans on the porch rail waiting for me. Thick iridescent turquoise lines her eyes as if crayoned. When we'd met a few weeks earlier at my library reading, her hair had been light purple. Now it was white and blond and reddish brown. Her brightness calming.

At the library, Melanie had told me about this shared house and rehab for mothers. The mothers stay six to nine months. Their children with them the whole time. Going to group together, meals.

Eight bedrooms upstairs, three bathrooms, kitchen downstairs. Living room. Typed poems written by the mothers are tacked to the Group Room walls. Big silver stars around them. Blue and red and yellow streamers hang from the ceiling as if we're at a school dance. At the library, Melanie had said, *It would be great if you could come read at the house, if you come back here.* I didn't mention that I still had a few more weeks in town. Wary of making promises I won't follow through on. *Email me,* I said.

She'd been in a staff meeting, and someone mentioned the next Family Night. A night when family members of mothers and alumni are invited to the house. May 15. Themed events, this one would be Poetry Night. *Who could we invite as a visitor?*

Melanie said, *I know someone.*

The women cooked all day. Tables in the Group Room full of dishes, pastas and salads, cut fruit and a giant cookie cake. Women and kids all around us. I don't know what the format is, what's expected of me. *You're not going to eat anything?* T asks. She's sitting at the end of one long table with her plate, Melanie eating from the plate in her hand. I realize how rude I'm being, pick up a paper plate, scoop two stuffed mushrooms on it. I'm too nervous to eat. Melanie hands me a fork. I eat a mushroom.

Melanie had introduced me to T whom she'd mentioned earlier in an email. She's new, she writes poems. She looks at me the way I look at other poets: breath relaxing, light-eyed, shy. Another woman in a white T-shirt is in the corner between tables. Melanie tells me that she's an alumni, that she's visiting. The woman asks, *When is the visitor going to speak? I want to go to the movies.*

She's right here, Melanie says. *We're just letting everyone get food first.* Melanie says, *I'll let you two talk,* and walks away. The woman is careful, guarded. Does not seem especially interested in talking to me. Pale, dark hair falls like rain in uneven sheets to her shoulders. Eyes far away as pebbles on the ground, but a little curious. The woman tells me she's worked for the same company fourteen years, that her boss let her do the payroll while she was in treatment here. She worked at the table of casseroles and rice and noodles. *Where do you live?* she asks. Plastic cup of apple juice in my hand. I say, *Stonington, in the poet James Merrill's house, to write for four months. When he died, he gave his house to the town, and they made it into a place for writers.*

I did a collage for a book of poetry at the prison, she says. She's coming toward me, a thread between us. *I was at the prison,* she says. Or if not a thread, through-light. Each of us a window on opposite sides of a room that light passes through. I wish I felt less stiff. Mothers are sitting in chairs in the living room, on couches, moving, standing, talking around me.

The kids are young. Infants and two-year-olds, three. A couple of kids may be four or five years old. One girl tries to put her finger in the white icing on the giant cookie. *Don't,* her mother says.

It's hard to resist, I said. Wonder why no one is eating the cookie, which says in icing, "Happy Mother's Day." The message nervewracking—aren't we safely past Mother's Day? Maybe the dessert is for later. But the kids are really well-behaved. No one crying, no one yelling.

The woman in the white shirt asks me, *Why are you here?* I tell her that I got pregnant before I got sober, and gave my son away. And he died. I wrote about trying to find him. The woman cries, but all the water stays pooled in her eyes. Little red veins appear. *I gave my son away too,* she says. She names the city where he lives. My eyes like hers. We stand looking at each other. I nod my chin toward her. Try to pull it together. Just nod. Swallow.

People find seats. Someone's boyfriend or husband is there. *Where should I sit?* I ask. Melanie points to an empty chair at the far end of the living room. Chairs spill out into hallway where Melanie stands. There's not enough room.

Everyone is so excited you're here, Melanie says, soft-faced, soft-bodied. A woman cradles a baby on the floor. T sits on the carpet beside my folding chair. She holds a kind of wooden abacus/alphabet for a little boy. He touches a letter, laughs. He and another boy and a girl in a rainbow tutu have recently learned to walk, stepping hard and bouncing forward. I want to reach out my arms. We go around, introduce ourselves. A girl comes in late. Takes the chair beside me, holds my books on her lap like a child. Her hair curls and shines as if wet. Eyes night-sky bright.

A little girl twirls in small mirrors, a lark song. I hadn't really thought this out, that I'd be speaking and reading poems to adults and children. I want to say how much I admire them. Envy them for keeping their children. Not in a terrible way. But hungry, admiring. I want to say that they're brave. Good mothers. *The first time I drank I was afraid of it, what it could do,* I say.

I tell them about Tommy. *I gave him away. I kept drinking. I was disappearing.* When I say that he died, a woman gasps nearby or maybe it is all around. The feeling is the room of mothers has gasped. Surrounded by mothers with their babies and toddlers, some of them without some of their children. They know the weight of what happened to me. That gasp isn't the gasp of people looking at me as if I am on TV, a woman on fire. The gasp I'm used to. The circle is like arms. It's later when I realize that I feel not crazy with the mothers and children. My grief is not crazy.

And then I don't know if I can speak, how to speak after this. I am unfrozen. The only things I can see not black and white are the silver stars, streamers, Melanie's eyes. And the girl's tutu, flitting pink of new tulips and yellow net through the room. I almost can't bear to look at it, this openness to the world. The world opening.

Melanie said that she'd looked around the room as I spoke. Saw how the women's faces changed when I told them about my drinking. My son. Saw that I wasn't there to judge them, talk from some helping profession. That I hadn't been able to do what they were doing.

I'm going to read a few poems, I say. The mothers nod. When Melanie had invited me, I'd asked if others would read poems too. But I didn't know that this was also a Mother's Day celebration, that the mothers would read poems about their children. The little boy who touched the wooden letter ran toward T. The little girl in her tutu ran into the middle of the room. The children a chorus.

A dark-haired boy comes to sit on the floor in front of me, smiling. Face to face. *This poem is Sister Goldenhair,* I say.

Did you have a sister with golden hair? the boy asks.

No, I had a friend. It was a song we sang. A boy with light brown curly hair comes toward T and me. The center of the room a dance floor the kids can't resist. Every few lines, I look up to smile at a child making his way toward me. One mother reads a poem with her daughter on her lap. Over and over the poem says, *I love my daughter, I love you, I love you,* and her daughter, shy and thrilled, levitates in happiness. The woman holding her infant in her lap reads a love poem to her daughter. Her hair spun high above her face, a cameo, enameled. I want to see her baby so badly, I can't even look in her arms. Just quick glances to take in the length, thin blankets wrapping a body the size of shoebox. That kind of swaddling kept my baby safe, from scratching himself with his fingernails.

Another woman reads a love poem from her phone. T reads her typed poem that she's taken off the wall. When she talks about her poem, she glances at me though her eyes are down, but I know I'm being spoken to. *I have another one, if you want to hear,* she says, and we all nod. She reads the handwritten one with the bird flying inside it, in her strong voice. Her father is in there, someone lost, wanting to live.

We clap for each other. The shiny-haired girl says, *Here are your books.* The little boy is before T again.

That was beautiful. Do you write a lot? I ask.

Yes, T says. *I have notebooks too.* She tells me she has two children she gave away. That when she sees schoolyards, she wonders if they might be there. If I hadn't given Tommy to relatives, I would do the same thing, scan schoolyards. All yards. She has two children with her. Is the little boy hers? It's hard to tell as all the mothers greet all the children so warmly. Why didn't I ask? *And no one can take this one,* she said. *Not DCF,* she looks down. I hadn't noticed before, how round her belly is. Due soon. I wonder if she or he can hear us talking, if we sound like water.

Can I go to my room and get my art to show you? T asks.

Yes, I say. It gives me a chance to catch my breath. She comes back with three drawings, sits beside me. It wrecks me, her *Can I?* Her drawings full of bodies and words next to each other. Letters hidden between the people, but she takes me through them. Makes sure I see.

Do you see? I do. In the third drawing, people don't have faces, but the arrangement is similar, all the bodies connected to each other. Her need to be seen, to be recognized, so familiar, my own face bare to writers I admire. Writers who I can hear, who I wish could hear me.

One of the other staff members comes by and hands me a bag. I say thank you with such surprise, she looks surprised. As if rethinking the appropriateness of it. A Mother's Day gift. All the mothers receive the same sparkly flowered bag with sheer white ribbon handles. Inside the polka-dot tissue paper is a plaque. On the left of the black frame, MOM is spelled out in raised silver letters. The remaining two-thirds of the plaque is a photograph of a woman leaping in sand, beach grass around her. Ocean in the distance a line under white sky. The woman's feet are in the air, one knee bent, foot kicked behind her. She holds an umbrella high though the clouds are white cumulous. Arm and umbrella hover over the words: "I choose to be unstoppable. I am bigger than my concerns and worries." *Mom*. I've never been called Mom before. Turn back to T sitting beside me, lean over her pages. She's letting me be the one who can see, a mother.

*

AFTERLIFE
JANUARY—MAY 2014

In Mystic, "Discover Heaven" is the headline on *TIME Magazine* at the grocery store. As if heaven were Antarctica or Bora Bora or Cleveland. What are they selling? Time would make sense. Drive by the harbor graveyard, lucky rich dead in Connecticut with a water view, but who stays with their body?

Very late last summer in Provincetown, with fall on the way, I sat at a picnic table. Green leaves of childhood overhead. We ate lobster that Mark and his brother brought, corn, raw fennel. On a strip of land in the middle of the ocean. Salt skin from swimming, hair billowing. Light still, but lowering, sparks of tiny insects. A calm as if an infant had been laid across my chest, slept. Maeve teaching her dad to fly over and over from this table, patiently, knowing how it's done.

My family house sold in Wellfleet, the place I thought I'd

die when I was very old. Its existence like a hand I couldn't let go. But here at the table, Nick said, *It's like heaven. The kids running around...,* his hand opening to the air, children laughing in the grass. It was. For once I had nowhere to go. Needing nothing except my dead, who seemed not far. For once there was nothing I could do or buy or beg for that was more.

*

In my apartment, there's a half-gallon of dark whiskey under the sink between silver pots and pans, smaller glass bottle I've shoved beside the strainer. I hate touching the caps each time I reach for a pot to heat soup, fry an egg. Brush of *death-deathdeath.*

At the Big Y they're selling *The Loves of Marilyn.* On the cover, she's in a white spring blouse, cotton, both dead and alive. Hair curled in a soft blond hat. Snow's piled high as hazmat suits for giants on the corner of Water and Union. I heard a few notes of an Irish song that made me homesick for somewhere. But now the piped-in music at the grocery store smothers, stuffs over-frosted cakes down my throat. Gagging, I want to ask the cashier how she stands it. How she doesn't run out of the store screaming. The girl bagging my groceries asks, *Is that your natural hair?* The five thousand curls. I nod. *You can just go,* the cashier said, flipping her hand in a flying motion, as if I'm free. Her hair a soft chin-length like Marilyn's. *What I would give for that,* she said, handing me the ribbon of receipt.

Rain is coming, I said.

I don't mind rain while I'm sleeping. We need it, the cashier said. What would it be like to consider the needs of trees and grass. My own body thirsty with the dirt, lowered river. Or the kiss we give the dead, body gone, love blown through open fingers into air. Once I stood corralled behind a cash register in Florida. After my ten-hour shift, I ran circles around a lake downtown, unsafe near midnight. Air steamed as if ironed—almost drinkable. Ran as fast as I could, lunging. Desperate. Shin splints burning, so drenched in humidity and sweat, I was clean. My body pushed, chose how far to go. The surprise of it—as if I were in a cartoon. Legs moving so fast, a ride that, once I reached a certain speed, carried me. I'd slow before I blacked out, if I saw stars.

*

Painted girl on animal skin like ruby silk. Girl with blue eyes in black on brown paper. Both damaged, on Sarah's table at her Velvet Mill studio where chemistry will restore them. *Isn't she beautiful?* Sarah says, not really a question. Two girls who each sat for a painter four hundred years ago in another country. Their beauty collected across centuries, and someone with money owns these images of bodies now all bone. Sarah with her thick farina hair, evening-primrose smile could have been in one of these paintings. She unfolds a Revolutionary War map of New York which disguised points of interest in case it fell into British hands. The land cotton balled with flowers, parasols, Miss Mary, violets. Still lives in the sleepy colors of pencils I drew with as a child, a green you'd have to bear down to make darker and even then it appeared as through a cloud.

In the 1800s, people made velvet in this room. For clothing, jewelry boxes, coffins. Shiny pillowing at the waist, under a head for all eternity. We want our dead comfortable nestled underground. Though it still seems unbelievable that my hands will simply stop as theirs did. And the living box my body up. Bury me in earth as if I am a kind of flower or seed.

STAR TABLES

Q. What do you suppose the fixed stars are?
A. I suppose they are suns to other worlds, as they shine with their own light.

My downstairs neighbor lets me hold a sextant from 1778. Dark wood sheen, it almost looks new. Kept in a broken box under a table. A triangle with an arced bottom. Square mirror at the top center is on a moveable arm that connects to the arc, its scale of numbers. Another smaller mirror, size of two thumbnails, is off to the side. To navigate, look at the horizon through this mirror.

My neighbor has two more lenses, one rosy sepia. These fit one on top of another as in an optician's test, slide into place. We guess it is like sunglasses for an eclipse or just very bright sun. Light reflects off the top mirror connected to the moveable arm. The arm can be moved so that it then reflects off the side mirror and through the eyepiece. Turn the sextant to view the sun over the horizon. Read the angle between the two from the scale. A boatlike arc at the bottom of the sextant.

For celestial navigation, measure the angle between the

horizon and the sun when the sun is at its highest point. Then, your tables tell you which line of latitude the sun should be above on that particular day. The tables contain the stars. The sun could be above the Tropic of Capricorn. So that star's latitude is yours. I never thought of the sun above the stars before—in the sky it's one cloak. A star tables book seems crucial.

Longitude is harder. Every hour the Earth rotates fifteen degrees. *This means that if the sun is above the longitude of zero degrees at noon, one hour later it will be above fifteen degrees west.*

You need a very accurate clock. It helps to have the sun right overhead. Easy to get lost. My neighbor told me that a woman's boyfriend had been out to sea, on his way back to the harbor when his boat went down. Into the downslope of a wave. Instead of coming back up, it went straight down into the ocean. *They all drowned,* he said. I've never heard of such a thing. But if a wave is very high, trench low, I could see how a ship might not make it back up.

The nineteenth-century white window frames are rattling. Sixteen panes per window—eight on top, eight on the bottom. Five sets look on the bay at night. My neighbor and I are both here temporarily, in the house that once belonged to the painter, Hans Hofmann. I rent the attic apartment from friends—Hofmann's painting studio; my neighbor rents the main house with a friend. Across the courtyard, an architect rents Hofmann's painting school studio, fronted by glass, a wall of fireplace, thick dark beams, planked floor. Soon a famous TV producer will buy the house and studio. His white couch will wrap around the room. A chandelier will hang. Soon we'll be gone. Wind so cool today, a cold I could drink.

Sky pinking, baby blue over the ocean, a houseboat blinks amber light when the night darkens. Wind like someone trying to get inside tonight.

*

On the street, white roses and white gladiola spill over the fence. Petals cool and dense. All I have to do is breathe. If ever I am ungrateful let me remember the cold air and opened flowers in June, early evening, when I was lucky enough to live here. *Look,* my neighbor said, when I come home. Birds dark against the deep sky, flying toward the ocean. Flowers like white tulle dresses all over the front yard. Peonies.

Orange poppies so short-lived they're almost gone before summer even arrives. On the other side of the brick sidewalk leading to our front door, a slightly different longitude means a little orange still lives, though the petals are sleepy. Bachelor blue flowers just born, indigo soft spiky. Tonight, the white peonies smell like roses. Forty-five sunflowers planted on either side of the sidewalk, so by the time I return from Florida, they may line the walk again. Rise up like yellow footmen from the earth.

The distance in longitude from Provincetown to Orlando is only about ten degrees. My body magnetically aligned with true north along these parallels. I'll fly there soon, drive to the beach. Live with friends until I can see where to live on the map.

The visit to the funeral home in South Yarmouth is tomorrow, half-way up the Cape. The cemetery, a restaurant my uncle Dean liked, where I'll be with people who love him. Dean, Dean. He still feels alive. I worry that tomorrow at the funeral home, that he won't. That it will be like that too-high wave, that we will be in the deep trough, and how will we come up again?

When I heard my aunt Penny's voice on the phone, I thought the same thing as with Dean's, how no one has her voice, how I'd know it anywhere. I've been hearing it my whole life. If this is what sky looks like, trees, everything seen/heard for the first time named inside my body, then these are what voices sound like. The voices of my family, relatives, like Penny and Dean who divorced long ago, but she's stayed beside him all this time. Organized his medication in the calendar of boxes on his kitchen counter, did his bills. *Do you remember the birthday parties we used to have at the house?* she asked. It's part of my wallpaper inside. I don't remember separate parties, but the being there, their voices. My shy cousin Gretchen madly riding a plastic horse as if to kick-start it, bring it to life. Or, as if she were already going somewhere.

At Dean's memorial, I hadn't expected to see Young Peter, my cousin. Last time I'd seen him, his father had died in Naples, Florida. I drove from Orlando, my voice hoarse from singing into the highway wind. Peter's sister Janey there too. Janey who'd taken me riding on her horse when we were kids. Peter, who when I was fifteen stood with me in his front yard, where it meets the tar, said, *You always live in warm places.* He had a new wife who had a little girl. Lived on a cranberry bog on the Cape. I'd wondered how to have a life like that. So drawn to both Peter and Janey, both a few years older than me. How they lived on the Cape all their lives. How steady they were on their feet, the ground theirs.

In the Naples funeral home, Janey had said, *I remember when we visited you in Weymouth, and your mother gave us gold stars.*

It's funny what you remember, Peter said.

Q. What is their distance from the earth?
A. It is not certainly known. It is supposed, however, they are, at least, a hundred thousand times farther from it than the Sun is.

My brother drove down from Virginia for Dean's memorial. *I'm meeting Gretchen at Hallet's Funeral Home at 10:30,* he said on the phone. My brother who I'd lived with every day, and now see once a year. *I can't be alone,* he said when I visited him and his wife-to-be, her girls. But I leave him alone. I don't know what to say.

Okay, I'll be there too. But the drive up the Cape from Provincetown took longer than I'd thought. I meet them at Ancient Cemetery in South Yarmouth just after 11 a.m. Stricken as everyone has already arrived, standing at the edges of a tent. Waiting for me. Park on a narrow cemetery road, I hurry over. Stand on the thin fake grass blanket over grass. Penny smiles, Gretchen smiles. Andrew his son. Deanie in his wheelchair. *Do you remember Kelle?* And Deanie leans forward and says my name with all the extra sound in it, as he always has, as if I'm more than I am. Is he the oldest grandchild or am I? I no longer remember.

I stand by my brother who reads a story of Dean's life. My mother wrote the beginning, my father the end. They were here with Dean in Cape Cod Hospital, here for the induced coma, the dying.

*

When Dean was dying in May, I was living in a town of stones, in a house donated by the poet James Merrill. I had a four-

222

month writing residency, and this was the end. From here, I'd go to Provincetown, to live again in the Hans Hofmann attic for a month.

The stone town had a stone church. A stained glass window for Annie and her infant daughter Annie who died over 150 years ago. On the sidewalk outside the church, a woman with ocean waves of brown hair on either side of her head had smoked a cigarette. *Can I go in?* I asked.

The church? I don't know. Try it. Unlocked. Inside, I saw the altar. Dean doesn't want a service, doesn't want anything, my mom said on the phone. They're going to have a memorial in a restaurant. With a buffet. It made me sick, the idea of lined-up food. How could we eat after Dean dies? Good to me my whole life, loved me my whole life for nothing, for existing.

I'd left my jeep at his house in South Yarmouth in December and January, when I had to fly to stay with Cory in Virginia. I'd been in the Hans Hofmann attic all winter, but my friends were returning for the holidays. I had to leave for a few weeks.

At Dean's house, I had been embarrassed at my situation. My nowhere-to-live, my overstuffed suitcases I lugged to a cab, belongings so jigsawed in my jeep, they covered the windows. Who lives like this? Living nowhere? My voice up a register, but Dean was just himself, funny, kind, helping me in any way he could. His voice the same. I hugged him once, so glad I did. Fast because I don't know how to be with almost everyone. *You're like me,* he'd said when Nana died, his mother. *Come out of there,* he'd said from the doorway of her apartment, when I was trying to help clean out her things. I'm like Dean.

Church empty. But, I stared at the stained glass like a tourist in case I was being observed. Almost 7:30 p.m. Sat in the second pew. Ahead, satin white over the altar, gold, the letter A beginning a word. What is the word? No one here. Cried for Dean. For my family. For my mom—his sister. The hymn printed in front of me is *Gloria*. I remember singing that song as a child. Sing it inside my body in the pew.

Dean's heart beating triple time. Failing. Hospital. Kidneys shutting down from the congestive heart failure treatment. Induced coma. MRI to see if there is brain function. There is. He's in there. But then the C.diff—that infection made organs shut down—liver, I don't know everything. But the doctor said it was time, and there had been a family meeting. His daughter Gretchen had to make the final decision to take the respirator off, take all the machinery off. They said he could die in two hours or two days. He was still breathing that afternoon. They gave him morphine. *He looked peaceful* my mom said. *Better without the tube in him.* He never came out of the coma.

In the church, I don't know if he's still alive or not. Purely good to me since I was a kid. One person in the world let me leave my old jeep in his yard for a month last winter. Sick himself, and it was no problem. The plastic case on the counter with boxes for all his pills a kind of calendar. Each day, a handful. So much snow fell in the month I was gone, worried my jeep would be buried. Locks unworkable—they'd frozen in Provincetown.

I'd returned to Dean's in January, exhausted from cancellations, re-routings, and after days of trying, was back in Boston. Bus to Hyannis. And then what, I wondered? Start shoveling? Would the jeep doors even open? Dean couldn't drive, so I took a cab to his house. In his yard, my jeep green and cleared of mountains of snow. Lock opened as easily as summer. Dean had asked or paid someone to do this for me. It was the last time I saw him. I was a child in this house, a flower girl. Wore my blue ocean dress in his living room. I hear him laughing when we'd visit, low laugh, rolling—how can I even help you hear it? Like it had water in it, and love, and he could laugh at things in a way that grounded you in the world. Made it good. Made the bad bearable. He was funny. Could make you laugh with just the look in eyes, his smile beginning. I was always happy in this house.

I'm mourning with the colored glass. Jesus with a triangle of light behind him. I wish Dean could just wake up, be well, start again. This ending makes so much feel useless. On the phone, Mom kept forgetting everything. Just quiet. Dad said, *You wake up tired, and you go to bed tired*.

There's nothing I can do but feel it.

Keep is to continue, go on. I think of Dean's infant son who died, his much younger brother, my uncle Jeffrey who died at seven. Nana. Gramp. Dean told me he often went to the cemetery to Gramp's grave. *He was my father,* he said. So they are there, somewhere, for him. Tommy too, my son. All the dead. The whole church opened for me to grieve. Keep is the strongest, innermost part. Keep is to continue to have and to hold, to not give up.

His heart will probably give out first, Mom said. *It's beating three times as fast.* I wish I could fix him. Steady his heart. What can we do but love who we love? What did I pray? Please comfort him. Please give Dean all my love. Certain that it is something he can keep. Rain falls out of a sunny sky this afternoon, as if this is Florida. Then the harbor is all fog.

After the stone church, I walk into the fog that now covers the streets. Breathe the cool water air into my lungs, let it fill my hair. I'll miss that breathing.

*

In the cemetery, at Dean's funeral, Cory is crying beside me. He's 6'2" in a black suit, a commander in the Navy. A specialist in nuclear power. We have the same eyes as each other, as Dean. He can't read the words. We're all standing around the edges of the canopy and carpet, in a square, except for the top which is where the graves are. Dean's white box is a small sculpture. Dean isn't in there. It doesn't seem real. I knew Andrew when he was an infant in Nana's arms, the youngest of Penny and Dean's children. *Can I stay home with you?* I'd asked, one summer day. It was the only time Nana said no to me. Told me to go on the boat with Gramp and the others. She wanted to be alone with the new baby. I understand now. How nothing else is like that.

I take the pages from Cory's hands and read as if I were reading to a class, an auditorium. But then I come to the names of Dean's children who are with me in the square. I almost say *Gretchen* before my throat closes. Look up at Andrew who stands with his wife and small son. He smiles a little. *We could pass it around,* he says quietly. But I'd handed the pages back to Cory, whose voice is strong again, gets him through.

It all goes so quickly. Fifteen minutes? Half an hour? We are all surprised, it seems we've been here forever. We walk under the canopy. It took us all that time to feel okay about stepping on the carpet, entering this space. As if it is the grave itself we step on, are inside. In a way, it is, all our spaces, our own graves, under our feet. Bought and marked for us long ago.

I mention Jeffrey's grave, how we'd just noticed a few years ago that his name had been misspelled. Andrew beside me says, *It's strange.* We all turn. *When we got married, the DJ at our reception was there. The day Jeffrey was killed. He said it still haunts him.* A sled down a hill, hitting a tree. That's all I knew. Jeffrey was seven, my uncle, Nana's late-in-life baby. His older brother there, and his brother's girlfriend. Teenagers. The girlfriend's brother pushed the sled down the hill.

Dean's memorial is in a nearby restaurant. In the bar, my cousin Peter says it was a toboggan, not a sled. A little impatient with my lack of winter sports equipment knowledge, as if I'd grown up beside him. Not in Hawaii and Spain and Texas and Florida where we did no sledding. *Jeffrey was in the very front,* Peter says. *It was the first time they let him sit there.* The other kids piled in behind him. But that front spot, it was like a kayak seat I imagined, because Peter said you couldn't get yourself out. You were fitted in there. So when the tree came at them all, the kids jumped out. But Jeffrey couldn't get out. Hit the tree head on. Gramp carried him home in his arms. Someone must have had to find Gramp, tell him what happened.

My life was tragic, Nana said, late in life. After all those years of her laughter and bells and arms around me. And this was why.

A blond woman sits next to Peter at the bar. She asks me, *Isn't your mother here? I came to see her.*

No, I said, *she was here while Dean was in the hospital, and when he died. She's in Florida now.*

I remember how she'd put baby oil on and lie in the sun, the woman says. This doesn't sound like my mother. But she'd been young. The woman had lived near my grandparents. She said she remembered when Jeffrey died. She said that Nana stood on her front porch and screamed night after night. On the barstool beside me, Cory keeps saying he'd overheard something when we were kids. When we stayed at Nana and Gramp's house. The house they'd sell to Penny and Dean, where Dean continued to live after the divorce. Where I parked my jeep last winter for a month. Cory said Nana's sister Marguerite was on the couch with her. He heard Marguerite tell Nana that Jeffrey died because she was a bad mother. Why did Cory keep telling me this? Who would say such a thing? *Nana cried and cried,* Cory said. How could he remember or understand? He'd been three years old.

Even if it's true, what could Marguerite have meant? I ask.

Letting Jeffrey go sledding with teenagers in charge.

Didn't everyone do that? We all played on our own. No supervision. It seems unimaginably cruel. I loved Marguerite, and it sounded unbelievable.

In the bar of the restaurant, Peter says, *I remember when they told me. I remember crying at the window.* He was long divorced now. I'd heard that he'd left the cranberry bog house, moved to North Carolina to start all over again. Lick his wounds. I'd wanted to send him the poem I wrote about his dad's wake. Did I send it to mother? When he walked into the restaurant's banquet room, he'd looked right at me as if he knew me. Walked right toward me without breaking eye contact. I had no idea who he was, looked away. The stare too direct, too knowing of me. Then, *Peter, it's Peter.*

He said, *The last time I saw you was in Naples, the wake.* Foolishly, I mention the poem again. But it seems the only way I ever get anything true is in writing, and I want to get something true to Peter. Not this avoidance, my looking away as if he's a stranger.

My memories of Jeffrey are of him alive, gray split-wood under our palms, balancing on a fence. Feet skimming the log below. Summer in the round plastic pool that we just fit inside with water toys. Laughing. But is that because I saw pictures of these moments? Or did the moments become photographs in my memory?

At the funeral, a military man I'd not noticed before had an American flag folded in a triangle and walked over to present it to Andrew. Andrew gave the flag to his son. *Be careful with that,* Andrew said gently, his hand on the boy's back. *Don't drop it. It's special.*

Do we tip the minister? Penny had asked. None of us knew. *He got paid, but do we tip?* It would be weird, all of us handing him a dollar. We decide you don't tip at funerals. I wish Dean could come with us for lunch. All of us together. John and Diane arrive at the restaurant. Lots of people. The round tables full. It's a place where Dean liked to hang out years before, when he was still well. One neighbor comes to shake Gretchen's hand. The man who'd last cut his hair came. *We were out, and I'd asked, Wouldn't you like a haircut?* And Dean had said, *Yes.*

Photos of Dean are in the back of the room, and the front. Along with a slide show of photos on a small screen. Dean still doesn't seem dead. Here we all are. Everyone who loves him. Even an older woman whose mother had taught my mother in school, who had been in love with Dean when she was young. Apparently still is. But Dean married Penny.

How did you meet? I ask Penny when it was all over, when

she and Gretchen are going out the door. *He went to a different school, and my girlfriends would sometimes go for a ride with boys from his school. One day I got in the car with Dean. A convertible.* I could see them in the roofless car, Penny and Dean, laughing teenagers. They both laughed so beautifully, easily, as if it were the most natural thing. Everything still ahead. I don't know how to talk to someone whose ex-husband has just died. Which sounds so cold—*ex-husband*. I don't know how to talk about Dean now. Partly because he seems not dead. Because he had been in the world with me my entire life. Peter and Cory in the bar, wait for me. I watch Penny and Gretchen go toward the door.

That's when Gretchen turns to me and says, *No one knows you like family.* It isn't what I said or didn't say, it is just my existence that matters. I belong to them. From a far distance, this traveling looks random, an abstract map. But here, very close, I see I'm looking at the tiny lights of home.

INTERSTATE

I-95/NEW SMYRNA BEACH, FLORIDA
2014

> *...and grew myself / to fear and love until they
> became like children, mine, twins,*
>
> —Kasey Jueds, "To Swim"

I still have a terrible sense of direction, the place cells in my hippocampus misfiring or not firing, or maybe, not even there. I get lost in towns where I've lived for years. Turned around in an instant. Even with a GPS, I need a back-up. A cross-check. Because if there's a glitch in a meeting of highways that frazzles the GPS system, an outdated map, or an instruction to go north, south, east, west, I'm utterly lost. Folded, paper maps are useless to me, decorative. Printed written directions are necessary, to be read first, before following the GPS. It feels shameful, this inability to take myself from place to place. The panic and fear of being lost. It is childlike, and I am not a child. I am at the very end of Cape Cod, in Provincetown, preparing to drive south. I'm hoping that with a phone GPS, and an outdated mounted GPS, and written directions, I will find Florida. I will make it to Atlantic Center for the Arts, where I'd been in residence many times, been on the staff, and returned over the years to teach in the teen writing program, and to write. And where I am now being welcomed back for a writing retreat.

231

This May and early June, I'm living again in Beth and Kiki's loft in Provincetown's West End. I've been traveling for three years, teaching and living in residency programs across the country to research and write a book I'd thought was about home. Where is home? What is it?

I print out a TripTik from AAA. But my printer ink is almost gone, and I can't really see the little maps. Printed Google Maps directions are light too. Hard to see where I'm going. Packed all my paper before printing the directions, but I find flyers Kiki made advertising her body sculpting classes. A former body builder, her black and white photo on the flyer is so defined it's like one of those maps of the human body showing all the muscles. Biceps, triceps, pectorals. Obliques and quadriceps. Usually red-orange in diagrams, the texture of tightly-woven basketry. But here is a living woman being strong. I print my driving directions with Kiki on the opposite side. Lug the printer under one arm down the attic stairs to the long boat-like landing painted robin's egg blue, another flight of stairs, out the back door of the house. Shimmy it into the back of the jeep, among the books. Slam it shut. Everything fits somehow. High winds, but fair, a seventy-five-degree late June day. A day for arriving, not leaving.

I can't get the jeep checked out at Pete's repair shop. A sign on the door, "Family Emergency." *It's been up since yesterday,* says a boy in a garage next door. *And Pete's sciatica has been acting up,* the boy says. Well, I had an oil change in Connecticut this month, had the tires checked. Now, I buy a jug of coolant at a convenience store. Try to pour the green liquid into my jeep's plastic reservoir, just in case. It's getting hotter, sun high. A man watches in a black SUV parked beside me. *Does it matter if it spills?*

You need a funnel, he says. *But it'll be okay, it'll burn off. Where are you going?*

Florida.

Florida? He laughs long and quiet. *By yourself?* He could see the passenger side full with my red suitcase. He looks toward the back of my jeep. *You've got a lot of books in there.* His speech and laugh seemed to not quite end, spooling out as if considering something. I don't answer. Close the hood. I am driving over a thousand miles by myself. It might be best not to tell strangers everything.

Before I leave, I phone my parents. *Stay the first night in the last city in Connecticut,* my mom says. But what city is that?

It's not the last city, but I do stay in Connecticut, finding a hotel after driving only four hours. My first day. It seems extravagant, stopping so soon. But I'm grateful to be here, near Mystic—somewhere familiar. I'd grocery-shopped here during my residency, visited the seaport museum.

Day two, I head for New York and the Tappan Zee Bridge which I have been told I must find. Though my out-dated mounted GPS and my iPhone GPS both insist on the George Washington Bridge. Which means going through NYC. *No, no,* my parents had said. *Whatever you do, don't do that.*

*

When I'd phoned a friend to tell her my driving plan, she said, *Whatever you do, don't go on the Bronx Expressway. Hell on earth.* I can only find my way with the GPS, can't improvise. Can't cross-check the TripTik while driving. *It's a big sign for Tappan Zee,* my mom said. But at the last rest stop in Connecticut, a woman behind the counter says, *Take exit 21 for Tappan Zee. It's easy.* I do. It does say Tappan Zee and White Plains. But no bridge appears. Just drive and drive until the GPS recalculates me toward the George Washington Bridge, and with horror, I read the sign I am approaching: Bronx Expressway. *Hell on earth.*

There is no sign that says: *If you can't handle it, turn this way.* There is nothing to do, but go forward. Or give up, go back. But where, to what? I keep going, straight into it. I hear my friend Nick's voice, *Okay, be scared, but you still have to do it.* In front of me, a line of trucks spirals up. A vehicular circle of hell. Panic attack building the higher I go. Purgatory smoke rising, bumper to bumper. It takes my breath. I normally drive in beach towns, not major cities, on expressways. But people do this all the time. Why am I falling apart? The whole way up, down, I make myself breathe. Here's air, here's my friend Larry's calm voice: *You can make it.* Here's a prayer, here's me turning all of this over with my hands on a black steering wheel flaking hot bits of rubber against my fingertips. Rising up with all the others.

A man stands to the left of all the cars with a cardboard sign. How did he get up here? Did someone drop him off? If I were the person I want to be, I would at least unroll my window, give him my bag of tangerines. Too afraid to take my hands off the wheel.

And then I'm on the George Washington Bridge, a suspension bridge over the Hudson River to New Jersey. A cat's cradle, riding on the strings. Two weeks before, Harold Olivares jumped from this bridge. I'll read this in a newspaper when I later do an internet search on the bridge, to understand where I've been. He was a forty-nine-year-old man who lived in the Bronx. He left a 1998 Taurus parked at the top of the bridge. It was the same day two tractor trailers hit each other head-on up here and killed one of the truckers. Before or after, Harold Olivares got out of his car, and jumped from these strings. In a movie, the actor Jeremy Irons grabs the girl in the red raincoat before she jumps off the bridge. But Harold fell. The bridge towers 604 feet above the water. Remind myself to keep breathing. As if I am a separate person trying to keep another calm.

Over the long bridge, into the hand of the New Jersey Turnpike, at first just a heaven of flat road, blue sky. Held there, my body calms. I exhale. Peaceful until all the cars jam together. Then the shaking begins. *Oh no,* only day two on the road. I'm only through Massachusetts, Connecticut, and New York. My jeep shakes as if all the doors will fly off, hood rise up and clank to the roadside. As if the steering wheel itself will come off in my hands. So that I'll be driving nothing, as in a make-believe scene in a movie. *No no no.* Over so soon. Why did I think I could drive this old jeep for twenty hours down the East Coast? My hands shaking, arms shaking, legs shaking. All of me, all I have with me. Surrounded by lanes of bumper-to-bumper cars. I cross to the far right lane, head for the breakdown lane. Insist my way between other stuck drivers creeping along. And then, it stops. The shaking stops. Released or calmed. The jeep makes its slow way with the others.

*

I keep going. In the hotel at the exit, I find Delaware has child baseball teams. Boys everywhere, transfixed before TV screens in the lobby. Expensive rooms. So, I drive on, through

Baltimore. Signs say a tunnel is ahead: Fort McHenry. So many weaving roads surrounding it, like another planet. At the toll, I ask, *Is the tunnel very long?* I'm claustrophobic in tunnels, enclosed spaces. Can't even drive a car into a car wash. Panic in parking garages, desperate for any window, square of light.

The toll taker laughs gently, *No,* she says. Windowless, like a tomb, like being buried underground. *Not far, not far,* I say to comfort the suffocated girl in me. The girl who died. *Not far.* Is that light, is that sun and sky? Or lighting around the corner? It's the way out. *Breathe breathe breathe.* Fort McHenry goes underneath Baltimore Harbor. *The tunnel is the lowest point in the Interstate system under water.* Underground because it's underwater. That's why no windows. They would have looked out on water.

I drive in an underwater tunnel. One and half miles. Lights bedroom dim. At its lowest level, 107 feet below the harbor water surface. I do not know this at the time. Getting late, though not yet dark. Can I make it to Silver Spring? That sounds nice. My dad had said that when I saw a "2" or "4" before "95", it would take me around a big city. I am on a road around Washington, DC, but crazy and jammed and fast moving. When night falls, the lights confuse me. I keep looking for a hotel sign, not knowing there aren't any on this road. That I will drive and drive nearly to Fredericksburg, Virginia, before I see a hotel sign. Eight hours of driving. The farthest I've ever driven the jeep.

The next day, I have a hard time accelerating on small hills. I'm moving from static to motion, the drivers in their newer cars impatient with me trying to rev back up to fifty-five miles per hour. Overheat needle rises. Is this it? Will my jeep keel over here on the Capitol Beltway with no emergency lane? Hot, late afternoon. Feeder lanes from the left clog up the fast lane. An accident, motorcycle overturned. Man on the road, another man in a camouflage uniform bends over him. Sirens. An ambulance comes from behind for another accident. By the time we inch our way forward, the injured man is lifted, carried away.

Virginia is big. I sleep in Chester. I sleep in Lumberton, North Carolina, and Port Wentworth, Georgia. The many miles of uninterrupted driving trigger my dream panic of not being able to control a car. Trigger dissociation. Have to tap the brake to reassure myself I have the power to stop. This isn't a dream. My limbs work.

I arrive in New Smyrna Beach, Florida. Just after dark, I drive through the gate at Atlantic Center for the Arts. Drive the sand path around to the laundry room. Park and walk back into all that green. Everything waiting quietly for my return. The door of a corner unit left unlocked for me, gold key on the bedspread. It smells like the ocean even though the shore is three miles away. A white desk looks out on the woods outside my window, a sixty-nine-acre ecological preserve. I always breathe more easily here, as I do at the beach. These one-room apartments feel large to me, space made for writing, for something new.

Twenty years since I first came here. That sign I saw then: "Artists at Work." The feeling that here I am an artist, and my writing is work. That this whole place is here to support our work. It is as if the trees themselves hold me, the atmosphere. I plan to stay a few weeks until I leave for Virginia. (While still in Provincetown, I sent a panicked last-minute application to a residency program in the foothills of the

Blue Ridge Mountains. Before I left for Florida, I received word that a space had miraculously opened up for me. Two months. When the director called to let me know, she said, *You must be living right.*)

In my room at Atlantic Center, looking at my blue photos of Provincetown makes me feel hollowed out. I wanted to stay. The Cape has always been home, the place where I'm from. Place of my childhood, my family. Though many of my relatives have died or moved away, I keep looking for them. Hear my uncle Dean in the voice of the man behind the fish counter at the Stop & Shop, see my grandmother's powdery soft face in the lone woman passing me on the winter beach.

That night at the welcome dinner in Atlantic Center's common room, I tell Jim, ACA's co-director, about my two-month residency in Virginia. He says, *Why don't you come back after Virginia? Stay here until the new year. Okay,* I say.

At my table, I meet the wife of a visiting composer. She tells me that a couple of years ago, she decided to do things she'd always wanted to do. Like fly in a biplane. She'd already gone up in a hot air balloon. As a kid she used to hear the balloons going over her house, with fire whispering, propellent. She wanted to go up too.

How do you land? I ask.

You can't really plan it, she says. *It depends on wind speed, things like that. You could land on a house. We almost landed on the corner of one.* But somehow, they kept going and landed in a cornfield. No one had traveled the muddy road in for fifteen years. A truck had to bring them out.

You weren't afraid? I asked. *You didn't freak out?*

She said, *People who are too afraid think of things like, I'm in a wicker basket.* But she didn't focus on the mechanics. Or on possible disaster scenarios. Instead of thinking what could go wrong, she just let the balloon lift her up. Stayed in the experience, the feeling.

At dinner, her husband says, *You have a long history here.* Nick, the residency director, says, *You are many things to ACA.* When I hug Jim, he pulls me closer and says, *Don't halfway hug me.* I think of my uncle Dean's memorial last May on the Cape, my cousin Gretchen turning to me as she left the restaurant: *No one knows you like family.*

It's a kind of home, I say to the composer at dinner. *They are a kind of family.*

Kiki sends me an email to say I can move back into the loft apartment in Provincetown in October. Asks if I can start paying rent then. Last winter, the rent was waived, a gift from Beth and Kiki. I'd survived on a can of soup a day, noodles, some vegetables. If I made the food as hot and watery as possible, I felt less hungry. They've been so generous, their request so reasonable, but I'm still without a job. I can't pay rent. I'll have spent the money from a National Endowment for the Arts fellowship grant by then. I have to live as economically as possible, look for work in the new year.

I tell Kiki I'm scared to live in their Provincetown loft this coming winter, scared what it means to spend all my money on rent. Then have no job, no money, no place to live at the end of the land in winter. There is something helpless in that plan, an abdication. As if the chance to write in peace transcends my need to be alive. To take care of my physical self. What kind of work could I find in Provincetown in the winter? I belong in this body. I need to house it. But I'm not done with the book. I still don't know where home is.

Atlantic Center has welcomed me for twenty years. Maybe it isn't a kind of home, but a home. If the Cape is my home, and Atlantic Center is my home, maybe there's another one somewhere. It's the Fourth of July. Last night was the anniversary of my death.

In between my stays at Beth and Kiki's loft last winter and spring, I had that four-month residency, January through April, in Connecticut. I was the sole resident of a historic house with an incredible library. I read and wrote. Snow fell and melted. I was feeling alive, sitting in the yellow room in the house. Harbor out the window. Prior to my poetry reading at the town library, a reporter called on the phone. Had read my memoir. I asked if we could talk about poetry. He ignored my request, wanted to talk about rape and murder. The male reporter mentioned my abduction, gang rape, attempted murder so casually in his article. He made the violence that happened when I was twenty-one years old the focus. As if I needed to be punished for writing about this. As if I wasn't human because I wrote about this. Not the same as other people. As if I could be shamed into silence. Too late.

Once, a boyfriend's mother said it was surprising I was still alive. Rape always the taking of something. A yellow field. When I read of my own body taken or of another's, I'm emptied out. It's automatic, filling with darkness. If I try to see through my attackers' eyes, I think I should die. That I am nothing, a thing to be used. When I complained about the article to the woman who was my contact at the Connecticut residency, she said, *We don't want anything salacious connected to us. Salacious.* When rape is salacious, there is nowhere for me to go. When three men suffocated me until I stopped breathing, struggling, was that salacious too? The newspaper article was printed just prior to my end-of-residency reading at the library. A man from town ran up the aisle to say, *We know all about you now,* laughing. As if I were a character, an entertainment.

When I was dying, I worried they'd throw my dead body in a dumpster, that I'd be ground up, compacted with garbage, those solid cubes. And no one would ever find me. They'd think perhaps I had run away.

During that Connecticut residency, I read newspaper articles about women who had been raped. And women raped who died. It has to do with making a person not a person, a man doing whatever he likes with the body, anything—he could eat her small finger or just bite right through to bone. Men carry a woman like a doll between them on a bus, in a cab, rape her in public. Last summer, a telephone operator was gang-raped for a month. Then, in August, these men found someone new, a photojournalist in an abandoned mill.

December 16, 2012, a twenty-three-year-old woman who was a physiotherapy intern rode a bus with her friend. Six others were on the bus, including the driver, all of whom raped the woman for several hours and beat her friend. They used an iron rod on both of them. Bodies dumped from the moving bus, they were found by passersby. She died two weeks later. Her name was Jyoti Singh. My hand shakes writing that down. Like someone being shaken.

In December the year before, a sixteen-year-old girl was gang-raped. After she told authorities, the same men raped her again and set her on fire. The turquoise cloth that covers her body is mostly folds—her body beneath curled up like a child. A bag of fluids hung above her gurney. Surrounded on all sides by men who watched to see what she would do next. She died. After her death, doctors learned that she was pregnant. At first, authorities said the girl set herself on fire. But in her dying statement, she said two of the men *set her alight.*

That spring in Connecticut, after I read these articles about other women raped, I had trouble driving too. My hands felt like they didn't work, a dead girl's hands. Remind my muscles I'm not a ghost, not full of darkness. Reattach my hands, my arms. Inflate my flattened lungs. My soul, which never left, turned lights back on. Outside the air smelled like gasoline. The boy in the deli couldn't hear my voice, leaned closer. I tried to find it. On a drive with the poet Leslie Mc-Grath, who befriended me in Connecticut, I learned the name for this. *It's disassociation,* she said. In my search for home, I missed my own body. It's the place I keep leaving, like a city, a town. As if, after being forced to give it up, I never settled back in.

In the years after I came back to life, I thought, *This is all extra time. You can do anything.* When I first came here twenty years ago, I'd been alive again for almost nine years; being respected as a writer felt like yet another birth. Where I could be who I most wanted to be, a writer.

This Fourth of July I drive from Atlantic Center to the ocean and walk on the hard sand, watch stars explode around me. I want to let myself be at home in this second life. Let the balloon lift me up. Alive. Breathing.

MARS

> *...I had made up my mind now,*
> *I would appear before I disappeared.*
>
> —W.S. Merwin, "The Dwelling"

The gate makes a little clang of arrival and goodbye. Leaves in the pool, tiny legged black creatures I scoop to concrete. I'm in the Blue Ridge Mountains of Virginia for three months, late summer to early fall. Down the hill, past the gardens, there's a swimming pool.

Swimming, I get rid of something I don't need. At breakfast, I'd heard that Mars will be visible tonight. I've never seen it before. A question my whole life: Is there life on Mars? The planet so close as if it could blink a message to me. A planet not white but red, what could be more alive? Rivers on Mars meant there was water once, life at one time. The all-night diner sign *hello* of our first meeting.

We're a half-mile from the highway, down in a valley. Little green house we pass, stacked wood. Slope, blue mountains in the distance. Boxwood maze to the left. I swim in underwater silence. To get to this mountain, this pool, I drove through pouring night rain on the wrong roads. Two-lane country roads with only churches and fields, signs that read "Peaches." Through South Carolina, North Carolina –

one gas station where I filled up not knowing the emptiness ahead. I couldn't find a hotel, any place to rest. Just rain and darkness. Played songs I'd loved when I was twenty, no idea what was ahead. "Spirits in the Night," over and over.

Rain everywhere, everything. I kept driving. Nowhere to go to give up. Further than I thought from Florida to these foothills in Virginia: 690 miles. Stopped to buy a flashlight and water before I left. In the night, I felt myself rising, but couldn't see how high up, just felt the darkness around me. A slight floating. *Are we high up?* I asked a woman a few days after I arrived. She knew I was afraid of heights. Gave me a sideways look as if I might panic, fall off if I knew. I still don't know how high we are, up and down of hills a kind of holding. No precipice visible.

When I arrived I drove to the Visitor Center, asked for a map of Virginia. Tacked it to my wall like a piece of art, a drawing. I can see the blue of the ocean, but it's far away. *This must be what I wanted to be doing.*

In Ruzica's studio, a mirror is covered in crossed blue tape. Underneath: "Do Not Believe Me." I can only read the words when I'm reflected. Maybe I'm not what I see. I swim in the hills of the mountains almost every day. The tree outside my bedroom is American Holly, leaves thick and sharp as cut plastic. Evergreen, pollinated by night moths. Whip handles from this pale wood.

Birds that appear: Cardinal, bluebird, mockingbird, crow. Ruby appears out of the rain, I wait for her. She's from Pakistan, lives in Bushwick. Ruby said the crow is a witness. They gather. She'll draw fifty crows. Long black eyelashes. She fed her paralyzed mother for eleven years. Mouth open. Ruby carries a spoon. She gathered sticks for three years. Everything she made fell apart. In the honeysuckle she went unseen. *Three blue speckled eggs. You don't know what you'll find,* Ruby said. Gathering twigs.

Her father didn't celebrate her birth and so she made a work of art called, "My birth will take place a thousand times no matter how you celebrate it." It's made of twigs, a seated mother and a child who lays her head in the mother's dissolving lap. Becomes twigs again. She'd had a fellowship in England with a stipend of 5,000 pounds, but she'd been too shy to buy food and lived on peanut butter. Laughed. I know what it is to be shy in a new place.

Ruzica here from Croatia. *This strange day,* she said. *I just want to lie down,* hands folded in the air beneath her cheek. Rain. Thistledown in the air, milkweed, the sky full of floating puffs, baby hair. Spilth, to spill profusely. On my fingertips it's almost nothing, then gentleness. What can I feel? Stand on the road of sparky down in blue air. Did it settle in the dark when I couldn't see it? I don't think so, wind still lifting it unseen while we walk down the grassy hill to the pool. Past the old green shed. Blue mountains watch so quietly, as if anything can be done, accepted. A strange wind blew through here—a *derecho,* sideways hurricane, knocked down trees, power gone for weeks. Thistledown not nothingness but tiny seeds, sowing.

An English boxwood maze hides the pool in evergreen. Sunken garden with a lily pool. Chinese elm leaves are see-through, like lace. Elm rises straight up. Reaches like a living creature, arms outstretched as if in praise. Seventy different trees . Lawns of up and down. Down to the pool.

The train is going by again. Down in the air around me falling. I don't mind so many in the water even when I swim, the stars and dark make room. And they cluster in the shallow end. So my legs can kick, I can be underwater. Days ago, I'd feared Nicole and I would not be friends because I couldn't join the lake swimmers who swam in the murky lake across the highway. Afraid of my dream of being underwater in a lake, unable or unwilling to rise. On the brink of drowning, not knowing if I could swim to air. Even now, since that dream, even in the bright afternoons, I panic a little when I dive beneath the surface. Swim a stroke, at most three. Will I have the strength, the will to push my way up? Kick my feet hard, push up like a fish. Surely if I sunk someone would notice I was below, water filling my lungs, surely they would cease their talk, but maybe not. I push up hard, break the surface.

*

Saturn and Mars within three degrees of each other this night. Nicole and I see them as we walk to the pool. Stop on the path of trees, absent horses to our right. Above, the red spark is Mars' neon sign on and off. Saturn beside, all in Libra. Someone made a picture of the sky long ago, and we still see it.

Sometimes a person sees me, but I saw Nicole's light. Even though I never swam the lake, we took a night walk. Then we were the walkers. Field and highway wide, laughing in the dark. I'm still afraid, but walking anyway. In Florida, this is how a person could get killed, this is asking for it. But in Florida, I was always alone when the car slowed behind me at dusk, sidled next to me. When a man pulled a knife on me. I'm still too afraid to go right, lore of biting dogs and no leash law. Left we go, but Nicole says, *Soon you won't be afraid.* Over bridges, train tracks, overpasses at midnight. And after a few weeks, walking beside me she said surprised, *You're not afraid.* I was on the dark road without a flashlight. Towers of kudzu high as buildings beside us, like giant green men. Stars and moon enough to see by.

When the lake swimmers swam at the boatyard across the street, I swam in the pool down the hill. Slow laps. One woman wore flippers and a bathing cap. Another did the butterfly as if she were propelled. Churning.

*

No pressure, Nicole said. *No pressure.* Nicole graceful as a bird in her yellow dress. *Let's all go skinny dipping,* she'd said, joyful. All I felt was panic. On the sidewalk beside the four barn silos, dark already falling. It was completely beyond me now. Nakedness. Play. No more leaving my bathing suit on the beach, walking into the ocean. No more. Forgetting how to live in my body instead of just hauling it around.

But as we walk on the dirt road toward the pool, my terror rising, Nicole said, *Wait, wait.* Silos behind us, silver and empty, used for nothing but beauty now, skyline shine. *I want to see the stars, I want to see what's there. Mars,* she says. *Saturn.* Each planet comes into focus as I look up, follow where she points. Indistinguishable lights in the night sky, and then two worlds appeared.

In the outside swimming pool cut into the foothills of the Blue Ridge Mountains, we're a gyroscope of unsynchronized swimmers. We try to spin as one. Clothing strewn on concrete around the pool built by the rich years ago. In 1979, the mansion burned down when men used propane to burn off old paint. A renovation that destroyed the whole house.

Something happened when I stepped into the pool, under stars. *What's the ratio of naked to un-naked people in the pool,* I asked. I don't remember the number called out to me. Sixty-five percent naked? Eighty-five percent? I just wanted to be one of them. Free of my fear, unsticking the elastic tight to my skin. I lift my arms over my head, strings of my top in my fingertips, bikini bottom slides off. What did I need them for? I swim the length of the pool. We hold hands and do Esther Williams kicks and waves. Blue other, blue least and frontal, blue apprentice. Blue house. Blue indefinite, blue constant. Blue refrain.

I think Kelle's naked, one bathing suited person called to another, indecisive about nakedness. Kelle's naked. Water blank enough for all of us. I'm not the same, the yellow seen in leaves. But I can walk into water. Our knuckles in each other's wet palms, grab tight to hold on. Slipping, falling back. Underwater, spitting chlorine. I don't want to carry fear, become old with it, die with it. I take two strangers' hands, kick as high as I can. Spin. I swim the pool end to end, touch the bumpy concrete with the soles of my feet, push off.

Mars blinks above. Saturn close. My voice hoarse from laughing, calling out in the dark.

Around us old hickory forest, wildflower garden. Green canes curving with down. The spigot is a green garden hose emptied into the pool. Constantly filling. Where does the excess water go? Why aren't we drowned by now?

It's as if they tried to plant one of everything here. Copper beech. Catalpa with long pods, shiny brown-black of coffee beans. Sour gum, spruce. Is the cedar of Lebanon covered in vines? Peonies, chrysanthemums. Ginkgo, Cherry. Path to my bed strewn with fuzzy green balls, soft underfoot, walnuts inside. Black Walnut tree, *Robinia pseudoacacia*. The male flowers catkins from old Dutch *katteken* for kitten. Female the green tennis balls that fall, nut inside. On the night-dark walk, you hear a little thud. Walnuts rain down. Figs. Magnolias.

A train goes by through the woods behind us. At night it sounds like rain on stones or windows. Blue mountains black in the distance. Nicole had pointed to Mars in the sky, red blink from so far away. As if it were alive. Long green lawn around us, quiet trees, horses gone. No one can see us here—strangers to each other a few days before. I swam among them. Threw a little pink float, hand to hand. Caught it when it came my way. End of August, night still hot. Lindsey pregnant, just beginning to show, said, *I feel like I'm doing what my baby is doing,* reclining in warm water. As if we could be born from this.

*

MAP OF THE BODY
AUGUST—OCTOBER 2014

> *Body my house / my horse my hound / what will I do*
> *when you are fallen*
> —May Swenson, "Question"

One summer in Hyannis, I worked the counter at Tiffany's Bakery in the Cape Cod Mall where we could eat all the broken cookies. So we broke them. Piled them into tall white bags. Ate the cool white dough, chocolate chips until we were sick. At a party at a co-worker's house, I met a boy. After a couple hours, he and I walked to the nearby beach. The boy stripped, ran into the water, looked back over his pale ass as if I'd follow him.

I wasn't that interested, stayed clothed, sand strangely cold, scratchy. Back at the house, we had sex in a dark room on the first floor. But it was another boy I wanted. My co-worker's brother, the blond. Later, I fell asleep in his bed.

It was the other guy who called, drove me one afternoon into the woods where we had sex on the hood of his car, tree overhead, sun. I had no real interest in him, but liked sex. Liked being wanted. I murmured something about coming back to Cape Cod sometime. A politeness. Car hood hot on my bare skin, raised spine down the center making me arch my own. I rolled to the left of it.

He said, *You'll be in Florida. Why would you come back? I'd never come back.* I don't know where his mirage of Florida sprung from—spring break, a magazine. Sun through leaves on us, two naked kids in the woods. Like the prelude to a murder scene, like we're asking for it. Florida's hot, but it's not paradise, not like he thinks. This boy I'm with because he pursued me. My tan stomach flat, breasts outlined in triangles of white from my bikini, white string around my neck like a necklace. I've just turned eighteen. My boyfriend from school stopped calling. I'd seen another girl put her arms around him at a concert, and let it happen. He was one of the boys who'd come toward me too. No one I chose. Easier to let go. A year later, I'll be not-in-love again. Pregnant. Why not choose? Why not be with someone I care about? Love?

In Virginia, at dinner, a poet from Cleveland tells me the history of turns. Turns can be emblem or ironic or a filibuster, he said. *A filibuster?* I asked.

You keep from saying what you need to say, he explained. I thought a filibuster was more of a delay. He recited lines from poems to help me understand the turns. Everyone else had left the table, dining room. One of these fragments he recited—I can't recall the words, or even the poet, or kind of turn. But he sat beside me, looked into my eyes, and said that he was flawed in many ways, but he would always love me. I had to stare at the tablecloth because when he recited the words of the poem, unblinking, they felt true. As if there were another life where we would also sit at a round table with a white tablecloth, a wall of windows like tall doors behind us. Blue of the mountains turn into the dark of night. Until it is all one thing.

The poet touched me on the arm once or twice as he spoke. *You keep from saying what you need to say.* All my talking a disguise. Don't show fear. All my life I've been hiding my fear. Trying to keep my face blank. Because if others could see what I want, need, fear, they'd have power over me. Don't I trust anyone?

The German stone sculptor at lunch tapped my shoulder in the barn kitchen, beside the silo where the composer sang for me and four other people. The white silo door within the Normandy barn, on the far wall of the artists' kitchen. Walls white too, with the door blending in, so you might not even notice it's there. Or dismiss it as a closet. But inside is a sixty-foot tower with glazed red brick walls, and a black ladder to the conical roof.

Only five of us could enter the silo because that's all the space can hold. We sat on benches on either side of the composer, Ayesu, who stood in the center. With the door shut, and the light switched off, it's pitch black. When my fear of enclosed spaces is triggered, I lose all sense of direction, of exit. That's when Patricia, sitting across from me on the other bench, had said, *You'll be okay. You'll hear the music.*

In that perfect dark, his song circled us and rose. I breathed it. The silo held corn in the years before the artists arrived, a cylinder of gold. Really, I was afraid I'd cry. A church song. Live music. Kept looking toward the door, the crack of light along the floor, to keep from falling completely inside the song in the silo. If I started to cry, I might not be able to stop. *The one who can sing, sings to the one who can't.* The song a kind of touch. I save it inside.

*

When Nana had been very ill, we were worried she'd die, but she'd recovered. I went to visit, helped her into bed. Her gown shifted as she settled into bed: *her legs are so young.* She had the legs of a girl. It was winter, my aunt and uncle's house on the Cape. Nana had been in the hospital. She needed care, so she was at their house instead of home alone. I wished I could care for her. When I murmured something about this, Nana said, *You've always been this way.* This way. And it was said with great love. But this way means I don't take care of anyone. Maybe not even myself. How do I become a person who can take care? Even now, after all these years, I live no-where, all my furniture in storage. I couldn't even feed a cat. Debt piled around me like buildings, a city. How can I be my son's mother now? It seems the most basic thing is to live. He would want me to live. How?

After Nana's death, my aunt had said it would be good to do an autopsy. So the rest of the family would know what diseases to look out for. Nana had heart attacks, diabetes. Been stuck with needles so many times, she'd told me she couldn't stand it anymore. I'd said *No, no autopsy.* And they'd listened to me. Later, Nana's will was found. She'd written <u>NO AUTOPSY</u>. Underlined. After death, after she couldn't feel anything, I took care of her body.

*

What does a map of the body look like? Nicole asked. *Do you remember making maps in school? Drawing the states and then coloring them in?* A rectangle shape outlined in dark red, a garnet pencil. Then the shading lighter, a rain of red inside. For forty thousand years, people have drawn maps to see themselves in the world. *Maps as much about existence as orientation.*

"The Map of all Under Heaven," is Korean, made in 1800. In it, the land is a body. Mountains and rivers are veins and arteries. Energy transport. A map of my body would help me see myself in my body. Night sky of sharp stars. I can see them so clearly in Virginia, up high in the hills. Mountains higher still and darkness all around. Nothing to hide the stars. I'm surprised there are so many, that this light is always here even when I can't see it. A sense that there are even more, a bright existence. That these are the sparks. A white butterfly shows up often when I'm out walking. It makes me feel not alone, walking in the right direction.

*

When Ayeshu sang in the silo, in the pitch black, on this old plantation in the foothills of the Blue Ridge Mountains, I was afraid. I had a panic attack just thinking of the door shutting behind me—just a hidden door in the kitchen, into the old silo now empty. The only way out was up. You'd have to fly. *Go into the music,* Patricia had said. I did, on the bench in the 100 percent darkness, I went into his song and my fear was held in it instead of inside me. Later I mistakenly erased it—the whole song that I'd recorded with my phone. Gone.

But two years later, I'll synch my iPod with songs from

my computer, and "Silo" will appear. Silence, no song. But then, I'll hear myself clapping, I'll hear my thanks, my voice inviting the next group of people into the silo—*This is your time,* I'll say laughing. And then I'll hear the water rushing—I'm washing a glass at the sink. Patricia there. I'll say, *It worked, going into the music.* I'll say, *I have panic attacks in closed spaces.* Patricia will say, *Sometimes the darkness can be a gift.*

Fourteen minutes on my Silo recording. I'll tell Patricia, *See you later.* My voice will sound like someone I know. I'll hear the grass under my feet, the stones. Hear myself walking in Virginia. To my studio, keys jingling, falling to the cement where the black fur coat caterpillars curl uncurl all night at my front door. Inside I try to hear the song again, and erase it forever. Some things only happen once. Maybe everything.

CALL YOURSELF ALIVE

I learn by going where I have to go,

—Theodore Roethke, "The Waking"

I.

I dance drunk at twenty on a dark gray concrete slab, Ronnie plays a painted black Stratocaster above me, long yellow hair, shiny shirt. Loud. Distortion a shade I can rest in. Melanie a maid for Halloween, Ronnie in a corner with us, angel face bent toward ours. Even up close, he's hard to see, as if I were looking into a light. This October, it's eighteen years since he shot himself. That night, he's twenty-two. Orlando, Florida.

Shirt ripped open as if his chest expanded in rage, deflated. Chin like the underside of gorse petals. We have the same shag haircut. But his and Melanie's lie down, shine. He kisses me, pink puffy lips, goodbye, an old name for something. Maybe I remember that kiss so well because there was nothing after. He walks toward the bar to get a drink. When he plugs back into the Marshall, my sandaled foot taps like a sewing machine needle. Red, white, and blue Budweiser sticker on the back of his guitar. The root of *suicide* is *apart*. An undersong. He's buried with the black guitar in South Carolina. Blond hair a shambles as he plays.

At twenty-eight I dance for hire, sober, with Billy at Downtown Disney. We're in a New Year's Eve television commercial promoting Pleasure Island. We have to dance all night in the street. I don't know what to do with my hands, my feet. Freezing cold in a strapless cotton mini, toes bare in black straps, high heels. Eventually, I just move my body against the cold and dark, blend into the crowd.

Dance for years in my sublet on Howell Branch Road, second floor, all the lights off. R.E.M. incantatory in the dark, dancing so long and fast I have to take off my clothes. Bra, panties. Sweating in Florida, the humid nights. Dance in my body and out of it. Skin deep, skin tight. Under my feet, a person downstairs is trying to sleep. Under death is the mandible, zygomatic bone, occiput, clavicle and carpals, tibia, tarsals, the skeleton of a woman. My bones carry me, are carried, the last to go.

John in South Carolina for his PhD. Too broke for a phone, I walk from my pink apartment on Lake Ivanhoe, up Virginia to the gas station booth. Stand behind the glass, sweating. His mother paid for movers to take everything from his Cocoa Beach condo to Columbia. Massive bookcases, desk that belonged to his father. His father died by suicide at the house on the lake. Years later it still reverberates, ripples out. I wondered if it was there, at that desk, wood a black forest. A place where you couldn't find a way out. My grandmother, Nana, died earlier that Spring. I'd flown to Boston, arrived too late. *Kelle's coming,* my aunt told her. They shocked her back. She died again. Hospital elevator going down crowded, shoulder to shoulder with white coats. Doctors avert their eyes from me, my uncontrollable crying. *None of you could save her?*

In Florida, I'm silting up. No desire to move. Can't count the cash drawers at the bookstore I manage. Can't work.

Can't care. Suddenly unemployed, I sleep until John leaves for work. Float in the ocean all day. So tan, I'm nearly orange. My family, John, worry I'll never work again, never come back to myself. Like a spell was cast.

The first time I'd slept over at John's house, we'd gone for Chinese food. The red and white menu told us who we were, who we should love. Red rooster, crow, snake. All the animals red. I'd kept my apartment in town, stayed at John's beach place four days a week. We talked of marriage. Then Nana died.

Coming out of the Orlando Publix with a grocery bag in each arm, the task of finding items on shelves, paying, walking out the door, it seemed enough. I wanted to drop the bags in the parking lot. Let the soup cans spill, milk cartons split. Drove home. When I got out of my car, bags in arms, I saw the white butterflies over the grass. Between me and my red door. *Nana's here,* I thought. Let myself fall into the grass, slid as if air's water, bags balanced. Sat there, white fluttering all around. A neighbor called from his red doorway, *Are you all right?* I nodded. Stayed a long while. Darkness came, tiny frogs called on the manmade pond beside the parking lot. *Don't they know it's not real?* Soap bubble sacs like amplifiers at the corners of their mouths, under their cold throats. Male frogs called for female. Females called back.

At John's beach house, sometimes it was early afternoon before I could throw off the sheet, put my feet on the floor. Grab a towel, apple, water, keys. Bikini on, flip-flops. Drive I Dream of Jeannie Lane. White butterflies on the boardwalk, in the trees. One night near dusk, as I was leaving, a peacock appeared on the sidewalk. Fanned out against the dark like a blue and green solar system. We stayed together. Was he preening for me? Peacocks not native to this place. No one knows how they got to Cocoa Beach, Florida. Crest on his head like a Spanish crown. A black-edged mantilla.

For hours, I floated in the ocean. If I stayed in one place, moved as little as possible, I could stay close to Nana. Where she'd stopped in this world. My parents came to visit. I drove all of us to a fish restaurant, John beside me, parents in the back seat. After dinner, we walked on the beach. My mom and I walked ahead. I heard my dad say, *You need to treat her right. You need to take care of her. Can I count on you for that?* John said, *Yes*. They talked about me as if I were an invalid. It was like walking underwater. Air not just humid but heavy. Surface somewhere above. *Nana, Nana.*

If I hadn't been underwater, I could have said, *I'm grieving.* I could have worn a black mantilla. Could have been like the peacock not native to this place. Appearing, disappearing. Then stomping on someone's roof, terrifying people.

I went to visit John once in South Carolina. Drove nine hours on the highway surrounded by truckers squeezing me between rigs. Behind his house a brown river I feared held alligators. Bumpy prehistoric bodies crawling up the grass, to the windows.

He was in class all day, so I went looking for a woman I'd read about in a discount book on South Carolina travel. Just a brief mention of a woman buried in a glass-topped coffin. Someone loved her so much, he couldn't bear to cover her face when she died in 1853. But then the Civil War came, Sherman burnt the town, and the church beside her. When the town rebuilt, they put the church right over her grave. Covered her up.

I was desperate to find her. She's under the Washington Street Church. On a weekday afternoon in September, I drove the quiet streets until I saw a long brick building. Parked in the empty lot. Walked alongside the brick, until it darkened into older brick with crumbled edges. A brass Washington Street Church plaque attached.

Inside the church is a broom closet with a hole in the floor. To find the woman, I would have to get permission. Have someone open the closet, let me drop through the floor to a narrow passageway. Close on all sides. Need a flashlight. Crawl a few dozen feet until I came face to face with the woman buried under the church. Imagine my head jerking up, hitting the dirt above me. Nearly burying myself. Panicking. Forgetting how to turn around. How to crawl. How to get out. Just me and the dead woman. I walked back to my car.

In his kitchen, I read John's translations of Old English on a yellow legal pad until he came home. *I found her,* I said. *Will you go with me, before dark?*

With John, I felt less afraid. *Let's go around the back,* I said. We turned the brick wall corner, passed the plaque. Ground mushy and rocky. As if in the dark, we were walking on unearthed bodies. Sharp, bony edges under my arches. My toes hit unyielding bumps.

Afraid I'd fall into a kind of slough, quicksand that would suck me in among the long dead. John kept walking though his voice shook. We climbed over air-conditioning pipes the size of small cows. *Where are we going?* We climbed a wire fence surrounding a playground. Empty swings in the dark. A slide. Black windows lining the wall on our right. A bird flew quickly by, and we both jumped at the darkness in flight.

Maybe it was enough, maybe this is all I could do. Just be beside her. Know she's here. Loved even with this building on top of her. Even in death. A man's face appeared in the window beside us. Glowering. He didn't move or speak. Terrifying, but also shaming. I don't remember any body, just his long face behind glass. We're trespassers.

A few months later, John's neighbor gave him a banjo. Moved in with him. When I called him collect from the gas station pay phone in Orlando, she answered. Wouldn't take my call. Her laugh a cackle. No job, very little money left. Phone cut off. Walked back home. Tiny frogs called all night.

Even frogs respond to extreme conditions. Stop moving. It looks like they've given up, but they enter a state of torpor. Don't move for months. Sometimes they dig, make a little cave and live underground. If a frog isn't good at digging, he just buries himself in dead leaves. Some frogs sink to the bottom of the pond. Even in mud they can find enough oxygen in water to stay alive. Some frogs freeze, appear dead. Sugar protects their internal organs. When things improve, their hearts start back up. The woman not there anymore, not buried under the church. Gone before the coffin maker placed the sheet of glass over her face. Free of her funeral dress and fallen skin, free of the night pond inside.

I finally get a job, at the opera, the old water tank for the city. Janean, the other assistant, wants to see Steely Dan in Tampa. Our cars not reliable for a two-hour highway drive, we borrow her boss's. Dance side by side in the aisle. *We're the youngest people here,* she yells, joyous. Her boyfriends are wan and dark, off-center, broken and glued back together. Janean's breakups like spring cleanings.

Bruce Springsteen comes to Orlando, and I spend what

seems an incredible amount of money to see him in concert. Ninety dollars. Janean doesn't want to go. I go alone. Since the breakup, I've been freezing up. Disconnecting from my body. As if I'm just hauling it around. No dancing. But I've been listening to Springsteen since I was seventeen. *Darkness on the Edge of Town* helped keep me alive. His poster over my dorm bed a guardian. *Greetings From Asbury Park*—fast words inside. In the Orlando Arena, he keeps yelling, *It's okay to have a good time.* Over and over, until I believe him. Dance.

Surprised to fall in love again in a summer writing workshop in Provincetown, Massachusetts. To stay in love. Get engaged, move north. Dance in a living room in Rome, New York. My snow angel in the backyard waving her arms. All the flowers we'd drawn on little white cards lean on the glass cupboards, china. Lie flat on the long table where we drew petals all night like prayers. We dance near the window, my hands in his. He's as graceful as a man in a ballroom, black and white suit. Holds my hands so lightly, as if they could be crushed, ruined. An enchantment. Makes my body lighter. I forget to be heavy. I am devastated to have it not work out. I don't know how to live with his unmedicated depression, mood swings. Cycles of darkness and joy. Running around Green Lakes, I think about drowning. Becoming a lake. I don't tell him about this. But I have to leave. Say I'll be back, but he cries like a child in the airport, as if I am going to war, as if I am dying, as if this is over. This is over. Even though I love him. He loves me.

I move to New Smyrna Beach to work at an artists' residency program, create a summer writing residency for teenagers. Two of the teachers, Alan and Denise, dance with the kids in the black box. By then, I can barely walk into the theater. Lean against the doorjamb as if I am part of the architecture, a stone woman, a caryatid. Ready to bolt. Flee. *Why aren't you dancing?* A girl asks, mystified.

When I was a girl, I loved to dance with my friends. Jackson Five songs. Three of us dancing on top of the picnic table or in front of the big living room mirror, singing.

Dans Maen, the Stone Dance, is a circle of stones in Cornwell. A spell cast five thousand years ago on nineteen girls, turned to stone for dancing in a field. Almost nothing human about the granite blocks, rectangular, tilted. But one has the swayed back of a spine, a body in motion.

I'd left Florida in the fall of 2011. Spent four years teaching and writing in places I've never been before. Where I knew no one. Summer in Lake Tahoe. A dance for teachers and students. June, the chair of my department, tries to lure me onto the floor, makes her arms into a scarf. Self-consciousness jangling, jabbing me like a chain mail of paper clips. Pillar of salt, of stone, becoming stonier. In junior high, instead of going to our school dance, we drank beer at Satellite Beach with tall dune grass scratching our arms. Hair blowing, salting.

I pull away from June, and then it's the DJ calling me out on the dance floor. I try to hide behind other bodies. But she calls my name over the microphone, crackle-boom through the air like the pour of gasoline, small explosions. *KELLE GROOM,* she calls again, emphasis on my last name. Her board lights up with flashing colors: yellow, pink, blue, like the panel on my record player in sixth grade. I watch one of my students flee and understand—he can't dance either. Why is she calling me? In the crowd of faculty and students, heads begin to turn, and look for me. Aspens outside. Even the trees are different here. Someone said, *The wind sounds different through these branches*. I leave before I can be identified. Find the dark cutout door.

II.

It was the end of my fourth year of traveling, fall of 2014, when I was in Amherst, Virginia, out of money, lucky to have a ten-week writing residency. One night, in the dining room of the Fellows Residence, Adelbert from Germany suggests we have a dance party. Both words terrify.

A white flyer appears on the glass front door of the building. *We're rolling the rug back*. Is this metaphor? What kind of dancing is inhibited by carpet? I plan to hide in my studio. The dance is Friday night in the Fellows' living room, and I have a recovery meeting at 8 p.m. at a church in town. I'll come back, rush through the hall, hopefully unseen, and out the back door. Walk up the gravel path to my studio and work. But after dinner, Simon, a writer from Malta, reaches an arm toward me as I go toward the door. *Come see us for a little while tonight?*

Yes, I say. I could just walk into the room, I think. At least do that. But what I want is to dance, to break this spell. *Can't you just snap your fingers?* Alan had asked years ago. No, no, I couldn't then. But now I think I am willing to move my body, live in it. Let myself want it.

In Amherst, I've been living with a constantly changing group of thirty people for over two months. Upstairs, our tiny rooms with little monk beds side by side. *The things I've done in that little room,* the guy from North Carolina said, mock-horrified. Shaking his long, narrow head like a horse, nearly snorting. Even his big-toothed smile horse-friendly. Our bedsheets of faded flowers, stripes, pinks and yellows like Nana had at her house. At night, I secretly turn on the fan for the whole floor. White noise to drown out the sound of so many people breathing.

When I return, no music plays in the foyer of the Fellows' Residence. Turn left into the first living room, walk through into the adjoining living room. Brick wall at the far-end. The guy from North Carolina is on the cushy beige couch. I sit beside him. He's always easy in his body, windblown, loose. Wall of sliding glass behind us. White slatted blinds shut. *They're still getting set up,* he says. A computer to find, speakers. The rug IS rolled back as if for ballroom dancing or ballet. Serious dance. Wonder if NC's ease tonight is fake like mine. Even he seems a little nervous—slight rigidity to his hands clasped in his lap.

The shelf over the TV has been made into a bar—square tequila bottle with an H on it. Four or five people proclaim it the best they've ever had. Beer bottles and wine in ice cubes in a big blue plastic tub. Salted chocolate squares, Doritos, popcorn. My bathroom mate—I share a bathroom with a composer whose room adjoins mine—hoists the tequila bottle in my direction: *This is so good.* I nod and he remembers I don't drink. *I'm such a dick,* he says. I smile. I'm out of water, find someone's liter of Sprite in the laundry room fridge and pour some in my water bottle. Hold it in one hand for a long time. Something to do, drink, while my feet turn in different directions as though I can't decide where to go, hips swaying. The composer is shoulder bumping North Carolina. *You have to use more force,* he says.

I'm really impressed by the level of not-giving-a-shit dancing, NC says to me. He's tall—I have to look up. Later, he'll pat my hair, becoming even more curly in the overheated room. *I have to touch it.* We're standing outside the circle (my head nodding slightly), bar behind us, stolen Sprite sweating in my hand.

Show me how, I say to Tyler who shoulder bumps NC again. I leap as if making a basket, smack his arm with mine. It seems like something to only do once, so I stand in the circle of dancing people. Do my little black boot turns as if cranked by an invisible hand. A woman from New York turns to me, says, *I haven't felt comfortable dancing since I quit drinking.* I blink. I'd just seen her dancing. Sometimes when I walk Stage Road alone to the Sweet Briar College gym, I see her going the other direction.

How did it feel? I ask. Her hair long, silvery. *Strange,* she says. We might be the only two sober people in the room. She's braver than I—she can say it. I have to keep my fear hidden, or think I do. What if I just admitted to her that I feel the same? Exactly the same? I see her again later, dancing an elegant box on the floor.

Do you dance? Sarah asks. She's wearing a red peasant dress. I'm dancing when she asks me this. I say, *No, but I like to do it for fun.* Which isn't untrue. I just leave out the not-dancing years. The not-fun. The fleeing.

The composer asks, *Do you want to see me breakdance?* He's moving thickly through the air. I don't realize he's drunk. Just slowed-down.

Sure, I say. He throws himself down on the bare wood floor, shoulder-first. Thud. A tumbling feat with no spring-back. The composer's in his twenties, not heavy, but solid. A lot of weight pounded his shoulder. He does it again, lands on the footstool. Then, I lose sight of him.

Have you heard of the red shoes? Sarah asks. *A woman*

is poor and gets these shoes, and every time she puts them on she can't stop dancing. A fairy tale. I dance in my short black boots with zippers up the back, in old red-and-black-plaid jean leggings and someone else's gray V-neck sweater from Goodwill.

Do you think "Smells Like Teen Spirit" is okay to play? Dana asks me. A wall of books behind him. Exit sign above a door I've never seen anyone use. He's very concerned about picking music everyone will like. There are already complaints.

Yes, I say, though I can't remember the song, only a cassette tape's aqua cover, a baby swimming underwater. I'm just glad to be spoken to, glad not to be ostracized for dancing like a shy lumberjack unused to humankind. Glad he thinks music will have any effect on me. As if I have moves beyond these little waves and nods. My hands like fledglings trying to lift up off the ground. Room very warm. I slide a glass door open a little. Cool October air on my face. *Thank you,* Ruby says, breathing it in.

But when the Nirvana song begins, I know it. Feel it. Something happens. One of the German guys, Roland, locks eyes with me. The song a live battery. He bends his knee as if doing warm-up lunges before a run. Then he jumps.

The quadriceps, femoris, sartorius work together, raise my thigh. Soleus, metatarsals, cuneiform bones lift me off the ground. Not like when I was seventeen, and a man took both my hands and drew me onto the dance floor of a bar, kept my hands in his like double ropes that kept me upright, moving. This time, no one takes my hand. This time I jump. Shaking my hair the way I shook it in some dark long ago. Roland and I are jumping. And, then, who knows who else. All around us people are in the air.

Beautiful Ruby sits on the couch alone, so Roland and I grab her hands. And she leans back, away, the way I would. Roland and I plead, dance on either side of her. She laughs, lets us pull her in. We are jumping, hold hands until it's hard to breathe, laughing. Gasping. Her hand cool and sweating. I turn to see her incandescent. The opposite of flight.

I rise up from the bottom of myself. Identical squares of light brought closer and closer together until they meet. Little rivers of sweat down my neck, spine. Back of my scalp. We dance until we have to bend at the waist, panting. Our bodies heat the molecules in the air. Draw them out, like blue heat in metal. Electron charge.

Before I got sober, when I cut my right forefinger on a broken glass while bartending in Orlando, an emergency room doctor sewed my finger together. It healed white. Even now, it's white as if filled with light. My whole body like this tonight.

Midway through the night, a slow song plays. *Ugh, this song,* Brandel says. *This is a hang-on-a-boy's-neck song.* She flung her head back, and her arms over Lu's head, dances as if drugged. Hair piled in a loose Mary Poppins bun.

Do you want to hang on my neck? Simon asks. He writes children's books. His big eyes behind his big glasses are kindly. Normally I would want to hang onto another person for help. But this time, I don't even answer, just smile and move a little away, sway.

The composer appears, holds a hand to his shoulder. *I had to pop it back in,* he says. *My arm fell out. I dislocated it.*

You put it back in yourself? He shrugs with the other shoulder.

In the middle of my body, it's calm. Long into the night I

watch Lu and Dana do a dance like a walk around the room in S curves. I silently wish I could do that, let myself want it. And then there is Adelbert smiling, offering his hand. I rest mine at his waist, his cotton shirt wet and a little cold, and we do the same dance-walk around the room.

Adelbert beams all day long, some kind of German angel. Cooks strong coffee with cardamom on the stove for everyone at lunch, every day. Even though there are two coffee makers, even though there are so many of us. He beams and wears a black beret and digs red clay out of the ground at Sweet Briar College because all his sculpting supplies from home as well as his espresso machine have been lost in the mail. He buys plaster at Home Depot and unscented soap at CVS to melt down for the plaster. *I thought you had sensitive skin,* I say. He beams at that in the drugstore aisle.

The next day in the kitchen, Ruby who is perfect, told me that she'd been too shy to dance. How can someone so beautiful be shy? *But when I saw you doing that, I thought, I can do it,* she says. My Nirvana dance. Days later, she will email me: *What a dance night it was. It still makes me laugh.*

At dinner that night, a man who'd arrived during the Nirvana song, who'd hung back by the bar as I would have, says, *That was bacchanalian.* I wake to moaning outside my bedroom window in the early morning. The composer's dislocated arm has fallen out of the socket again. Hangs there in the dark like a long sock.

III.

Thich Nhat Hanh said the shortest Dharma talk he ever gave is *I have arrived, I am home.* He said it means *I don't want to run anymore.* The moment you're in is home. When I walk at Sweet Briar, the road has a green flag that reads,

You are home. Everywhere I've travelled, people say to me, *This is your home now.* People I'd just met, in Provincetown, in Florida, in meetings, here in Amherst over dinner in the Fellows' Residence. I'd thought them compassionate about my lack of a home, attempting to comfort. But it was true. Each place is home while I'm there.

Three people in my small recovery meeting in Amherst tell me I can come live with them. They all have room. Two women and one man, who has a crush. Who always walks me to my jeep across the street in the bank parking lot. Asks me to hike on weekends, gives me a framed photo he took of the Shenandoah Valley so I can remember the green in winter. I broke down in that church. Thought I was just talking, and suddenly, couldn't stop crying. When I tell them I'm leaving, an older man with very little breath takes my hand, hugs me. Will I ever see any of them again? The man who always smiles and asks what I wrote that day, kisses my cheek says, *You're a beautiful woman.* His kiss a gift.

The red dictionary I've carried with me everywhere says that *an isolated place at the outmost limit of human habitation* is a jumping-off place. *The starting point of a trip.* This is my home. They are my home. All of us in the blue hills. Ghosts of the horses that run beside me days and nights walking alone on the dirt and gravel road. Back to where the others sleep. Waking with them.

I'm leaving for Florida again, headed back to New Smyrna Beach to stay in a borrowed house. Look for work. Along the way, I'll lose the ocean ring my brother, Cory, gave me when I didn't die from ovarian cancer in 2005. Two thousand and five: before I get the artists' residency job in New Smyrna Beach. Before a friend suggests I imagine the life I want to live. In 2005, after surgery, after my doctor discovers

269

that I don't have cancer, my brother travels from Norfolk to Orlando to give the ring to me. My incision-stapled skin bandaged. Propped on the couch in my pink apartment. He'd read a poem in my first book called "Ocean Ring"—about women who wear rings, how it seems they're loved. How I'd bought a ring for myself. And when Nana was sick, I mailed the ring to her, as if I could marry her to me, to life. Found the ring in a dresser drawer in her apartment after she died in 1998, along with her wedding band. My uncle Dean stood in the doorway of her apartment, said, *Come out of there. You're like me.* He knew how much I loved her, how wrecked I was.

Terrible weather had delayed my brother's flight when Nana died, and he'd missed the funeral. When he read "Ocean Ring," I saw him wipe tears away. Cory in the brown easy chair in the Wellfleet house. I can still see him there if I turn to the right, weeping for Nana. Head bent over my blue book. The ring he bought me was a blue sapphire with two diamonds on either side. *It's your ocean ring,* he said. The most beautiful thing I've ever owned.

Before I leave Virginia, I take the ring off to pack and clean my room. Always so careful with the ring. Lurch of panic any time I misplace it for a moment. To keep the ring safe, I think to put it in my glasses case. I discover it's gone later, on the road, in a South Carolina hotel room. Empty my purse and suitcase over and over. Dump everything on the bed. Repack. Empty it out again. Disbelief that I could lose something so precious to me. The one material thing I'd let myself want without reservation has completely disappeared.

No one can find it in the Fellows' Residence. Maybe it'll show up one day, a sparkling ring. Someone will feel lucky. Sick over it for two days. Then, start to let go of it a little.

Weeks later, in Florida, I still touch my ring finger to be sure it's there—a habit—and find only bare skin. I'm loved without the ring. Bare skin enough. If home is the moment it's also the body.

IV.

Leaving Virginia, I won't know that my conversation with one of the painters in residence, in which I learn that her best friend has resigned from her summer arts job in Provincetown, will bring me back to Provincetown in a few months. Arriving between snowstorms in early February 2015, to live there for the next seven years.

If the appearance of the destructive voice I first heard in DC, its flare-ups and levelings were graphed, like population growth or snowstorms, the timeline of the chart begins in the fall of 2010. Before I got sober in 1984, I'd struggled with suicidal thoughts, and in early sobriety I'd been hit more than once by a depression that was like a crater, and I was slipping down the walls. I'd been terrified of the bottom, if I couldn't get out. But once I'd been sober for a while, I was mostly grateful to be alive. There were those two difficult relationships that triggered suicidal thoughts in 1999 and in 2002, with John and with X. Having to sit with my friend, Laurel for two days the first time—knowing I couldn't be alone.

In the intervening years, I'd had challenges. But DC was different. The voice that began talking to me on a regular basis. Standing on the Pennsylvania Avenue median, waiting to cross. After I'd given up my job as an arts administrator, given up teaching, stored all my belongings, and traveled to a place I'd never been. Where I knew no one. A grant to do research and write for a year. What I had always wanted. Dome of the

Capitol to my right so bright like a spaceship appearing. In front of Starbucks, the man who will sing in baritone, ask me for money. Who will call me, *Baby*. Say, *Maybe next time*. Everyone else moving very fast, eyes elsewhere. The store where I eat a salad from a bowl almost every night, looking out the glass at this sidewalk. Stood on the median, cold in my yellow coat, buckled black boots, I'd thought, or the thought came: *Walk into traffic*. The voice coming from outside. Like a furious ghost. *Your life is over*. Why then? Why there?

The voice came and went. Came back. Three years later, in 2014, at a writing conference in Seattle, I'd gone to a recovery meeting. A woman said, *My disease is trying to kill me*. It was the first time I understood that the voice I heard was my addiction, my alcoholism. Even sober, my disease was trying to kill me. A floodlight.

In 2015, when I moved to Provincetown, the peaks on my graph rose in the summer, working an around-the-clock job that I loved with hundreds of people, but little rest or quiet for three months straight, few recovery meetings. In early June of 2018, my graph spike was mountainous. I heard the voice every morning. Sometimes twenty, thirty, forty times between the time I woke up and walked to work: *You should die, you should die. Your life is over.* My workbook on fear and anxiety had said that repetitive thoughts were random noise, nothing. Is this murderous, haranguing voice nothing too?

The voice had waxed and waned over the preceding years, but the stress of summer always heightened it. A hammer I woke up to, expected. Beating me as I put my feet on the floor, made coffee, dressed: *You should die*. Put my arm through a sleeve, find my sandals. *You should die*. Keys. *You should die*.

I never told anyone. I went to work six days a week, I

smiled, I greeted, I ran nightly public events, I hosted BBQs and readings for students, concerts, exhibitions. Smiling. No one knew. Like my student in Orlando, M, I was fine. Appeared calm. I kept a card by the bathroom from one of my friends, so that I could see it every day while I brushed my teeth. Counter the hammer of the suicide voice. It read: *No one is more kind, empathetic, funny than you.*

Anthony Bourdain, the beloved chef and travel documentarian, died by hanging on June 8, 2018. It was unbelievable to hear that this easygoing, kind, beautiful man would die by suicide. In 1972, he'd gotten his first dishwashing job in the now-closed Flagship Restaurant in Provincetown. Bourdain came back to Provincetown to film *Parts Unknown,* his show on CNN exploring food and the human condition around the world. While there he said, *I cannot tell you how frequently I dream about Spiritus Pizza. I'm walking down Commercial Street, and I'm sort of dimly aware that Spiritus has moved, and there's a sense of dislocation and a loss as I stumble around this sort of Provincetown dreamscape of forty years ago. I was still here and living in hope.* Not *on* hope, but in it.

Nine days later, my friend Nick posted a link to an NPR opinion piece by a woman, Joelle Hann, who had been surprised by and at the mercy of her own suicidal impulses a decade prior. She interviewed a psychotherapist, Nicole Lewis-Keeber, who said, *OCD talks to you, anxiety talks to you, depression talks to you—but it lies to you. ...what that little voice is telling you to do is not true.*

I read the NPR article on June 19, 2018, while eating breakfast. Desperate for distraction from the constant voice. The funny thing is I read it wrong. I was sure that the psychotherapist had said, *The cruel things the voice says aren't true.* I cried all morning from the compassion of "cruel," of some-one understanding, *knowing,* that what the voice said was cruel. And yet, when I finally re-read the article nine months later, she'd never said "cruel," I'd come to that on my own. Been comforted by it for almost a year, the solidarity of it.

But what made all the difference was the psychotherapist's statement that *what that little voice is telling you to do is not true.* Even that I'd misread. Yes, what the voice is saying to do is not true. But I understood it to also mean that what the voice said was not true. The voice that said, *Your life is over.* It hadn't occurred to me that it wasn't true, that my life wasn't over. I thought okay, I just have to endure it. I have to try to live even though my life is over. But what that article told me—that voice—is those cruel things aren't true. Even if it was a misreading. My life isn't over. I don't have to die. It was news to me.

From that day on, June 19, 2018, the dozens upon doz-ens of suicidal instructions stopped. The incessant voice stopped. Once in a while, I hear it. A one-timer. Low-level peppering. Trying me out again. But it's lost its power, clam-or. I know it's not true. I'm still an alcoholic, my disease is still trying to kill me, even sober. I have recovery meetings, a program, steps, a sponsor. I know things can cycle, wheel around. But in reading that article, I'd heard a counter voice, *"What that little voice is telling you to do is not true."* As if the psychotherapist was in the room with me, opening the windows. Letting sanity in. I didn't feel alone with my secret anymore. Twenty years ago, I hadn't been able to tell M. But another person, a stranger, wrote down what had happened to her. Shared it. That writer's voice freed me.

V.

The first time I made the long trip south, Provincetown to Florida, then to Virginia, I'd been overwhelmed by fears— breakdown, bridges, tunnels, unfamiliar cities, being lost. *Okay, be scared, but you still have to do it.* Unable to believe I could keep myself safe, be safe. But it was also a shedding of something. I felt it fall off, not even heavy. I kept hearing my friend Larry's deep, calm voice: *You can make it.*

That first time, before I drive out of Provincetown, I go to the Methodist Church on Shank Painter for a recovery meeting. Sit in a little room with others. After the meeting, two strangers hold my hands. But I still shake with terror at driving away. *How will I ever make it?* My old jeep had overheated on three-hour drives in Florida. When the jeep was newer. Teaching in Lake Tahoe, petrified of driving the jeep ten thousand feet down the winding, cliffside Mount Rose Highway, I never did. Instead, I rode a bus from Incline Village, on teetering hairpin curves. Hired a woman at the college to drive my jeep off the mountain. For all my other cross-country trips, I'd paid a transport service. But there was no money for that now. I stand near H. Wait for her to finish a conversation, even though I feel self-conscious, not really knowing her. Every time I hear her speak at meetings, her words always wash away my shyness and isolation. When she speaks, her words are clear and practical as apples. I can carry them with me. I understand that I can not know how to do things. I can ask for help, then do those things. H makes it seem possible, normal.

It's what M taught me in Orlando so long ago: *Go to a new land. Learn to ask for what you need.* Learn the language. Learn to speak. I don't yet know that I will make it to Florida and Virginia and back to Florida. Then six months later, I'll arrive right back here in Provincetown between the snowstorms of 2015, with a job, with that terrible voice by my side growing louder and louder for three more years. Until someone I don't know tells the truth about her life, about wanting to die. Writes it down. And someone else shares it. Lets me hear it, and frees me. Helps me learn how to live.

So, in the early summer of 2014, in the church on Shank Painter, I stand until H turns toward the door. Tell her where I am going. I'm trembling the way I did in the early days, when I'd just stopped drinking. I wonder if I'm about to drive into my own death. If I'm never seen again, will H be the last person I speak to? But H says, *Take it slow. You can stop when you want. Get a hotel. Get a map.*

I can't read a map, I say. *The flatness is confusing.*

I can't read one either, she says. *That's why they're so great.*

Let me give you a hug, she says. As if it has to be done. Even my voice trembling by then. M alone on her first day twenty years ago, everything new. Red shoes swinging beneath her desk. I have my friend Larry's words: *You can make it.* I have H's voice, her arms around me. And the kind man at Provincetown Bikes, who after securing my bike to the back of my jeep, doesn't even ask. Just throws his arms wide as if he might fly, and gives a little nod to invite me in.

NOTES & SOURCES

Mirror City

Paula M. Marks, *In a Barren Land: American Indian Dispossession and Survival,* William Morrow, 1998.

This Used to Be an Ocean

Federal land owned in Wyoming:
   https://ballotpedia.org/Federal_land_policy_in_Wyoming
Fracking & fracking accidents across US:
   https://earthjustice.org/features/campaigns/fracking-across-the-united-states
Fracking accidents/explosions in Wyoming: (click on each skull for city/source/details)
   https://earthjustice.org/features/wyoming-and-fracking
Sublette County, WY: Source: "Buried Secrets: Is Natural Gas Drilling Endangering U.S. Water Supplies?" (http://www.propublica.org/article/buried-secrets-is-natural-gas-drilling-endangering-us-water-supplies-1113) Abrahm Lustgarten. *ProPublica*. November 13, 2008.
Pavilion, WY: Source: "US test shows water problem near natgas drill site." (http://af.reuters.com/article/energyOilNews/idAFN0116496920100901?sp=true)
   Jon Hurdle. Reuters. September 1, 2010.
Fremont County, WY: Source: "Flash fire at compressor injures man on Christmas". Katie Roenigk. *The Ranger*. December 26, 2013. Web. Accessed July 16, 2015.
   http://dailyranger.com/story.php?story_id=10585
Opal, WY: Source: "Fire rages at Wyoming natural gas plant; town's evacuation lifted". Paresh Dave. *Los Angeles Times*. April 24, 2014. Web. Accessed July 14, 2015.

Rock Springs, WY: Source: "Oxy agrees to major fines for contamination of springs." (http://www.gjsentinel.com/news/articles/oxy_agrees_to_major_fines_for/) Dennis Webb. Grand Junction Sentinel. April 26, 2010.

Officials Urge Wyoming Residents Not to Drink Water: https://af.reuters.com/article/energyOilNews/idAFN0116496920100901?sp=true

Trump rescinds the 2015 final rule on hydraulic fracturing (2017): https://www.blm.gov/press-release/blm-rescinds-rule-hydraulic-fracturing

Fracking Booms on Public Lands (WY) 2018: https://www.nytimes.com/2018/10/27/climate/trump-fracking-drilling-oil-gas.html

Wyoming Mineral Rights: https://www.tsln.com/news/mineral-rights-and-what-they-mean-to-landowners/

Wyoming/Gillette Coal Mining Boom 2012: https://www.oregonlive.com/environment/2012/06/coal_clash_out_of_the_gigantic.html

'The Harms of Fracking': New Report Details Increased Risks of Asthma, Birth Defects and Cancer 2018: https://www.rollingstone.com/politics/politics-news/the-harms-of-fracking-new-report-details-increased-risks-of-asthma-birth-defects-and-cancer-126996/

Trump 'turns back the clock' by luring drilling companies to pristine lands 2020: https://www.theguardian.com/environment/2020/feb/12/trumps-legacy-drilled-public-lands-and-the-resulting-carbon-emissions

Black Mountain

Joanna Bourke, *Fear: A Cultural History,* Counterpoint 2007.
O my terrified   my obdurate/my wanderer   keep the trail
   –Adrienne Rich, "Axel, in thunder," *Tonight No Poetry Will Serve: Poems 2007–2010,* W.W.Norton, 2011.

Occidental

Libby Larsen, "Songs From Letters: Calamity Jane to her daughter Janey, 1880-1902": https://libbylarsen.com/works/songs-from-letters-calamity-jane-to-her-daughter-janey-1880-1902/

"Les Goddesses," Moyra Davey: https://www.theparisreview.org/
blog/2020/05/28/les-goddesses/

Les Goddesses, Directed by Moyra Davey, color video, with sound, 61
minutes, 2011: https//www.guggenheim.org/artwork/33586

"Consider for a moment those hummingbirds who did not
open their eyes again today...a brilliant music stilled." "Joyas
Voladoras," Brian Doyle.

Law of Similarity

The "book of fear" is Daniel Gardner's *The Science of Fear: How the
Culture of Fear Manipulates Your Brain,* Plume, 2009.

The Cartographer's Assistant

Edelman, Peter. "The Worst Thing Bill Clinton Has Done," *The
Atlantic,* March 1997. Web. 4 June 2014.

Edelman, Peter. "We (And This Includes You, Democrats) Have
Blown a Huge Hole in the Safety Net," *Common Dreams:
Building Progressive Community,* 3 June 2014. Web. 4 June 2014.

Stan, Adele M. "Poverty Expert Peter Edelman Explains How
Low Wages and Racial Politics Line the Pockets of the Rich,"
AlterNet, 9 April 2013. Web. 4 June 2014.

Ward, Beverly G. "Related to the Federal Personal Responsibility
and Work Opportunity Reconciliation Act of 1996." *Center for
Urban Transportation Research,* USF, 2000. Web. 4 June 2014.

Billingsgate

"I am not the body. But I am." —*I Am Not This Body:The Pinhole
Photographs of Barbara Ess,* Guy Armstrong, Michael
Cunningham, et al., Aperture, 2001.

"body everywhere"—James Merrill, "Losing the Marbles," *Selected
Poems.*

"because in this space between spaces/ where nothing speaks,/ I am
what it says."—Denis Johnson, "Now," *Inner Weather,* Graywolf
Press, 1976.

Hans Hofmann House

"The fortnight ending, I lingered on, and as the year lengthened into autumn, the beauty and mystery of this earth and outer sea so possessed and held me that I could not go." Henry Beston, *The Outermost House,* Henry Holt, 1928.

Smallpox House

"the trees/are turning/their own bodies/into pillars/of light"
—Mary Oliver, "In Blackwater Woods," *American Primitive,* Back Bay Books, 1983.

Though the gravestones display only numbers, the numbers are assumed to correspond to the numbers as recorded in the Book of Deaths. The names and the numbers are reported in *The Advocate* March 17, 1994.

"Like the people of color in Ancient Cemetery in South Yarmouth?" Yarmouth Selectmen voted on March 7, 1826 "That all the people of colour shall in future, bury their dead in the Southeast corner of the burying yard." Town Records state that two Selectmen visited my Wampanoag ancestor, Thomas Greenough and told him to move two Wampanoag burials to the Southeast corner. On May 25, 2021, GPR/LiDAR surveys were conducted to identify unmarked graves in the Southeast Corner of Yarmouth's Ancient Cemetery. A public presentation of the results is still pending town approval.

"Being thus arrived in a good harbor and brought safe to land, they fell upon their knees," William Bradford, *Of Plymouth Plantation,* 1630-51.

Wilderness

"We enter solitude, in which also we lose loneliness."
—Wendell Berry, *What Are People For: Essays,* Counterpoint, 2010.

"The plainest summary of all the natural law is: to treat other men as if they were men. Not to act as if I alone were a man, and every other human were an animal or a piece of furniture." Thomas Merton, "A Body of Broken Bones," *New Seeds of Contemplation.*

Bourne, Edmund J. *The Anxiety & Phobia Workbook,* New Harbinger, 2009.

A Sailboat on a Tiny Sea

Campbell, Timothy C. *Wireless Writing in the Age of Marconi,*
University of Minnesota Press, 2006 (pg 211).

Hanh, Thich Nhat. *no death, no fear,* Riverhead, 2002.

Math, Irwin. Morse, *Marconi and You,* Charles Scribner's Sons, 1979.

Journals in Ice

"You said the only cure / For anxiety was fear. / Now solitude undoes
loneliness / Like a ribbon from your hair." James Galvin, "It Just
So Happens," *Elements,* Copper Canyon, 1988.

"Some things that go are gone." A.R. Ammons, "Eyesight," *Collected
Poems 1961-1971,* Norton, 1972.

"Pledge your flag and sing/slightly out of tune/ 'for spacious fields of
grain.'" Philip Levine, "Who Are You," *Not This Pig,* Wesleyan,
1968.

Liner notes, Anton Dvorak, "Stabat Mater" op. 58, Deutsche
Grammophon Gesellschaft.

"how we will someday / (right now!) be together," Matthew
Zapruder, *Come on All You Ghosts,* Copper Canyon, 2010.

"the strangest, the most unnerving of all his country's poets," Harold
Bloom, *The New Republic,* 1976.

"in the reflection of each other's faces these thirty birds...did not
know if they were still themselves or if they had become the
Simurgh," Farid ud-Din Attar, *The Conference of the Birds,*
Penguin, 1984.

"In the game, someone has to touch you to free you/then you're
human again," Marie Howe, "The Mother," *What the Living Do,*
W.W. Norton, 1998.

Star Tables

"How a Sextant Works," "Navigation by Sextant," *Shackleton's Voyage
of Endurance,* PBS NOVA. Web. 11 June 2014.

Mars

"This must be what I wanted to be doing," W.S. Merwin, "Air," *The
Moving Target,* Atheneum: New York, 1971.

"The one who can sing, sings to the one who can't," Ellen Bryant
Voigt, "Song and Story," *The Atlantic,* May 1992.

"Map of all Under Heaven," (Cho'onhado) Korean map, 1800, maker
unknown, *Great Maps,* Smithsonian, 2014.

"Maps as much about existence as orientation," (see above).

Call Yourself Alive

"I cannot tell you how frequently I dream about Spiritus Pizza. I'm
walking down Commercial Street, and I'm sort of dimly aware
that Spiritus has moved, and there's a sense of dislocation and a
loss as I stumble around this sort of Provincetown dreamscape
of 40 years ago. I was still here and living in hope," Anthony
Bourdain, "What Provincetown Meant to Anthony Bourdain,"
Boston.com, June 8, 2018: https://www.boston.com/culture/
restaurants/2018/06/08/what-provincetown-meant-to-
anthony-bourdain/

Joelle Hann, "At My Darkest Moment, I Reached Out For Help And
Chose To Live," NPR, June 17, 2018: https://www.npr.org/
sections/health-shots/2018/06/17/620561421/opening-up-
about-depression-and-suicide-could-help-someone-else-on-the-
brink

Nina Cassian, translation by Brenda Walker and Andrea Deletant
"Call yourself alive," "Temptation," *American Poetry Review,*
March 18, 1988.

If you are having thoughts of suicide, call or text 988 to reach
the National Suicide Prevention Hotline or go to

SpeakingOfSuicide.com/resources

for a list of additional resources.

ACKNOWLEDGMENTS

Thank you to the editors and magazines who originally published these essays (sometimes in slightly different forms): "Call Yourself Alive" in *AGNI;* "Interstate" in *Another Chicago Magazine;* "Billingsgate" in *Bennington Review* as "When I'm Dead I'll Learn to Travel"; "Black Mountain" as "How to Cure a Fright," in *Bluestem,* and anthologized in *Making Essays: 20 Creative Nonfiction Essays and Interviews with the Writers;* "Hans Hofmann House" in *Brevity: A Journal of Concise Literary Nonfiction;* "Journals in Ice" in *The Common;* "Law of Similarity" in *Frank Martin Review;* "A Sailboat on a Tiny Sea" in *Gulf Coast* as "Antibody"; "Emerald City" in *Hunger Mountain Review;* "Smallpox House" in *The Literary Review: An International Review of Contemporary Writing* as "Destroying Angel"; "Lake" in *Lumina;* "The Cartographer's Assistant," in *New Orleans Review;* "This Used to Be an Ocean" in *Orion* as "You Can't Drink the Water"; "The City Beautiful" in *Ploughshares* (Nick Flynn, Guest Editor) as "How to Live with Uncertainty"; "You Grow in a Meadow" in *Provincetown Arts Magazine;* "Nauset House" in *Superstition Review* as "Dear Baby"; "At Sea" as "Ezra Baker" and "Mars" in *StoryQuarterly;* "Star Tables" in *River Teeth: A Journal of Narrative Nonfiction;* "Occidental" in *Punctuate: A Nonfiction Magazine* as "Live Music"; and "Stone Baby" in *Zone 3.*

Thank you to Jeffrey Levine, Kristina Marie Darling, David Rossitter, Ann Aspell, and everyone at Tupelo Press for their dedication to the literary arts, vision of experimentation, beautiful books, and for their great care with this book.

Thank you to Michi Meko for his stunning painting, "Into the Vast," his own explorations in navigation and wayfinding, and his generosity in allowing his work to be the cover of this book.

Thank you to the people and institutions whose kind support helped me to write this book: American Antiquarian Society, Ann

Brady, Atlantic Center for the Arts, Black Mountain Institute, University of Nevada-Las Vegas, Dr. Carol C. Harter, Maile Chapman, Bill Clegg, Larry Collins, Jim Frost, Nick Conroy, Djerassi Resident Artists Program, Sharon Dynak, Nick Flynn, Linda Frysh, Beth Greenfield, Kiki Herold, Library of Congress, James Merrill House Residency, Tom Johnston, Joshua Kryah, Margot Knight, Leslie McGrath, James David Moran, Nancy Lowden Norman, National Endowment for the Arts, James David Moran, Nicole Parcher, Sheila Gulley Pleasants, Myra Slotnick, Susanna Sonnenberg, Terry Ann Thaxton, Amber Flora Thomas, Trish Thompson, Brian Turner, Ucross Foundation, Sierra Nevada University, Virginia Center for the Creative Arts, Gillian Whittle, Richard Wiley, Joan Wickersham, Amber Withycombe, and Lisa Zimmerman.

KELLE GROOM is the author of the award-winning memoir, *I Wore the Ocean in the Shape of a Girl* (Simon & Schuster), a Barnes & Noble Discover selection, *New York Times Book Review* Editor's Choice, and a *Library Journal* Best Memoir. Groom's work appears in *AGNI, American Poetry Review, Best American Poetry, The New Yorker, New York Times, Ploughshares,* and *Poetry.* She is the author of four poetry collections, most recently *Spill* (Anhinga Press). An NEA Fellow in Prose and Massachusetts Cultural Council Fellow in Nonfiction, her honors also include two Florida Book Awards. Groom is a nonfiction editor at *AGNI Magazine.*